Britain and the Middle East in the 9/11 Era

D1496113

CHATHAM HOUSE PAPERS

Chatham House (the Royal Institute of International Affairs) in London has provided an impartial forum for discussion and debate on current international issues for nearly ninety years. Its resident research fellows, specialized information resources and range of publications, conferences and meetings span the fields of international politics, economics and security. Chatham House is independent of government and other vested interests.

Chatham House Papers address contemporary issues of intellectual importance in a scholarly yet accessible way. The Royal Institute of International Affairs is precluded by its Charter from having an institutional view, and the opinions expressed in this publication are the responsibility of the author.

Already published

Vladimir Putin and the Evolution of Russian Foreign Policy
Bobo Lo

Through the Paper Curtain: Insiders and Outsiders in the New Europe
Julie Smith and Charles Jenkins (eds)

European Migration Policies in Flux: Changing Patterns of Inclusion and Exclusion
Christina Boswell

World Trade Governance and Developing Countries: The GATT/WTO Code Committee System
Kofi Oteng Kufuor

Exit the Dragon? Privatization and State Control in China
Stephen Green and Guy S. Liu (eds)

Divided West: European Security and the Transatlantic Relationship
Tuomas Forsberg and Graeme P. Herd

Putin's Russia and the Enlarged Europe
Roy Allison, Margot Light and Stephen White

The New Atlanticist: Poland's Foreign and Security Policy Priorities
Kerry Longhurst and Marcin Zaborowksi

Britain and the Middle East in the 9/11 Era
Rosemary Hollis

Forthcoming

America and a Changed World: A Question of Leadership
Robin Niblett (ed.)

Lands of Discord: Central Asia and the Caspian between Russia, China and the West
Yury Fedorov

Pax Bruxellana: EU Global Power and Influence
Richard Whitman

Islamism Revisited
Maha Azzam

Britain and the Middle East in the 9/11 Era

Rosemary Hollis

A John Wiley & Sons, Ltd., Publication

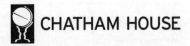

This edition first published 2010
© The Royal Institute of International Affairs, 2010

The Royal Institute of International Affairs
Chatham House
10 St James's Square
London SW1Y 4LE
http://www.chathamhouse.org.uk
(Charity Registration No.: 208223)

Blackwell Publishing was acquired by John Wiley & Sons in February 2007. Blackwell's publishing program has been merged with Wiley's global Scientific, Technical, and Medical business to form Wiley-Blackwell.

Registered Office
John Wiley & Sons Ltd, The Atrium, Southern Gate, Chichester, West Sussex, PO19 8SQ, United Kingdom

Editorial Offices
350 Main Street, Malden, MA 02148-5020, USA
9600 Garsington Road, Oxford, OX4 2DQ, UK
The Atrium, Southern Gate, Chichester, West Sussex, PO19 8SQ, UK

For details of our global editorial offices, for customer services, and for information about how to apply for permission to reuse the copyright material in this book please see our website at www.wiley.com/wiley-blackwell.

The right of Rosemary Hollis to be identified as the author of this work has been asserted in accordance with the Copyright, Designs and Patents Act 1988.

Wiley also publishes its books in a variety of electronic formats. Some content that appears in print may not be available in electronic books.

Designations used by companies to distinguish their products are often claimed as trademarks. All brand names and product names used in this book are trade names, service marks, trademarks or registered trademarks of their respective owners. The publisher is not associated with any product or vendor mentioned in this book. This publication is designed to provide accurate and authoritative information in regard to the subject matter covered. It is sold on the understanding that the publisher is not engaged in rendering professional services. If professional advice or other expert assistance is required, the services of a competent professional should be sought.

Library of Congress Cataloging-in-Publication data is available for this book.

9781405102971 (hardback)
9781405102988 (paperback)

A catalogue record for this book is available from the British Library.

Set in 10.5 on 13 Adobe Caslon by Koinonia
Printed and bound in Malaysia by Vivar Printing Sdn Bhd
01   2010

Contents

Contents

Contents

About the author

Dr Rosemary Hollis is Director of the Olive Tree Scholarship Programme and Visiting Professor at City University London. Her research focuses on international political and security issues in the Middle East, particularly European, EU, UK and US relations with the region and the international dimensions of regional conflicts, and she has published and broadcast widely on these topics.

Dr Hollis was previously Director of Research at Chatham House (the Royal Institute of International Affairs) after ten years as Head of the Middle East Programme there. She has also held positions at the Royal United Services Institute for Defence Studies and George Washington University in Washington, DC.

Preface and acknowledgments

This book was originally inspired by Khair el-din Haseeb, the Director General of the Centre for Arab Unity Studies (CAUS) in Beirut. Thanks to his vision and determination, since its foundation in the 1970s the CAUS has grown into a major sponsor, publisher and promoter of scholarly works on Arab affairs. The challenge he set me was to write an account of how the British make their policies towards the Arab world in the contemporary era.

Since my initial discussions with Dr Haseeb in the mid-1990s, the goals and hence the substance and focus of the work I have undertaken have evolved. Even so, the finished product is still broadly in line with the study he originally commissioned as part of a series published by the CAUS on the major international powers and the Arab world. Accordingly, with some adjustments, this book is to be published in Arabic by the CAUS, in association with Chatham House, in 2010. I should like to take this opportunity to thank Dr Haseeb and the CAUS for granting me the funds to begin work on the book when I was Head of the Middle East Programme at Chatham House.

I originally saw the project as an opportunity to build on the research I had done for my doctoral thesis about Britain's adaptation to imperial decline, as played out in the Arab Gulf states between 1965 and 1985. As the work developed I realized that this was also my opportunity to achieve a goal originally proposed to me by Professor Bernard Reich, my PhD supervisor at George Washington University in Washington, DC in the 1980s. He urged me to write the sequel to a seminal work by another British woman, Elizabeth Monroe, entitled *Britain's Moment in the Middle East, 1914–71*, published in 1981. An earlier version of this work had been published in 1963 – and in both cases the author was fortunate, as I have been, to have the assistance of the library staff at Chatham House. In my case I should like to thank Susan Franks in particular for her incredible capacity to track down key sources and check the accuracy of references.

This book thus represents the fulfilment of two long-harboured personal ambitions. Some of the specific findings of my PhD thesis are presented here (notably in Chapter 8), but the whole is the synthesis of evidence, insights and observations accumulated over more than two decades – from the vantage points of Washington, London and countries across the Middle East.

Specifically for the book, in 1996 I began a series of tailored interviews of British officials and businessmen dealing with the Middle East. However, as soon as New Labour swept to power in 1997 I realized that a new era had dawned in the British government's understanding of Britain's place in the world – which had implications for the British policy-making process and policies in the Middle East. This realization shaped the substance of my research in the late 1990s.

The shock of the attacks on the World Trade Center and the Pentagon on 11 September 2001 (9/11) then transformed the global landscape. For the next three years I gathered material as events unfolded. As Head of the Middle East Programme and then Director of Research at Chatham House during this period, I was also a participant in the national, policy and media debates about the implications of 9/11 and the ensuing Iraq crisis.

Living through this momentous period prompted me to rethink the thrust of the work I had embarked upon. From an explication of British policy-making towards the Arab world, it became an examination of Britain's response to 9/11 and the government's decision to join the US invasion of Iraq, and all that this entailed for Britain's involvement in the Middle East. What follows, then, is an attempt to explain British policies and policy-making in a critical period, to those in both the Middle East and elsewhere who seek to understand the broader context of what changed with 9/11 and where that takes British relations with this complex region. The emphasis is on the British side of the story, written as much with a British audience in mind as an Arab one.

I am particularly indebted to those friends, colleagues and contacts who have generously afforded me the benefit of their insights. Among those from the Middle East I should like to acknowledge especially Prince Hassan bin Talal, Mustafa Hamarneh, Omar Nahar, Ghassan Khatib, Easa Al Gurg, Khalil Shikaki, Asher Susser, Mahdi Abdul Hadi, Yossi Alpher, Samir Al-Taqi, Mustafa Alani, Heba Saleh, Nabil Fahmi, Abdel Monem Said Ali, Prince Turki Al-Faisal, Saeed Badib, Khalid Al-Khater and a number of Iranians whom I shall not name for fear of causing them embarrassment. I have also benefited from the wisdom and experience of friends and contacts across Europe, notably Bassma Kodmani, Christian Berger, Volker Perthes, Svein Sevje, Johannes Reissner, Olivier Roy, Isabel Rauscher, Charlotta Sparre, Paolo Cotta-Ramusino, Mariano Aguirre and Richard Youngs. In the United States, in addition to Bernard Reich I should like to acknowledge Geoffrey Kemp, Nathan Brown, Dan Kurtzer, Jon Alterman, Mark Fitzpatrick, Patrick Cronin and Sam Lewis.

I owe a very special debt of thanks to those who read and commented in detail on drafts of this book: Sir Harold (Hooky) Walker, Richard Muir, Greg Shapland, Mark Heller, Tarak Barkawi, Kathleen Jordan and Roger Morgan. They were very generous with their time and gave me much encouragement. I should also like to thank and honour the late Patrick Bannerman, St John Armitage and Lord (Timothy) Garden, who were a great source of inspiration to me in my quest to better understand Britain and the Middle East. I also much appreciate the guidance and support I have received from Sinclair Road, Sir James Craig, Sir Mark Allen, Anthony Milton, Raad Alkadiri and Cho Khong.

To my close friends and colleagues who have been such a joy to work and debate with over the years, and who have kept me going in adversity, I thank Kathy Jordan, Tarak Barkawi, Nadim Shehadi, Robert Lowe, Maha Azzam, Rime Allaf, Mai Yamani, Yossi Mekelberg, Ali Ansari, Claire Spencer, Gareth Stansfield, Shane Brighton, Saker Nusseibeh, George Joffé and Toby Dodge. Finally I am very grateful to Robert Lowe and above all Margaret May who deserve special mention for helping bring this book to fruition. I alone bear responsibility for the end product, mistakes and all.

R.H.

Map of the Middle East

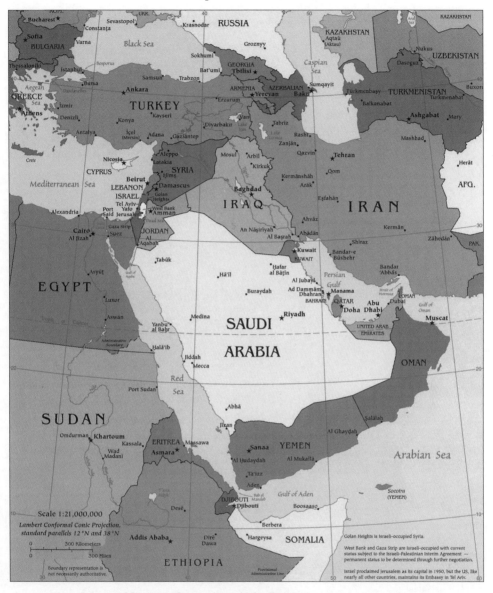

Source: Library of Congress, Geography and Map Division

Introduction

The decade of Tony Blair's leadership of the British government has proved distinctive in the history of Britain's involvement in the Middle East.[1] The story of this period is in many ways the sequel to an earlier account provided by Elizabeth Monroe in her book *Britain's Moment in the Middle East*,[2] which charts the rise and fall of British imperial power in the region, ending with the withdrawal of British forces 'East of Suez' in 1971. Thereafter, the United States assumed the role of principal arbiter of regional political and security arrangements while the British, though still active in the region, adopted a more modest and less influential profile.

So the situation remained until the late 1990s, when the British electorate delivered a landslide victory to the rejuvenated British Labour Party – the self-proclaimed New Labour – in May 1997. This proved a turning point, as successive New Labour governments began reordering Britain's foreign policy priorities, projected a new image and reshaped the way policy was made. Initially the Middle East did not dominate the agenda, but after the events of 11 September 2001 (9/11) Blair personally took the lead in developing a policy dictated by 'the war on terror' and focused on the Middle East. Britain's involvement in the subsequent US invasion of Iraq in 2003 and its aftermath delivered a bitter epilogue to Britain's imperial 'moment' in the Middle East.

This book offers an examination of Britain's policies and role in the Middle East during the Blair decade. The central focus is on how the British response to 9/11 – particularly the decision to join the US invasion of Iraq – affected British thinking about and relations in the region. Far from assisting the United States in remaking the Middle East for the better, the British ended up partnering the Americans in an endeavour that hastened the end of US regional hegemony, leaving President Barack Obama's administration to reap the consequences after both his predecessor George W. Bush and Tony Blair had left office.

Three key questions about Britain's role in the story are explored in this work. First, what was 'new' about New Labour and how did this affect the policy-making process and British policies in the Middle East from 1997 to 2001 – before 9/11? Second, what changed in British thinking as a result of 9/11? And, third, how did the British government's handling of the Iraq crisis and invasion alter its policies and role in the Middle East? The detailed analysis takes the story to the point at which Tony Blair handed over as prime minister to Gordon Brown – though the legacy of his period at the helm and the apparent implications are also discussed.

Given the genesis and development of this study, as outlined briefly in the Preface, the whole work is organized around the central focus of Britain's stance before and after 9/11 and the invasion of Iraq. The pivotal chapter (Chapter 5) is devoted to a detailed account of how the British government arrived at the decision to join the invasion of Iraq and presented that decision to the British public.

In order to understand what was new about New Labour thinking and policy with respect to the Middle East it is necessary to have a picture of what went before. Accordingly, Chapter 1 provides a historical overview to set the scene. An understanding of Britain's role in shaping the contemporary state system in the Middle East and the transition that took place from the era of British imperialism to US hegemony is also essential if one is to make sense of how Britain is perceived and received in the region today.

Chapter 2 opens with an assessment of Britain's place in the global order when New Labour came to power in 1997. An account follows of how Blair's government presented Britain's foreign policy priorities and goals during his first term and how the Middle East featured in its overall vision. The content of the government's first Strategic Defence Review is examined, as well as its initial policy pronouncements on the Middle East, including an early commitment to promoting democracy in the region. The chapter ends by assessing the rethink prompted by 9/11 and the US response to it. As a consequence of the 'war on terror' declared by President George W. Bush, and the invasion of Afghanistan in 2001 and then Iraq in 2003, the Middle East moved to centre stage in British foreign policy. It became the cockpit of US and allied British confrontation with the forces of al-Qaeda, its sympathizers and various other radical and anti-Western forces. The Strategic Defence Review was expanded with a new section on the threat posed by terrorism.

Chapter 3 is devoted to considering how the policy-making process changed under New Labour. Blair's government wanted to 'rebrand Britain', and design a foreign policy that would 'make Britain a force for good in the world' through promoting the values of freedom, tolerance, democracy and justice, confronting dictators and championing human rights. Crucially, how the government described its objectives became as important as its actions and achievements. A preoccupation with policy presentation – news management, or 'spin' – prevailed at the expense of policy substance. The prime minister adopted a presidential style of government and concentrated decision-making in Downing Street. He devised policy in consultation with an inner circle that included unelected advisers and officials, to the detriment of deliberations in cabinet and debate in parliament. Moreover, Blair and his team at No. 10 preferred informality to meticulous record-keeping. The combined effect was to undermine time-honoured processes and procedures, which had a bearing on how the government handled the Iraq crisis and planning for the invasion of Iraq and its aftermath. Chapter 3 concludes with some thoughts on the roles of the media and civil society, and hence government accountability and public trust in the 9/11 era.

In Chapter 4 a detailed examination of Britain's involvement in the Middle East peace process between 1997 and 2001 shows how the government sought a niche role in the margins of US and EU engagement. For most of this period the US administration of President Bill Clinton was in the forefront of attempts to revitalize the Arab–Israeli peace process, but events on the ground defied its best efforts and by late 2000 the second Palestinian Intifada and Israel's response heralded a return to intense conflict. British policy progressed from supporting US strategy – with periodic interventions by both Blair and the Foreign Office – to a series of desperate attempts to stem the tide of violence. British diplomatic dealings with Syria and Lebanon during this period are also discussed here.

Chapter 5, the pivotal chapter, considers in detail New Labour's policy on Iraq, before and after 9/11, culminating in the government's decision, approved by parliament on the eve of the invasion of Iraq, to join the US undertaking. Citing open sources – including a series of internal memos that would subsequently surface through the media and on the internet, and the reports of the Hutton and Butler inquiries – the account presented here traces the steps by which Tony Blair and his team arrived at the fateful decision to go to war, and discusses how their thinking was presented to the cabinet, parliament and the public. The chapter concludes with an examination of the justification that was offered and the questions surrounding this.[3] Chapter 6 analyses the consequences of the invasion of Iraq – for the country itself, the wider region and Britain. A summary of developments in Iraq following the invasion and Britain's role in the occupation precedes some comments on the costs incurred by Britain (and others) in the Iraq theatre. The rest of the chapter examines developments in British relations with Iran, Syria, Libya, Jordan and Egypt and how these were affected by 9/11 and the invasion of Iraq.

In Chapter 7 the focus returns to the Israeli–Palestinian conflict and Britain's involvement in efforts to galvanize the US administration of President George W. Bush to restart serious peace negotiations. The advent of the 'war on terror' and then the Iraq crisis significantly changed British thinking about the conflict as it became increasingly important to deal with it more effectively. Yet British thinking changed again after the terrorist bomb attacks in London on 7 July 2005 (7/7): there were indications of a hardening of attitudes in the British government and a change in the tone of British diplomatic dealings with the Israelis, suggesting greater appreciation of their position. The British government's reactions to the election victory of the Palestinian Islamist movement Hamas in 2006 and its stance on the war between Israel and Lebanon that summer also receive consideration.

Chapter 8 discusses British relations with the Arab Gulf states of Saudi Arabia, Kuwait, Bahrain, Qatar, the United Arab Emirates (the UAE) and Oman – the six Gulf Cooperation Council (GCC) states. The central issue addressed is the British defence agreement with Saudi Arabia, Al Yamamah, forged originally in the 1980s and the largest single defence deal in history. The chapter argues that Blair's government could not have rowed back on the deal it had inherited without serious damage to the British national interest. The significance of Al Yamamah is examined in terms of the secrecy and controversies that have surrounded the details of the arrangement and the implications for British policy options in future. The story of Britain's relations with the GCC states demonstrates how the British, as they wound up their empire, essentially paved the way for the United States to assume predominance in the region. Yet the British have not exited; instead they are still present in the Gulf – investing, trading, taking holidays and selling arms – and they count the GCC states as among their closest allies.

Some conclusions are presented in Chapter 9. The implications of policies adopted during the 9/11 era are apparent not only on the home front but in how Britain is generally perceived and received in the Middle East too. As a result of the decisions made during this period, many see Blair as having been Washington's unquestioning lieutenant. Yet the evidence throughout this study is that Blair was his own man, evolving from affable champion of good causes to a conviction politician confronting evil. But despite all that was new about New Labour, and all the changes it made in the policy-making process, it did not deliver Britain from the lingering legacy of empire. It merely encountered the latest manifestations of that legacy.

1

Historical Background: Stages in the Relationship

'Where the relationship between peoples is what it has been in the Middle East – one of self-confident force imposing itself upon resentful weakness – certain consequences are bound to follow, and they are not essentially different whether it is Westerners who are imposing themselves upon Asiatics, Christians upon Muslims, or one Western people upon another.' – Albert Hourani (1953)[1]

'Apart from general human benevolence, what has Great Britain ever wanted in the Middle East but stability and peace, and reasonable freedom to come and go and trade, and, if and when world strategy makes it imperative, some access to strategic points?' – Stephen Longrigg (1953)[2]

To understand British relations with the Middle East in the 9/11 era it is instructive to have in mind the successive phases through which those relations have evolved since the mid-nineteenth century. The advent of the New Labour government towards the end of the 1990s marked a shift in the British outlook on the world and changes in the policy-making process, yet a review of the historical context will demonstrate how much was actually new and how much was a product of underlying assumptions and connections built up over decades. A grasp of the historical context is also essential to understand the impact of 9/11 on both Britain and the Middle East.

For the purposes of this historical overview, the following sections delineate and examine four phases in Britain's relations with the Middle East over the last century and a half. Overall, these phases trace the evolution of Britain from an imperial power of unrivalled global reach to a much reduced but still significant power, whose continued prosperity and influence depended fundamentally on its relationship with the United States.[3] By the 1990s Britain still ranked among the major economies, allied to the United States and Europe within the framework of NATO and the European Union, in a world defined by globalization and the relative supremacy of the United States. Over the same period the Middle East emerged from the dominion

5

of the Ottoman Empire to become the single most significant energy-producing region of the world, divided into fractious states and characterized by territorial conflicts and competing ethnic and sectarian identities.

British involvement in the Middle East over the last 150 years has been continuous but variable in intensity. The relationship, although never symmetrical, has been formative for the Middle East and instrumental for Britain. On the one hand the contemporary state system in the Middle East was largely designed by the British (along with the French) in the 1920s. On the other hand, the energy resources of Iran and later of various Arab states maintained British naval power in the early twentieth century and fuelled the British economy thereafter. Following nationalization, the oil wealth of the Arab Gulf states has also sustained the British defence industry, buttressed the financial sector and provided a lucrative market for other corporate interests.

The historical summary below highlights how changes in Britain's power and global outlook have affected its engagement with and policies towards the Middle East. The first phase spans the late nineteenth and early twentieth centuries, when the British Empire was still expanding and Britain viewed the region primarily as a communication route to its imperial possessions and interests further east. As such, the Middle East was primarily depicted as an area to be mastered in the face of competition from other powers. By the early years of the twentieth century, it was also viewed as a repository of precious oil resources to be tapped, where possible to the exclusion of rival claimants.

During the second phase, from the First to the Second World War, the British, in conjunction with the French, divided up the remains of the Ottoman Empire into separate states and spheres of influence. Britain, with its League of Nations Mandates for Iraq and Palestine, among other areas, presided over the formation of the modern state of Iraq, maintained privileged access in Egypt, established the Hashemite monarchy in Trans-jordan and enabled a Jewish homeland to develop west of the Jordan River in Palestine.

The third phase takes the story from 1947 to 1971, when the last formal vestiges of Britain's imperial presence in the region were finally withdrawn. During this period almost the whole of what remained of the British Empire was dismantled in a retreat driven primarily by the need to adapt to Britain's economic decline and the rise of independence movements and nationalism across the globe. Meanwhile the Cold War and superpower rivalry became the defining features of the global order, determining the security agenda and British policy options in the Middle East as elsewhere.

In the fourth and final phase described here, from the 1970s to the mid-1990s, the British financial sector and industry adjusted to the new realities and capitalized on the opportunities afforded by the 1970s oil boom and attendant wealth creation in parts of the Middle East. In the 1980s Prime Minister Margaret Thatcher presided over a restructuring of the British economy which shifted the emphasis from production to services and finance as the keys to its prosperity. In the Middle East superpower antagonism gave way to unrivalled US influence as the Soviet Union collapsed and Washington became the leading peace-broker on the Arab–Israeli front and dominant arbiter of security arrangements in the Gulf.

BRITISH IMPERIAL PRIORITIES AND THE MIDDLE EAST IN THE HEYDAY OF EMPIRE: 1860–1914

Historians differ as to the exact date when the British Empire reached its peak, but most place it somewhere between 1860 and 1880.[4] Almost all identify the causes of eventual decline as implicit within the strengths that distinguished Britain among its economic and industrial competitors in the late nineteenth century. These competitors, notably the United States, Germany and France, would eventually overtake the British in terms of industrial production and share of global trade. In 1860 Britain accounted for 25 per cent of world trade, more than twice the share of its nearest competitors in Europe,[5] and even in the mid-1890s, Britain clearly led the world's league table of economic powers in terms of annual per capita income, but 'others were catching up'.[6] By the 1870s income from overseas investment had overtaken returns on overseas trade as a primary source of wealth generation for Britain. Thus 'net overseas assets grew from around 7 per cent of the stock of national wealth in 1850 to around 14 per cent in 1870 and then to around 32 per cent in 1913'.[7]

During the late nineteenth century, British foreign policy remained the preserve of the British upper classes and:

> For the Foreign Office it would have been vulgar ... to measure a country's importance by the amount of trade done with it. Nowhere in the world was more important than Europe: Europe *was* the world. The rest was periphery.[8]

In fact, the majority of British trade was with the rest of the world. However, trade was the concern of the middle classes and did not present a problem for foreign policy so long as economic opportunities abounded and the Royal Navy 'ruled the waves'. In any case, prosperity, social mobility and representation in parliament enabled a convergence of interests between the middle and upper classes during the heyday of empire. Successive prime ministers and their governments prevailed in pursuit of what they themselves deemed the national interest.

As recounted by Dahrendorf, Hobsbawm and Bernard Porter, in the mid-nineteenth century the British did not see themselves as empire builders in territorial terms, but rather as the harbingers and beneficiaries of free trade and capital generation through investment worldwide from which all, it was assumed, stood to gain. It was the essence of Victorian liberalism 'to believe that "interests", properly perceived, were not mutually exclusive but were common and complementary, so that what was ideal and what was practical really were the same'.[9] Curiously – and as will be discussed more fully in Chapter 3 – this notion that interests and ideals can be complementary infused New Labour thinking about foreign policy over a century later. As Tony Blair would contend: 'values and interest merge'.

This broadly optimistic worldview endured until it was increasingly challenged by countervailing interests and the resistance of others to British assumptions about the common good. Competition for market predominance, influence and territory, notably in Africa, gathered pace. Meanwhile, British trading interests demanded unimpeded access to communication routes. Among these, the Suez Canal was to acquire a central place in British calculations.

Expansion of Britain's interests in the Middle East

The term 'Middle East' made sense for British traders and imperial civil servants depicting the region midway between Britain and East Asia, or the Far East. That the term has become common parlance and has also entered the Arab lexicon is indicative of the strength of that legacy. Yet the name refers to a region on the way to somewhere else that was originally of far greater intrinsic interest to early British adventurers and merchants.

Britain's Indian Empire emerged in defence of commercial gains made by the East India Company. The British presence and thence colony at the port of Aden (in what is now Yemen) was established by displacing a rival Portuguese presence, in order to set up a coaling station for British steamships making their way to and from India and beyond. The British navy, operating out of India, imposed its presence in the Persian Gulf in the late eighteenth and early nineteenth centuries the better to protect its merchant vessels from piracy (see Chapter 8).[10]

British speculators and investors also made their presence felt in nineteenth-century Persia (modern Iran), principally in search of 'concessions' – favourable or exclusive entitlements in the trading of commodities and access to resources. For their part the Persians hoped to secure British support against Russian encroachment through Central Asia, but discovered that the British gave precedence to the protection of their own imperial objectives; and in 1907 the British signed a convention with the Russians, under which they agreed separate spheres of influence in Persia.[11]

Competition with the French, meanwhile, inclined the British to oppose the Franco-Egyptian idea of a canal linking the Mediterranean to the Red Sea to facilitate marine traffic between Europe and the East. Yet the strategic value of the Suez Canal was not lost on the British. Thus in November 1869, when they learned that the Egyptian Khedive was in financial straits and seeking a buyer for his 44 per cent share in the Canal, Prime Minister Benjamin Disraeli saw an opportunity. Overriding the opposition of both the Foreign Secretary and the Chancellor of the Exchequer, Disraeli quickly acquired the shares for £4 million, advanced by Rothschilds.[12]

This would prove a portentous turning point, since the Suez Canal subsequently became a crucial factor in British decision-making about the protection of British interests in the Middle East. In 1882 Britain took over the government of Egypt, sending troops in at Alexandria. The proximate justification was to save Egypt and thence the route to India in the face of a national uprising opposed to British and French financial involvement there. The decision was also influenced by the growing perception in London that the Ottoman Empire (dubbed 'the Sick Man of Europe' at the time) was crumbling and Britain needed to be positioned for its expected collapse. Britain 'was deeply involved in Egypt in any case, financially rather than politically, but with finance and politics getting harder by the month to keep apart' the die was cast.[13]

As Britain gained political control in Egypt it was also advancing its hold in the Persian Gulf. In a dispatch of 1899 the Viceroy of India, Lord Curzon, described the exclusive treaty arrangements that Britain had established with the Arab sheikhs in the Gulf as a *Pax Britannica*.[14] In 1903 Curzon visited Sharjah and made a speech to the assembled rulers of the 'Trucial States' which was subsequently described by the (British) India Office as follows:

> He [Curzon] had evolved a new and original conception of the Gulf as forming in itself a complete and distinct political entity; this idea, latent rather than expressed, dominated his own policy in the Gulf region and may now be regarded as having entered the domain of established political principle.[15]

The next significant move by the British in the region came in 1914 when the government, following the precedent set by Disraeli's decision to buy shares in the Suez Canal, committed public funds to secure a stake in a private oil company. Having presided over the conversion of the Royal Navy from coal to oil, the First Lord of the Admiralty, Winston Churchill, persuaded the British government (with parliament's backing) to buy a 51 per cent stake in

Anglo-Persian, a relatively small company founded in 1909 and engaged in prospecting, hitherto without much success. Making his case for acquisition of the controlling share in Anglo-Persian and thence an exclusive concession in Persia, Churchill argued that this would help free Britain and the Royal Navy from dependence on the two oil giants of the time, Standard Oil and Royal Dutch/Shell. In giving a boost to the fortunes of Anglo-Persian it was only reasonable, he argued, that the government should share in the rewards and in the process 'obtain the power to regulate developments according to naval and national interests' in the region.[16]

According to Daniel Yergin:

> the decision was driven by the technological imperatives of the Anglo-German naval race. Even as the Germans sought equality, the British navy was committed to maintaining naval supremacy, and oil offered a vital edge in terms of speed and flexibility.... Oil, for the first time, but certainly not the last, had become an instrument of national policy, a strategic commodity second to none.[17]

Thus it was that Britain initially acquired a pivotal position and attendant vital interests in the Middle East in the period leading up to the First World War. With a presence in Egypt and the Persian Gulf, and stakes in both the Suez Canal and Anglo-Persian, the British made preservation of these strategic assets their primary objectives in the subsequent carve-up of the region.

Anglo-Persian, later named Anglo-Iranian, was eventually to take over British Petroleum – a distribution company (originally German) acquired and nationalized by the British government in the Second World War – and adopt the name British Petroleum for the whole enterprise.

BRITAIN'S GRAND DESIGNS IN THE MIDDLE EAST: 1914–47

At the start of the First World War the British Empire was the largest in the world, encompassing nearly a quarter of the earth's population and landmass.[18] Britain owned an estimated £4 billion in overseas investments, compared with less than £5.5 billion owned by France, Germany, Belgium, the Netherlands and the United States combined.[19] Returns on those investments and other invisibles were the country's most important source of wealth generation and it was the world's largest lender.[20] In Hobsbawm's graphic image, 'The threads of the world's web of trading and financial settlements ran through London, and increasingly they had to, because London alone could fill the holes in it.'[21]

Yet in terms of other key indicators Britain had already been overtaken by its main competitors. The United States was ahead in terms of GDP per capita, and, along with Germany, had a greater share of world manufactured output.[22] Britain might have weathered the competition in relative terms had the 1914–18 war not cost so much and obliged Britain to liquidate a large proportion of its assets in the United States, to which it became heavily indebted as well. Investment income did recover after the war, but the slump of 1929 destroyed any illusion of a return to the pre-war heyday.[23] Meeting new public expectations for welfare provision by the state placed new demands on the Exchequer.

Even so, 'despite the signs of economic decline' at home following the war, overseas the British seemed to bounce back and the empire actually expanded after 1914, notably in the Middle East. Britain's 'moment in the Middle East', the phrase coined by Elizabeth Monroe, had dawned.[24]

In anticipation of the collapse of the Ottoman Empire and subsequent division of the spoils, in 1915 an interdepartmental committee was created in London to formulate British objectives in the whole region. This was unprecedented. The result, the *de Bunsen Report*, identified the following goals for British policy:

1. recognition and consolidation of Britain's position in the Gulf;
2. prevention of discrimination against Britain's trade by Turkey, the continuance of trading links with the area and/or acquisition of compensation for discontinuance of such trade;
3. fulfilment of pledges given to the Rulers of Kuwait and Najd and the maintenance of assurances given to other Arab leaders;
4. protection of projects in which Britain held an interest, including oil and water developments;
5. consideration of Mesopotamia as a possible area for Indian colonization;
6. security of communications in the Mediterranean with minimum increase in naval and military expenditure;
7. maintenance of the independence and freedom of worship in religious shrines;
8. a satisfactory solution to the Armenian problem; and
9. a satisfactory solution to the question of Palestine, i.e. one in which Britain would retain control of the Suez approaches.[25]

The goals were, in essence, to consolidate the British position in the region to the exclusion of rival powers and in protection of key interests, which included access to and exploitation of Gulf oil, but also control of the Suez Canal. Britain's acquisition of League of Nations Mandates (see below) in Mesopotamia (redesignated Iraq) and Palestine, linked by the British-created kingdom of Transjordan, provided geographic contiguity between the two areas of British strategic interest and marked the beginning of the contemporary state system in the region.

The British themselves recognized and capitalized on Arab nationalist sentiment to marshal indigenous support against the imperial Ottoman authorities. At the same time London had to maintain cooperation with its European allies. This led it into a tangle of promises and undertakings to different parties concerned with the region.

Imperial machinations[26]

In 1914 Britain declared Egypt a Protectorate and sent an expedition to secure the British position at the head of the Gulf in Mesopotamia. The following year Britain was obliged to clarify its position to its allies and in March 1915 the Constantinople Agreement, the first of a number of secret understandings on the future of the region, was reached with France and Russia. Russia's claim to Constantinople and the Turkish Straits was accepted, while France registered its interest in Syria (broadly defined). Concurrently, the British administration in Cairo was exploring the possibility of sponsoring an Arab revolt against the Ottomans under the leadership of Sherif Hussein of Mecca, the go-between in this endeavour being T.E. Lawrence (Lawrence of Arabia).

The import of the correspondence between Sir Henry McMahon, the British High Commissioner in Egypt, and Sherif Hussein between July 1915 and January 1916 retains significance in the region. The British purpose was to encourage the Sherif to instigate a revolt in return for British recognition and support, albeit subject to various caveats. The key McMahon letter in respect to the British position on both Syria and Palestine was dated 24 October 1915. A separate secret agreement negotiated by Mark Sykes acting for Britain and Georges Picot representing France, in May 1916, made different provisions.

The Sykes-Picot Agreement and the McMahon correspondence coincided on some points, including the expectation that the British would control southern Mesopotamia (now southern Iraq) and that the French would control the coastal zone of what are now Lebanon and Syria. Both documents provided for the independence of the 'Arab peoples' – subject to different but unspecified conditions. That the heartland of the Arabian Peninsula would belong to the Arabs was also taken for granted by both. The documents differed, however, on three main points: (1) according to the Sykes-Picot Agreement only, Britain was to have complete control of a small enclave containing the ports of Haifa and Acre; (2) Hussein was given the impression that Syria would be independent, while France was assured that it would be the sole source of 'advisers and foreign functionaries' – implying

French supervision there; and (3) with regard to Palestine the McMahon letter was unclear,[27] but the Sykes-Picot Agreement was specific – Palestine was to have an international administration, 'the form of which is to be decided upon after consultation with the other allies, and the representatives of the Shareef of Mecca'.[28]

The discrepancies between the McMahon correspondence and the British agreement with the French were revealed in November 1917 when, following the Russian Revolution, the Bolsheviks made public all secret agreements in the Tsar's records. At that point Sherif Hussein was soothed with British assurances, but controversy surrounding these documents was to surface again later.

The Arab Revolt against the Ottoman Empire was launched with British help in June 1916. In March 1917 the British forces in Mesopotamia took Baghdad and the following December Jerusalem was captured. In the meantime, on 2 November 1917 British Foreign Secretary Lord Balfour wrote a letter to Lord Rothschild stating the position of HMG on Jewish nationalist – Zionist – aspirations, which was to become known as the Balfour Declaration.[29] This stated that:

> His Majesty's Government views with favour the establishment in Palestine of a national home for the Jewish people, and will use their best endeavours to facilitate the achievement of this object, it being clearly understood that nothing shall be done which may prejudice the civil and religious rights of existing non-Jewish communities in Palestine, or the rights and political status enjoyed by Jews in any other country.[30]

This document has since become famous as a vital step on the road to the emergence of the state of Israel. It is still mentioned by Arabs keen to remind the British of their role in the genesis of the Israeli–Palestinian conflict.

After the triumphal entry of both regular British forces under General Sir Edmund Allenby and the Sherif's nationalists into Jerusalem (December 1917) and Damascus (October 1918), the French and British issued a statement on 8 November 1918 declaring their objective in the war had been the complete emancipation of the peoples oppressed by the Turks and the establishment of national governments and administrations deriving their authority from the initiative and free choice of the indigenous populations. For immediate practical purposes, however, Allenby turned to the Sykes-Picot agreement as his guide for allocating pressing administrative tasks.

The lines on the map

In the aftermath of war the priority of the victorious powers was to divide the spoils in Europe and it was not until 1920 that an international conference was convened at San Remo to consider competing claims in the Middle East. Final agreement on all the elements was not reached until the mid-1920s.[31] The British Protectorate in Egypt was abolished in 1922 and the country theoretically attained independence, but Britain reserved the right to maintain troops there to defend Egypt and the Suez Canal, to protect foreign minorities and to control Sudan 'until such time as it may be possible by discussion and friendly accommodation on both sides to conclude agreements in regard thereto' between the governments of Britain and Egypt.[32]

In Mesopotamia the former Ottoman provinces of Baghdad, Basra and (after much deliberation and bargaining) Mosul were put together to form the League of Nations Mandate of Iraq, headed by a Hashemite monarch, Faisal, Sherif Hussein's son. The device of the Mandate was a way to avoid the opprobrium of imperial rule and framed the role of the British as trustees until the state was ready for full independence.[33] The same formula was used to legitimize the French position in Syria and that of the British in Palestine. The Mandate for Palestine, confirmed by the Council of the League of Nations on 24 July 1922, made Britain the Mandatory power responsible for putting into effect the Balfour Declaration.[34]

By a decision of the League some months later, at Britain's request the territory east of the river Jordan known as Transjordan was exempted from the provisions in the Mandate relating to the establishment of a national homeland for the Jewish people. Transjordan, the eastern borders of which were drawn on the map by the British, became another Hashemite kingdom under Abdullah I, aided and advised by Britain. Meanwhile, the Hashemite kingdom in the Hijaz was conquered by Abd al-Aziz bin Abd al-Rahman Al Saud (Ibn Saud) of Nejd, and on 25 February 1926, following much wrangling between the British Foreign Office and India Office, Britain recognized Ibn Saud as 'King of the Hijaz and Sultan of Nejd and its Dependencies'.[35] He went on to consolidate these domains into the Kingdom of Saudi Arabia (see also Chapter 8).

The lines on the map were drawn. Not all borders were clear and many were disputed or ignored, especially by tribal herdsmen, traders and nomads. Yet the discovery and exploitation of oil gave the notion of fixed borders and sovereign territory new material and legal significance. Nationalities were defined, including the new Iraqi, Syrian, Lebanese, Jordanian, Palestinian and Saudi national identities. Kurdish aspirations were not thus recognized, while the Jewish people's right to a national homeland gained international, though not Arab, endorsement.

As mentioned above, some British officials and politicians, anticipating the collapse and carve-up of the Ottoman Empire during the First World War, contemplated colonization or at least the creation of protectorates in Mesopotamia and Palestine.[36] But, as Toby Dodge makes clear, that perspective did not tally with the theories of the US President Woodrow Wilson on how international relations should be structured in the aftermath of the war,[37] and Wilson's views reflected a new mood in the region as well as in America. It was the beginning of the end of colonialism as a way of organizing political space, though the British were in no hurry to concede real power to local leaders and elites.[38]

It should be noted that Britain also contributed to the development of regional trade, agriculture, infrastructure and the energy sector. Indeed, at the same time as resisting and suppressing local opposition to their presence, notably in Iraq in the 1920s and Palestine in the 1930s, the British essentially held to the view that theirs was a civilizing mission:

> ... whether it expressed itself as the idea of a superior civilization bring-
> ing a lower or a moribund one to its own level, or of the creation of justice,
> order and prosperity, or the communication of a language and the culture
> expressed in it. Such ideas, of which the logical conclusion was the ultimate
> absorption of the Arabs on a level of equality into a new, unified world,
> were crossed by others: a sense of an unbridgeable difference, of an innate
> superiority which conferred the right to rule ...[39]

In the Arab Gulf states, the British simply continued and reinforced the relationships they had forged earlier. With respect to the Gulf emirates of Kuwait, Bahrain, Qatar and the Trucial States (later the United Arab Emirates), the formal arrangement adopted was that of 'Protected States'. As discussed in Chapter 8, this gave Britain control of their foreign relations, including their dealings with international oil companies, without responsibility for internal governance. The Sultanate of Oman was not included in this designation and was formally fully independent, though the arrangements were similar in practice.

British representation in the Gulf and relations with the Gulf rulers remained the responsibility of the British Government of India from the nineteenth century until Indian independence in 1947. However, in the latter half of this period policy direction on all important matters came from London and all the treaties and engagements entered into by the rulers were with the government in Britain.

Control of Egypt, where the British had embarked on a 'temporary' occupation in 1882 which was to last for 74 years,[40] was always run from London. The British in Bombay, Cairo and London were not always in agreement, however, and they were particularly at odds over how best to recruit Arab help to demolish the Ottoman Empire in the First World War.

With respect to Persia/Iran, in both the First and Second World Wars Britain and Russia/the Soviet Union worked together to prevent it cooperating with Germany, in the latter case actually occupying separate spheres. Britain also monopolized the Iranian energy sector until 1953, through the Anglo-Persian Oil Company and its subsequent incarnations (as detailed in the next section).

In the interwar period, according to Albert Hourani, 'Britain's presence in the Middle East helped to maintain her position as a Mediterranean power and world power.'[41] British bases protected the strategic air and sea routes. In the Second World War colonial and British Commonwealth forces were deployed as part of Britain's global war effort, for which control of communication routes was so vital. By 1940, 'when there was scarcely strength to defend the home islands, the British were able to crack down on nationalists in India, Egypt and Iran and mobilize the Empire for war'.[42] At the end of the war, however, Britain was in no position to 'bounce back' and resume its imperial pursuits as it had after 1918. And the United States, to which Britain was again in debt, was not about to retreat into isolationism again. Over the ensuing years it was to assume a dominant position in most of the areas of the Middle East previously under British suzerainty.

IMPERIAL RETREAT: 1947–71

Even before the Second World War the rise of Nazism in Europe had begun to increase the flow of Jewish migrants to Palestine. During the war Jews from Palestine enlisted in the war effort against the Axis powers, but the British authorities in Palestine made attempts to curb immigration in the face of Arab hostility. By the end of the war this strategy had become untenable, when the full horrors of the Holocaust became manifest and pressure mounted, not least from America, to enable the Jews to find safety and a national home in Palestine.

In 1947, confronted by both Arab and Zionist resistance in Mandatory Palestine, Britain asked the newly formed United Nations to resolve the conflicting claims. The UN came up with the Partition Resolution of 1947 – a 'two-state solution' which would languish for decades until reinvented at the end of the century. The Zionist leadership accepted the UN scheme, but the Arabs rejected it. Lacking the will and the wherewithal to impose the partition by force, the British simply packed up and departed, leaving the Jews and Arabs to fight it out in the war of 1948. British forces did help the Jordanians, however, to hold the line at Jerusalem and maintain the West Bank under Arab control. In what remained of the Palestine Mandate (with the exception of the Gaza Strip) the independent state of Israel emerged victorious and quickly gained recognition from the leading UN powers, but not from the Arabs. The displacement of Palestinians from what became the Israeli state marked the beginning of the Palestinian refugee problem, which endures to this day.

In 1952 members of the Egyptian officer corps toppled the king and with him Britain's informal rule, opening the way for Colonel Gamal Abdel Nasser to assume the presidency of Egypt and leadership of a vibrant Arab nationalist movement across the region. The British perceived this as a challenge to their control of the Suez Canal. When Nasser subsequently nationalized this strategic asset, much depended on the position of the Americans, who were anti-imperialist on principle, but whose main concern was containment of the Soviet Union and its influence.

A nationalist government also came to power in Iran. Faced with the nationalization of Anglo-Persian by Iran's Prime Minister Mohammad Mossadeq in 1953, Britain colluded with the United States to topple him, reinstate the Shah and reverse the nationalization of oil. The price Britain paid was the loss of its monopoly over Iran's energy sector, and Anglo-Persian was absorbed into a new, Anglo-American (and French) consortium.[43] Even so, the deal enabled British Petroleum (BP), as it became, to hold on longer in Iran than the company might have dared hope – until the Shah himself nationalized Iranian oil in the 1970s.[44]

Commenting on the status of the company in the aftermath of the Second World War, Anthony Sampson observed:

> BP had emerged after the war with a far greater importance for Britain, as the cornerstone of Middle East oil. In spite of its remarkable failure to exploit Bahrain and Saudi Arabia, BP had spread out from its original territories in Iran and Iraq down the Persian Gulf to Kuwait, and it was reaping still greater profits for its shareholders, notably the British government. Ever since 1923 it had needed to raise no more outside capital, ploughing back its own profits to build up a world-wide market and fleet of tankers, and after the Second World War it regularly declared dividends of thirty percent.[45]

Comparing it to Shell, whose presence in the region was limited to a minority stake in Iraq, Sampson continued:

> But BP, with its Middle East strongholds, had acquired a confident regimental character of its own, happily combining a sense of public service with the fruits of huge profits, and untroubled by the political outbursts and antitrust crusades that embarrassed the American sisters. Sir William [Fraser, BP chairman as of 1941] referred to civil servants contemptuously as 'the gentlemen in Whitehall'.

Successive chairmen were knighted and then elevated to a seat in the House of Lords. The British government 'were told as little as possible'.[46]

It is probably immaterial to the peoples of the Middle East that BP paid little heed to the Foreign Office in its business dealings there, except when diplomatic intercession was needed.[47] From a regional perspective, Anglo-Persian and thereafter BP was a feature of Western imperialism in the early days and the pursuit of British material self-interest later. The latter characterization lingers on. The nationalization of Iranian and Arab oil turned the tables for the regional oil producers, but the caution, not to say suspicion, with which Arab and Iranian governments do business with the commercial companies in contemporary times derives from this history.

According to the historian of British imperialism Roger Louis, the Anglo-American action in Iran in 1953 was but one episode in a series by which the Americans worked with the British to transform what had been the British Empire into an informal or neo-colonial system of client states and commercial enterprises enlisted in support of the free market and capitalism and against the threat of communism.[48] However, as Louis points out, 'neither side cared to publish the fact, the one to avoid the taint of imperialism, the other to keep the prestige of Empire untarnished' during the transition and 'an imperial coalition was as unnatural for the Americans as it was demeaning for the British'.[49] Perhaps as a result, the British apparently took a while to adapt and they misjudged the Americans when it came to dealing with Nasser.

In what turned out to be the next in a succession of Arab–Israeli wars, in 1956 Britain and France colluded with Israel to try to wrest back control of the Suez Canal from Egypt and topple Nasser's Arab nationalist regime. The British Prime Minister Anthony Eden railed against Nasser as a menace akin to Mussolini, using language that would later be echoed by US President George H. W. Bush, who compared Saddam Hussein to Hitler. In 1956, however, the Americans did not share Eden's analysis or subscribe to old-fashioned imperialism. By forcing a run on the pound sterling, the US administration obliged Britain and hence France and Israel to abandon their Suez adventure. The French were allegedly furious. For their part the British understood the message and resolved to handle the 'special relationship' with the United States more skilfully thereafter.

The dismantling of Britain's imperial role in the Middle East then proceeded apace, though not always smoothly. The British-installed Hashemite regime in Baghdad was ousted in 1958. In 1967 Britain gave up its colony in Aden in the face of fierce local opposition assisted by Nasser. However, in the same year Arab nationalism also suffered a devastating reversal, when an Arab coalition suffered a crushing defeat at the hands of the Israelis, who captured the Sinai Peninsula (and Gaza Strip) from Egypt, the West Bank from Jordan, and the Golan Heights from Syria.

At the end of the 1967 war the UN Security Council passed Resolution 242, which:

> Affirms that the fulfillment of [UN] Charter principles requires the establishment of a just and lasting peace in the Middle East which should include the application of both the following principles:
>
> (i) Withdrawal of Israeli armed forces from territories occupied in the recent conflict;
>
> (ii) Termination of all claims or states of belligerency and respect for and acknowledgement of the sovereignty, territorial integrity and political independence of every State in the area and their right to live in peace within secure and recognized boundaries free from threats or acts of force.[50]

The British Ambassador to the UN, Lord Caradon, was instrumental in drafting the text. Calling, in essence, for 'the exchange of land for peace', this resolution established a formula for resolving the conflict that has been invoked repeatedly since. During the October 1973 war, UN Security Council Resolution 338 called for a ceasefire and immediate implementation of Resolution 242. Thereafter, successive peace initiatives have referenced *both* resolutions as the basis for achieving peace. Disagreement persists, however, on the exact amount of land to be traded.

The Arab defeat in 1967 dealt a devastating blow to the cause of Nasserist-inspired Arab nationalism and relieved some of the pressure on Britain to withdraw from its remaining footholds in the region. Thus Britain's departure from Bahrain, Qatar, the Trucial States and Oman was achieved by agreement rather than force, following the precedent set by Kuwait in 1961. As discussed in Chapter 8, the manner of their departure from the Arab Gulf states in 1971 set the scene for friendly treaty relations, defence cooperation and strong commercial ties to become the new norm. Meanwhile the United States, already entrenched in Iran and Saudi Arabia, became the new power to be reckoned with across the Middle East.

For the duration of the Cold War the Soviet Union competed with the US for influence and backed the Arab republics of Syria and Iraq, as well as the Palestine Liberation Organization (PLO), against the Israelis, while Washington became the latter's principal defender.

Struggling to adjust

On 15 October 1964 a Labour government took office in Britain for the first time in 13 years, pledged to revitalize the ailing domestic economy, champion new technological developments, cut defence expenditure and rationalize foreign commitments. Even though it was the outgoing Conservative government that had presided over the progressive disengagement from empire for over a decade, it was the Labour Party that was ideologically associated with anti-imperialism. A sizeable faction openly advocated a withdrawal from British bases 'east of Suez', including those in the Gulf, as a way to cut the defence budget. The efficacy of the British position in the Arabian Peninsula was also the subject of debate among academics and foreign policy commentators at the time.[51]

However, the government's main preoccupation from 1964 to 1966 was with avoiding a devaluation of the pound sterling (which by 1967 proved unavoidable) and the most likely source of rescue for sterling was assumed to be the United States. After a visit to Washington in 1965 Prime Minister Harold Wilson and Defence Secretary Denis Healey were convinced that President Lyndon Johnson looked to Britain to assist in protection of US and allied Western interests east of Suez by maintaining its military bases there, including in the Gulf.[52] Thereafter Cabinet members concluded that economic necessity and hence preservation of the special relationship required Britain to continue to operate as a global player.

According to Foreign Secretary Michael Stewart, Britain had to adjust to being a 'major power of the second rank' while retaining its 'position of considerable influence all over the world'.[53] This view was echoed in the report of a government-appointed committee on Britain's representational services overseas:

> Britain retains many wide responsibilities and a high degree of world-wide influence. We believe that the British people wish to sustain that influence and share Sir Winston Churchill's view that Britain should not be content to be 'relegated to a tame and minor role in the world'.[54]

With respect to the Middle East, in 1969 Sir William Luce, Britain's Political Resident in the Persian Gulf, identified Gulf oil reserves as of critical importance, given that Britain and Western Europe obtained over half their supplies from there.[55] He also saw it as essential that Britain resist any move by the Soviet Union to supplant its predominance in the Gulf. However, whatever fond hopes the British cherished of retaining a presence in the Gulf and beyond, by 1969 the need to economize had become irrefutable and by 1971 Britain's withdrawal from east of Suez was under way (see Chapter 8).

BRITAIN ADJUSTS AS AMERICA ASSUMES THE LEAD: 1971–97

The timing of this withdrawal was problematic for the Americans, for whom Britain's naval and military presence in the Gulf had served as a deterrent to Soviet expansion. Preoccupied as they were in Vietnam in the early 1970s, the Americans opted for a strategy of building up the Shah's armed forces to make him their surrogate policeman in the Persian Gulf.[56] The Shah was thereafter permitted to purchase almost any arms he sought from the United States. Meanwhile, as they departed, the British allowed Tehran to assert control over three islands in the Lower Gulf (Abu Musa and the Greater and Lesser Tunbs) at the expense of the UAE – thereby creating an enduring source of contention between the Emirates and Britain as well as with Iran.[57] Yet in neither respect would the British receive any lasting thanks from the Iranians, and subsequent US support for the Shah contributed to his downfall in 1979.

In the years preceding his fall, the Shah would both rely on British advice and harbour suspicions of British perfidy.[58] As Sir Anthony Parsons, the British ambassador to Iran in the 1970s, has recounted, the Shah would frequently summon both him and the US ambassador as the storm clouds gathered around his regime. Parsons found this irksome, since he was trying to keep out of politics and concentrate on trade at the time. Inevitably, both as confidants of the Shah (since 1953) and as beneficiaries of Iran's wealth, the British did not endear themselves to the revolutionaries who overthrew the regime (see Chapter 6).

Throughout the 1970s successive British governments struggled with economic difficulties, compounded by the oil crisis that followed resort to 'the oil weapon' by Arab energy producers in the October 1973 Arab–Israeli war. Arab producers and Iran also nationalized their industries in the 1970s, at the expense of oil majors BP and Shell, among others, and prices rose dramatically. In this context it became imperative for British companies to try to exploit their access to Gulf markets. In the mid-1970s Iran was Britain's largest export market in the Middle East and thence a valued source of foreign exchange. On the Arab side of the Gulf British companies joined others in the new rush for contracts. Yet Britain's privileged access was much reduced after its withdrawal in 1971, and only those companies with global reach and strategies to match could thrive in the competition for Gulf business (see Chapter 8).

Britain resurfaces

By the mid-1980s Britain was at last poised for economic revival. Since coming to power at the beginning of the decade, the Conservatives under Margaret Thatcher had introduced sweeping privatization, deregulation and restructuring measures, envisaging that these would lead to an increase in both British exports and influence abroad.[59] Among the state-owned companies sold off under Thatcher were BP, British Gas, British Aerospace and British Airways. While Britain's industrial sector contracted as a result of the Thatcher policies, those enterprises that survived performed more efficiently, new ones emerged and the financial and services sector began to flourish.

Meanwhile, victory in the Falklands War in 1982 gave a fillip to British standing abroad and contributed to Thatcher's resounding election triumph in 1983. The Conservative Party's campaign slogan that year was to 'put the Great back in Great Britain' – through economic revitalization and a more assertive posture abroad. Once returned to power, the government declared its intention to enhance UK defence; play an active part in the Atlantic alliance; meet British commitments to the European Community (of which Britain had become a member in the 1970s), and to its remaining dependencies; support the Commonwealth; and take a constructive role in the UN.[60]

The defence budget was increased. However, expenditure on the diplomatic service was reduced. By 1985 expenditure on the Foreign and Commonwealth Office (FCO) had been cut by 9.4 per cent over a seven-year period, by running down staff levels by 17 per cent and other cost-cutting measures.[61] In the process commercial work became the most well-funded diplomatic function. The progressive rise in the budget for the armed forces in real terms over the same period gave Britain the highest total and per capita defence expenditure of all the European members of NATO,[62] though the Ministry of Defence still faced problems meeting its full commitments.[63]

Around 95 per cent of the defence budget was devoted to security within the NATO area and the remainder was designated for the protection of trade routes and promoting stability in the world beyond.[64] Safeguarding British (and Western) interests in the Persian Gulf was one of the stated objectives of the government's out-of-NATO-area strategy, and the traditional concern with preventing Soviet expansion in the region intensified after 1979,[65] the year of both the Iranian Revolution and the Soviet invasion of Afghanistan. The combined effect was to prompt the United States to prepare to take the lead in Gulf security. Britain's role and influence thereafter could not and did not come close to that of the United States, but in diplomatic terms at least, British policies remained distinctive.

When the Iran–Iraq war began in 1980 the US administration pushed forward its plans for a Rapid Reaction Force for deployment to the Gulf at short notice. The British government acknowledged simply that it was in consultation with Washington on the possibility of British cooperation in the endeavour.[66] Responding to an escalation in the conflict in 1985, the British Foreign Office Minister Richard Luce said the government was coordinating with other European Community members to urge the protagonists to respond to UN calls for an end to attacks on civilian areas and the need for 'a just and honourable settlement'.[67]

Britain's official stance in the war was one of neutrality. Despite claiming it would not sell any offensive weapons to either side, the government did not condemn Iraq unequivocally for invading Iran in the first place and secretly supplied arms to Baghdad.[68] British diplomatic relations with Iraq continued throughout the war and high-level ministerial visits were exchanged in 1985.[69] Britain also maintained trade links and diplomatic relations with Iran, though only through an interest section at the Swedish Embassy in Tehran.

With respect to the broader region in the 1980s, Foreign Secretary Douglas Hurd linked the situation in the Gulf to that on the Arab–Israeli front:

> Our friends in the Gulf have always made it clear that the Palestine issue is enormously important to them, and that it is difficult for them to be counted as friends of the West so long as it appears that the West is simply supporting Israel. That's one reason why we Europeans, in the Venice Declaration last year [1980], tried to take an even-handed line and tried to advance matters.[70]

The Venice Declaration was a milestone for the EC, both as an agreed position on an important foreign policy issue and in terms of breaking new ground by recognizing the Palestinian right to self-determination and calling for the involvement of the PLO in negotiations. However, at the time it was denigrated by Washington, and Israel dismissed it out of hand.

In 1985 Britain took a unilateral initiative in trying to push forward dialogue. Following a visit to Egypt and Jordan by Margaret Thatcher, arrangements were made for a joint Jordanian–Palestinian delegation to travel to London to discuss a peace settlement on the basis of UN Security Council Resolutions 242 and 338 (see above). In the event, discussions were aborted when the Palestinian delegates announced on their arrival that they were not ready to endorse a statement which contained explicit reference to Israel's right to exist within secure and recognized borders.[71]

On the collapse of this initiative the government simply reverted to affirming its support for a settlement which recognized both Israel's right to exist and the Palestinian right to self-determination, along the lines of the Venice Declaration. This stance, together with Britain's support for EC and UN initiatives to end the Iran–Iraq war, spelled support for peaceful resolution of the two main conflicts in the Middle East, but also incapacity to achieve either without allies.

The way the Foreign Office defined British interests in the Middle East in the 1980s may be summarized as follows:[72]

1. maintenance of a stable and predictable flow of oil supplies from the region onto the world market;
2. preservation of prosperity in and access to lucrative commercial markets;
3. maintenance of as much stability and predictability as possible in world financial markets, to which Gulf surplus wealth was key;
4. protection of UK citizens and investments in the region;
5. enhancement of political stability;
6. containment and resolution of armed conflict;
7. prevention of incidents likely to produce friction between the UK and the US, and between the UK and other members of the EC;
8. blockage of Soviet intervention in the area; and
9. fulfilment of undertakings to friends and allies in the area.

Clearly Britain had found a new place in the world – within the Western alliance but with its own independent views and interests, some of them at odds with those of Washington.[73] As of Britain's withdrawal in 1971, the United States had become more directly engaged in Gulf security, but encountered competition for arms sales and other contracts from its European allies, including the British (see Chapter 8).

All the Western allies were also interested in access to Gulf oil, though as Britain had become a producer itself by the 1980s, the nature of its concerns had shifted. For domestic consumption, the UK relied on Gulf imports only for the kind of crude that could not be obtained in the North Sea.[74] However, as a producer it had a new stake in the stability and buoyancy of the oil market worldwide. Also, since British companies traded in Gulf oil, there was concern for the security of their operations.

Fears about Gulf security in the 1980s were twofold, focused on Soviet expansionism and spillover from the Iran–Iraq war, including attacks on Gulf shipping. When Kuwait sought protection by asking first the Americans and then the Soviets to allow it to reflag its oil tankers under their national colours, Washington obliged.[75] Russian withdrawal from Afghanistan and the end of the Iran–Iraq war then produced an interval of relative calm before Saddam Hussein invaded Kuwait and the United States intervened directly to lead the multinational coalition that liberated Kuwait in 1991.

From war to 'containment' in the Gulf

The Americans, who assembled and led the coalition that reversed the Iraqi occupation of Kuwait, dubbed the operation Desert Storm. At its height their commitment on land, at sea and in the air involved 500,000 US personnel in the area, a number equal to all the other coalition forces combined. The weight and sophistication of their armoury outclassed all the others. Victory on the battlefield was achieved with speed and minimal coalition casualties. From an American viewpoint, the Iraqis were so comprehensively thrashed that Saddam Hussein should not have been able to survive the humiliation. Yet he did and so post-war policy focused on disarming and containing Iraq – through a process that Saddam Hussein was also not expected to survive politically.

The British contribution to Desert Storm was small by comparison with that of the Americans, but it was the largest British commitment of forces overseas since the Second World War and second only to the Americans in the coalition.[76] The size of the British deployment was calculated to entitle British field commanders to a voice in the design of the battle plan.[77] The French came third in the line-up, but they did not operate so closely with the American forces as the British. Arab contingents were valued more for their political significance than military contributions and in any case declined to enter Iraqi territory when action was launched.

At the end of the war the US and coalition force presence was rapidly drawn down. However, in 1991–2 the United States, Britain and France instituted no-fly zones to constrain Iraqi forces from pursuing the Kurds in the north or approaching the Kuwaiti border in the south.[78] With allied assistance the Kurds were then able to establish an autonomous area in the north, but the no-fly zone in the south had less value to the predominantly Shia population there, who suffered terrible reprisals for their attempted uprising against the Iraqi regime in the immediate aftermath of Desert Storm.

Eventually the French were to end their participation in the enforcement of the no-fly zones, but the British continued to operate alongside the Americans, essentially in the name of containment of the Iraqi regime. Turkey and Saudi Arabia provided vital basing facilities for their air forces. A number of coalition members contributed to naval operations in the Persian Gulf, though the United States took the lead in intercepting suspect cargoes there, with a view to enforcing the sanctions regime that dated from Iraq's invasion of Kuwait and endured under the terms of the ceasefire. Britain also maintained a naval presence after the war, the Armilla patrol, which had been traversing the sea lanes, making port visits and conducting exercises in the Indian Ocean since the 1980s.

UN Security Council Resolution 687 of 1991 required Iraq to cooperate in the identification and destruction of its chemical, biological and nuclear weapons programmes and long-range delivery systems. Only when inspectors with the UN Special Commission (UNSCOM) to oversee the dismantling of Iraq's weapons of mass destruction (WMD) programmes pronounced

Britain and the Middle East in the 9/11 Era

themselves satisfied that this had been accomplished would the sanctions be lifted. Yet UNSCOM negotiations with the Iraqi government over access to certain sites proved tortuous and Iraq resisted other UN demands, including the return of Kuwaiti prisoners of war, and challenged the no-fly zones as an infringement of its sovereignty.[79] Initially the French joined the US and the British in the enforcement of these zones. In January 1993, for example, they bombed Iraqi surface-to-air missile (SAM) and command installations in Amarah, Najaf, Samawah and Tallil in the southern no-fly zone, killing several Iraqis in the process, and the United States launched a cruise missile attack on a factory and the Rashid Hotel in Baghdad.[80]

On this occasion the Iraqis backed off and declared a ceasefire, but continued on a course of resistance or minimal compliance with UN and US demands. As was discovered years later, the Iraqis themselves destroyed much of their own WMD arsenal without revealing or recording this for the benefit of UNSCOM.[81] Why they would do this and yet fail to claim their entitlements for full disclosure under Resolution 687 has been the subject of much speculation. The culture of secrecy and fear that permeated the regime may be part of the explanation. Distrust of UN and more particularly US motives also influenced Iraqi calculations (see Chapters 5 and 6). Equally, it appears that both at home and in the region, the regime could not be seen to cave in to foreign pressure or relinquish the means for its own defence.[82]

Whatever the explanations, a pattern was established whereby the Iraqis offered only minimal cooperation with UNSCOM, and the promise of an end to sanctions was either insufficient or insufficiently convincing to change their attitude. For their part, the United States and Britain came to rely on either the threat or the use of air strikes as a means of applying pressure on Baghdad, even when they did not have unequivocal UN Security Council backing for such measures.[83]

After the Clinton administration entered the White House in 1993 differences began to develop between the United States and other members of the Security Council, with the British trying to steer a path that would maintain cohesion. Washington held to the view that sanctions and containment would have to continue so long as Saddam Hussein and his regime remained in power.[84] In the background, the Central Intelligence Agency (CIA) set about trying to instigate a *coup d'état*, without success, and different US agencies adopted rival Iraqi opposition groups as clients to spearhead regime change in Baghdad.[85]

The government of British Prime Minister John Major shared the US distrust of Saddam Hussein, but held to the view that full compliance with UN demands was Baghdad's only way to relieve the burden of comprehensive

26

sanctions. Privately officials would argue that full compliance would very likely bring about the collapse of the Iraqi regime, but intimated that would not be unwelcome. So British diplomacy focused on keeping the promise of an end to sanctions credible in the face of Washington's outright rejection of any reprieve for Saddam Hussein, whatever he did (see Chapter 5). The French tended to the view that, since full Iraqi compliance was unlikely, to make progress at all, sanctions should be calibrated to recognize UNSCOM's achievements.

By early 1995 it appeared that the French position was gaining ground and some British officials began to voice concerns that the sanctions regime constituted a policy of diminishing returns. However, the situation did not remain static. In August 1995 Saddam's son-in-law, Hussein Kamel, defected to Jordan (along with his brother-in-law and their respective wives). Debriefed by the CIA and UNSCOM, Hussein Kamel revealed that Iraq had hitherto concealed much more extensive capabilities than had been thought.[86] Unmasked, Saddam Hussein handed over to UNSCOM a mass of data that confirmed the extent to which Iraq had been deceiving the inspectors. Outraged and alarmed at the way they had been duped, the Americans became more implacable and the British became more resolute about maintaining controls on Baghdad.[87] For its part UNSCOM went to work to put the newly disclosed facilities out of operation.

Thus the die was cast in favour of a policy of containment, in the name of regional security, for as long as Saddam's regime remained in place. Yet the British position rested on the conviction that UN inspections and the introduction of long-term monitoring arrangements were key to the success of the containment policy. With this in mind, Britain became the most energetic of the Permanent Five (P5) members of the UN Security Council in trying to find a formula that would maintain UN cohesion, or at least prevent France and Russia from breaking ranks. Renewed Iraqi obstruction of UNSCOM operations in 1997–8 (see Chapter 5) helped keep them on board, but both professed to be unconvinced that continuing confrontation provided a viable long-term approach.

Of equal concern to the British was the mounting criticism across the region and at home at the humanitarian toll on ordinary Iraqis. It was all very well to blame the regime for failing to put the needs of the population before its own, but the policy was seen to be backfiring. The instrument devised to address this problem, the so called oil-for-food deal, was initially rejected by the Iraqis, and even when accepted in 1996, the scheme was imperfect at best, increasingly open to abuse[88] and at worst counterproductive.[89]

If ever the sanctions policy had been expected to induce Iraqis to overthrow their regime, by 1997 it was seen to be a failure in this respect also.

What potential architect of a *coup d'état* could possibly want to take over the helm in a country under siege, impoverished, saddled with debts and reparation demands and in the process of enforced disarmament?[90] With encouragement from the UK officials, in March 1997 US Secretary of State Madeleine Albright was induced to promise economic and other assistance to a post-Saddam regime.[91] Initially, as it came to power in May 1997, Blair's government hoped to work with Washington to make the sanctions policy work better. Chapter 5 picks up the story.

The scene is set

The purpose of the foregoing overview is to set the scene for what follows. Neither the significance of the changes wrought by New Labour at the turn of the century nor the impact of 9/11 on Britain and the Middle East can be understood without reference to the historical context.

The above account shows that Britain's objectives and relative influence evolved over time in accordance with its changing global standing, adjustment to decline and recognition of US ascendancy. Having played the central role in the formation of the contemporary state system in the Middle East, Britain was also instrumental in the subsequent transition to US hegemony. By the time New Labour came to power, even though Britain's imperial moment in the Middle East had passed, it was still very much engaged in regional politics and trade, albeit in the shadow of the Americans.

As became apparent, the United States was the unchallenged architect of Gulf security, including 'Dual Containment' of both Iraq and Iran, and defence agreements with the Arab Gulf states (see Chapter 8). On the containment of Iraq, the British cooperated closely with Washington, but they preferred to go their own way on dealings with Iran, in cooperation with other Europeans (see Chapter 6).

On the Arab–Israeli front, the Americans also took the lead in managing peace negotiations. Following the liberation of Kuwait, the United States (and Russia – the Soviet Union having virtually collapsed) convened the Madrid Peace Conference of November 1991, which succeeded in bringing both the Israelis and representatives of all its Arab neighbours to the table. In the ensuing negotiations Britain was only a minor player, having to content itself with a supportive role and contributing to collective EU involvement.

Thanks to a Norwegian initiative, a groundbreaking agreement between the PLO and Israel to work for peace produced the Oslo Declaration, signed on the White House lawn in 1993. Thereafter the administration of President Bill Clinton assumed the lead in the resulting 'Oslo Process', and acted as mediator in Israeli–Syrian negotiations. The challenge embraced by the first

Blair government, therefore, was to identify a distinctive contribution for Britain to make to the peace process, as is described in Chapter 4.

On this and other issues, the New Labour government initially acted as though Britain had succeeded in putting the past behind it and was ready and able to assume a new role on the global and regional stage. As will be seen, however, it was not so easy to escape the legacies of history.

2

New Labour Worldview and the Middle East

'Foreign policy should not be seen as some self-contained part of government in a box marked "abroad" or "foreigners". It should complement and reflect our domestic goals. It should be part of our mission of national renewal.' – Tony Blair (1997)[1]

New Labour's sweeping election victory of May 1997 gave expression to a renewed sense of optimism in Britain, and this vibrant new force in British politics was well suited to the challenges of globalization. It is therefore not surprising that the new government's foreign policy, including towards the Middle East, should register a change from the patterns and precedents familiar to those in the region from their experience of Britain hitherto.

Before turning to the content of this policy, there are several points to make about Britain's relative standing in the world and the New Labour worldview, which produced significant changes in the way policy was made and implemented. As will be seen in this and the next chapter, the content of New Labour policy became entwined with its presentation and the process by which it was carried out. This was deliberate because the political leadership, along with those to whom it turned for advice and inspiration, was wedded to the idea that presentation, and hence image, were indispensable to effective policy-making and implementation.

BRITAIN'S PLACE IN THE POST-COLD WAR WORLD

For Britain in the late 1990s the imperial era was history and the travails of the Cold War were also seen as a thing of the past. The big issues affecting foreign policy were globalization, the role of the United States as the sole remaining superpower, the evolution and expansion of the EU, the transatlantic alliance (including the future of NATO), the role of the United Nations and the changing nature of threats to security within and between states.

Britain's place was firmly in the Western camp or alliance, and it ranked among the leading economies in the EU and founding members of NATO.

Its seat on the UN Security Council as one of the Five Permanent Members and its nuclear capability also afforded Britain a status ahead of other European countries (with the exception of France). The Commonwealth gave Britain a place in the network of its former colonies seemingly without the baggage of imperial responsibilities. In the global economic stakes, Britain was among the largest five, with commensurate clout in the top economic clubs of the G8, Organization for Economic Cooperation and Development (OECD), World Trade Organization (WTO), World Bank and International Monetary Fund (IMF). In 1998 it was the largest overseas investor after the United States and the recipient of significant flows of foreign direct investment (FDI).

With respect to energy resources, however, Britain was near a turning point. Its North Sea oil production peaked in 1999 at 2.8 million barrels per day and thereafter fell gradually as reserves depleted. In the mid-1980s British oil exports had been a significant earner for the economy, accounting for around 20 per cent of total exports and yielding a record £1.5 billion in May 1985.[2] Returns slid thereafter as prices also dropped. Price increases in the late 1990s gave a temporary reprieve but by May 2004 returns on exports were down to £206m. In June 2004 the line was crossed and Britain became a net oil importer again. By 2005 it had also become a net importer of natural gas.

In his book about British foreign policy-making John Coles, former Permanent Secretary at the Foreign Office, sought to characterize Britain's overall status in the global system at the end of the twentieth century. He thought the concept of 'middle power' did not suffice 'because that ground was already occupied by Australia and other similar countries' and he settled instead for the term 'a major European power with global interests and responsibilities'. The inclusion of responsibilities in his definition derived, he said, 'primarily but not exclusively from our permanent membership of the UN Security Council and membership of the G8 and our obligations towards our remaining overseas territories'.[3]

The writer Ferdinand Mount, editor of the *Times Literary Supplement* from 1991 to 2002, ventured the view that:

> Perhaps the British have at last found an answer to Dean Acheson's jibe that they had lost an empire but had not found a role. Perhaps all that has happened is that they have rediscovered the role they had before: that of a coarse, freebooting people whose licentiousness is controlled by a certain patriotic self-discipline.[4]

Mount postulated that the requirements of running an empire, in which the colonized vastly outnumbered the colonizers, required of the latter a level of discipline, self-denial and belief in the enterprise that resulted in the 'stiff upper lip' characteristic of the civil servant, and a taboo on displays of emotion. It took a while, he sensed, to throw this off after the end of empire, especially since initially the government continued to be responsible for running so many state industries and services in the public interest.

Anthony Sampson, who wrote several studies of the British political system in his *Anatomy of Britain* series starting in the early 1960s, revisited this subject in his last major work in 2004. Here he echoed Mount's view that Britain had retrieved its pre-imperial role as 'an international trading country competing with the world' and the English in particular had reverted 'to the much older English qualities of pragmatism and tolerance'.[5] The 'stifling post-imperial malaise' no longer stultified the spirit of enterprise and the country had become the richer for its embrace of immigrants from all over the world, he claimed.

Both Mount and Sampson credited New Labour with carrying forward a process begun by Margaret Thatcher. When Tony Blair and his party came to power they certainly enjoyed an enthusiastic welcome from an electorate that had become disillusioned with the tired unimaginative style of the last Conservative government, tarnished by accusations of sleaze and scandal. The accompanying loss of respect or esteem for politicians would resurface under New Labour – though only after a longer than usual 'honeymoon' for the incoming government. Perhaps irreverence among the electorate was an inevitable facet of the new or rediscovered Britain. In any case some commentators were worried by the consequences. Peregrine Worsthorne, the former editor of the *Sunday Telegraph*, claims he could have accepted the passing of the traditional British upper class – had 'aristocratic deference' been replaced with 'civic republicanism'. Instead, he sensed the arrival of 'egalitarian hypocrisy at the top and proletarian rancour at the bottom'.[6] Nick Cohen, a columnist for the *Observer* and the *New Statesman*, made a scathing attack on the rise of a new business and professional elite under the auspices of New Labour.[7] He argued that wealth accumulation had become the defining characteristic of that elite, rather than merit judged by the criteria of educational qualifications, community service or entrepreneurial skills.

Embracing globalization

Cohen also argued that New Labour simultaneously embraced and defined the phenomenon of globalization in an interactive and self-justificatory way. The age of the service economy – in which 'knowledge workers' could move effortlessly through serial career changes, equipped with laptop and ubiquitous mobile phone – was made to look like a panacea. Talent was to be liberated from the constraints of the old industrial age, in which protectionism and trade union obstructionism prevented individuals from realizing their potential and exercising choice. Cohen's sarcasm was biting, yet he provided a reminder of how the arrival of New Labour in government was celebrated among sympathetic commentators and academics as the embodiment of new thinking about government and society in keeping with the challenges of globalization.

On both the international and the domestic front this meant economic liberalization, while always working for 'a level playing field'. According to the Confederation of British Industry (CBI) in July 2000:

> UK business sees it as necessary to: improve the predictability of the environment in which companies operate; resist protectionism; and ensure that public opinion fully understands and supports open, liberalised markets and further liberalisation of trade and investment.[8]

The CBI argued that Britain should not only capitalize on the opportunities afforded by globalization, but work through the relevant international bodies, starting with the WTO, to refine and reform the rules by which all countries could enjoy the benefits of free trade.

This meant that Britain was not only predisposed to use its membership of the WTO, G8 and OECD to promote its interests, it was now also self-consciously a global player. In the late 1990s only America outranked Britain in the size of its overseas investments. Sampson's characterization of Britain as 'an international trading country competing with the world' seemed to be most apt. As such, the British outlook was bound to contrast with that of the United States, whose domestic economy was so big as to make it less dependent on the rest of the world. Nonetheless, the United States championed the values of free trade and the British followed its example on many facets of domestic economic policy.

The 'special relationship'

Turning specifically to Britain's relationship with the United States as a pivotal constant in its foreign policy, the economic dimension was clearly very important. At the end of the twentieth century Britain was among the biggest foreign investors in the US economy, rivalled only by Canada and Japan, until China outranked them all. The United States was Britain's largest export market, taking around £30 billion worth of British goods in 2001. In the same year, over 25 per cent of UK exports of services were generated in America.[9] What happened to the US economy and currency was of vital interest to the United Kingdom. US investment in Britain was no small consideration either, especially in the generation of jobs.

One of the attractions of Britain for English-speaking foreign investors was as a point of access to the EU market. Also, some of Britain's largest companies such as BP and BAE Systems, through mergers and acquisitions, had acquired sizeable assets, operations and partnerships in both the United States and Europe, to the point where BP at least could no longer be described as a purely British company.

As the unrivalled superpower in the 1990s, the United States had so much leverage in all the international arenas, such as the WTO, G8 and World Bank, that Britain's interests were better served by coordination rather than confrontation whenever possible. The same logic applied in other organizations, notably the UN Security Council and NATO. Pending establishment of an independent European defence capability – the subject of some contention with the United States – the possibilities for collective military action involving Britain were effectively bound to be subject to US influence if not participation.[10] Britain's capacity to undertake military operations overseas unilaterally was already very limited. Furthermore, as identified by Admiral Sir Michael Boyce, the Chief of Defence Staff, in December 2001, the British armed forces had capabilities in war-fighting, peacekeeping, counter-terrorism and 'nation-building' but had to make strategic choices to avoid spreading their resources too thinly and 'thus dissipating their effect'.[11] Thereafter, worries about 'overstretch' became a constant refrain among senior military figures.

In the 1990s Britain was perhaps the only one of America's closest allies with the ability to communicate and hence integrate with it in operations involving the most sophisticated US communications technology. Yet this status points to a key consideration in the so-called 'special relationship'. According to Douglas Hurd, the former Conservative Foreign Secretary, all British ministers and officials must remind themselves repeatedly that the special relationship depends on the usefulness of the United Kingdom to the United States.[12]

The United States worked against Britain's efforts to preserve its imperial possessions after the Second World War, and Washington humiliated the British over the Suez débâcle in 1956 (see Chapter 1). Thereafter fear of exclusion became a factor in Britain's dealings with the United States on intelligence-gathering. The intelligence-sharing aspect of the relationship (UKUSA – the UK–US signals intelligence alliance) was considered of fundamental significance by those with knowledge of what is involved (who were not willing to be cited by name). It seems the sheer volume and reach of signals intelligence which the United States is capable of gathering and sifting are without parallel; for Britain to be deprived of access to this would be like suddenly having to operate in semi-darkness.

To maintain its privileged access (to which only the Australians and Canadians have come close over the years), the British have apparently sought endlessly to make themselves useful in specific ways. As a *Financial Times* investigation claimed, this has resulted in Britain focusing on areas not otherwise central to its interests, such as North Korea.[13] But in that connection:

> A secret operation by MI6 was instrumental in gathering information to unravel a nuclear supply network run by Abdul-Qadeer Khan, a Pakistani scientist, which supplied Libya, North Korea and Iran and offered technology to other countries.[14]

These findings apparently were critical in persuading Libya to abandon its programmes for non-conventional weapons in 2003 (see Chapter 6).

In some settings, the British may even have had an edge over their US counterparts in human intelligence. Yet, as will be discussed, after the UN weapons inspectors left Iraq in 1998, Britain had little better access to intelligence there than the United States. Moreover, the fact that they were not specifically focusing on Iraq until it rose to the top of the policy agenda in Britain in 2002 illustrates how intelligence-gathering can be influenced by politics, and pressures to find material may influence the results.

Britain's handling of the special relationship has been much analysed in the light of its role in the invasion of Iraq in 2003. Lord Hurd believed that Prime Minister Tony Blair took the logical course after 9/11 in committing Britain to stand 'shoulder to shoulder' with its ally, since that gave him some prospect of tempering the actions of a wounded giant that might otherwise have lashed out dangerously. However, considering what transpired, both Hurd and Sir Malcolm Rifkind, another former Conservative Foreign Secretary, concluded that Blair could have been bolder in tempering Washington's stance on Iraq.[15]

Others, including American commentators, have been puzzled that Blair did not drive a harder bargain – given the political and other costs of his support for Washington.[16] Yet, as discussed in Chapter 5, that may be to misunderstand Blair's personal position on Iraq. Also, Blair's stance over both 9/11 and Iraq won him unprecedented appreciation as an ally and political orator in Washington and more broadly among the US public.[17] That said, even a prime minister who can impress the US Congress and 'bond' with two US presidents in succession may still lack decisive influence with a US administration fraught by feuds between different senior figures and departments.

In the run-up to the Iraq war British officials in both the Foreign Office and Ministry of Defence found themselves caught up in these turf wars.

Veteran Middle East hands at the US State Department were broadly in agreement with their British counterparts and were not above seeking their assistance in trying to temper the determination for war apparent among civilians working for Defense Secretary Donald Rumsfeld and Vice President Dick Cheney.[18] Personality clashes also had a bearing on diplomacy at the United Nations (see Chapter 5).

Bridging the Atlantic

In his biography of Tony Blair, Philip Stephens, the Associate Editor of the *Financial Times*, discussed the friction that developed between the British Prime Minister and French President Jacques Chirac. Blair told Stephens that Chirac saw the transatlantic row over Iraq as an opportunity to curb Blair's influence in Europe, which had threatened to undermine his own. By all accounts Blair never intended the special relationship to work to the detriment of Britain's relationship with Europe. On the contrary, the plan was apparently for Britain to be the bridge or pivot (Blair's term) in the transatlantic alliance.[19]

Given the stakes – for the British economy, Britain's place and influence in the running and development of the EU, and relations with America – Blair's government could not but seek maximum leverage in decision-making about the expansion and constitution of Europe. The so-called Eurosceptics in Britain would claim that Europe was becoming a bureaucratic superstate to which members would have to relinquish ever more sovereignty. The onus on the British government, therefore, was to counter this charge by exercising leverage in Europe while at the same time demonstrating that other interests were served, not compromised.[20] As long as the United States was seen to value Britain in part for its role in Europe, the path for Britain was clear, if complex. However, once a transatlantic rift opened up, as it did over Iraq, Britain's position became infinitely more difficult.

Europeans grew progressively more wary of US power and especially the unilateralist tendencies of the Bush administration. By 2002 the United States was reportedly less enthusiastic than it had been about a united Europe, if not actually hostile.[21] European attitudes towards Britain changed as a result of its stance on Iraq. While the President of the EU Commission, Romano Prodi, expressed appreciation for British 'pragmatism, common sense, a tradition of administrative excellence and a long expertise in international relations', he summed up the suspicion and confusion in Europe over Britain's position thus: 'Britain's attitude to Europe contrasts with many of its EU partners. It is a source of fascination, perplexity and sometimes frustration for your friends elsewhere in Europe.'[22]

The whole drama of the Iraq crisis and rift in transatlantic relations made a palpable impact on British public opinion too. An opinion poll conducted in April 2003 found that 73 per cent of respondents deemed the United States to be Britain's most reliable ally and 55 per cent saw France as its least reliable ally.[23] That said, the public was almost evenly divided over Britain's decision to support the United States in Iraq, with 43 per cent agreeing that Britain 'just does what the US tells it to do', and 44 per cent disagreeing. Approval for the United States was markedly down from findings the previous year, and opposition to joining the euro area had increased.

NEW LABOUR: NEW VISION

As soon as he took office in May 1997, Foreign Secretary Robin Cook issued a mission statement – itself new terminology more familiar in the business community, which declared that policy would be conducted in pursuit of four 'benefits', namely: security, prosperity, quality of life and mutual respect.[24] The pursuit of security was to involve promoting international arms control initiatives. Prosperity meant trade promotion. Protecting the quality of life meant combating illegal drugs, crime and terrorism as well as tackling environmental degradation and global warming. Mutual respect was to be built on defending and advocating human rights, civil liberties and democracy.

The strategic aims of foreign policy in New Labour's first term were to:

- make the United Kingdom a leading player in Europe;
- strengthen the Commonwealth; and
- secure reform for a more effective UN.

According to Cook 'the Labour Government was also committed to fostering a people's democracy to increase respect, understanding and goodwill for Britain among nations as well as governments'.[25] The vehicles for achieving this goal were to include the British Council and the BBC World Service. The role of the Department for International Development (DFID) – which soon assumed an importance to rival that of the FCO – was to concentrate on poverty alleviation and thence 'good governance'.

These objectives reflected both the 'ethical dimension' that Cook said he intended to give to British foreign policy and the notion that Britain's influence could be enhanced through a 'rebranding' exercise to better represent it as 'a force for good' in the world, as discussed in Chapter 3. The media reacted by focusing specifically on the notion of 'an ethical foreign policy', and hounded the Foreign Secretary thereafter when policy delivery fell short of this ideal.[26]

These and other criticisms of the Foreign Secretary undermined his reputation and detracted from his foreign policy achievements, including in the Middle East. The personal attacks might not have been so vicious had Cook not already set himself up to deliver a more ethical approach. His intention was that Britain should become a more self-conscious defender of human rights and would not sell arms to governments with a poor record in this respect. That objective rebounded on him when he was unable to prevent the sale of British arms to various regimes accused of human rights abuses, among them Saudi Arabia, China, Kenya, Zimbabwe and Indonesia. The problem started in summer 1997 when human rights groups lobbied against the shipment of Hawk jets, armoured cars and water cannon to the Suharto government in Indonesia, famed for brutally suppressing the East Timorese. The orders had been placed before New Labour came to power and cancellation would have raised legal problems. At stake, however, was a core British domestic interest, namely jobs in the defence sector, or so it was argued, and that sector depended on exports to keep the production lines running.[27]

Consequently, the ethical dimension in Cook's foreign policy was put to the test. It placed him at odds with No. 10, where the priorities were to deliver a better standard of living to the electorate and hence win a second term in office. Lobbying by the defence industry was also instrumental and the Prime Minister was convinced of the need to go ahead with the arms deliveries.[28] Thereafter Cook won a minor concession from No. 10 on the rules governing defence sales, such that these could not be licensed if they 'might be used' for internal repression.

Under Cook's auspices Britain also helped introduce a new voluntary register among European arms exporters and an EU code to try to prevent sales to oppressive regimes. However, the effects were limited and Cook's initial stance was undermined. He disappointed his erstwhile supporters in the human rights lobbies and was attacked by his opponents. The Conservatives were delighted to extract revenge for the acerbic attacks Cook had launched on the previous government, with great effect, over the 'arms to Iraq' scandal relating to secret weapons supplies to the Iraqi government in the 1980s. As discussed in Chapter 5, the whole experience may have helped to toughen the Labour government's stance on Iraq in the name of upholding ethical standards where possible.

If Cook's efforts suffered setbacks, these were minor in comparison with the blow dealt to New Labour's ethical stance in December 2006, when the Attorney General called off a Serious Fraud Office inquiry into bribery allegations against BAE Systems in connection with sales to the Saudi government (see Chapter 8).[29] Claiming responsibility for a decision that, strictly, he was not legally entitled to make, Tony Blair cited both economic and security reasons for the move.[30]

The first Strategic Defence Review

The term 'force for good' was used in the government's *Strategic Defence Review*, presented to parliament by the Secretary of State for Defence George Robertson in July 1998. In the introduction Robertson said:

> The British are, by instinct, an international people. We believe that as well as defending our rights, we should discharge our responsibilities in the world. We do not want to stand idly by and watch humanitarian disasters or the aggression of dictators go unchecked. We want to give a lead; we want to be a force for good.[31]

The review exercise was conducted jointly by the Foreign Office and the Ministry of Defence and involved consultations with and submissions from a variety of sources, including former members of the armed forces, civil servants, academics and others with defence-related experience and expertise (this author included). A team from industry, the armed services and the consultants McKinsey were also asked to study the best ways 'to learn from companies in areas as diverse as oil exploration and car production'[32] in the interests of improving defence procurement.

This extensive review was considered necessary, as relayed in the resulting White Paper, 'not only to meet the challenges of today's complex international scene but also to provide the flexibility to respond to those we may face well into the new century'.[33] The goal was to enhance Britain's capabilities to fulfil the role envisaged in New Labour's manifesto, namely that Britain be:

> strong in defence; resolute in standing up for our own interests and as an advocate of human rights and democracy the world over; a reliable and powerful ally; and a leader in Europe and the international community.[34]

Britain's intervention in Sierra Leone in 1997 had demonstrated how special forces – in this case mercenaries – could help topple a brutal regime, creating an opportunity for British forces to build on their initiative. The initial foray had its farcical elements and was at first cast as a case of means and ends not matching.[35] However, the outcome enabled the Blair government to claim the virtues of humanitarian interventionism.

Subsequently, Blair was to become the champion of troop intervention in Kosovo. In the midst of NATO operations there, he laid out five considerations that he proposed should guide policy-makers when deciding whether to intervene militarily in a foreign conflict:

- Is the case for action clear?
- Have all diplomatic options been exhausted?
- Are there military operations which can be 'sensibly and prudently' undertaken?
- 'Are we prepared for the long haul?'
- Are national interests at stake? [36]

According to some analysts, not only were these criteria not met in the Kosovo case, but they were not necessarily the correct criteria on which to base an ethical foreign policy.[37] Yet the perception of a virtuous cause appropriately defended triumphed over counter-arguments and Blair was reinforced in his convictions about the importance of benign interventionism.

Initial thinking on the Middle East

On the subject of the Middle East Tony Blair personally was not particularly forthcoming during his first years in office. Providing a clue to what would come later, however, he did articulate his thoughts on the connection between national 'values' and foreign policy:

> We use power and influence for a purpose: for the values and aims we believe in ... Foreign policy should not be seen as some self-contained part of government in a box marked 'abroad' or 'foreigners'. It should complement and reflect our domestic goals. It should be part of our mission of national renewal.[38]

In a speech about foreign affairs in December 1998, Blair developed his notion of Britain's role as 'pivotal', particularly with respect to the transatlantic relationship.[39]

While Blair concentrated on 'the big picture', the Foreign Secretary filled in the specifics. Speaking at a Foreign Office reception on 5 March 1998 to mark the fiftieth anniversary of the Anglo-Arab Association, Robin Cook gave a speech entitled 'The Arab–British Partnership'. This partnership, he said, was flourishing:

> The global economy is now a reality, not just a slogan. In 1997 Britain did almost £12 billion in trade with the Arab world. British companies are busy right across the Middle East ... transferring technology, creating jobs and spreading prosperity ... Our governments are working together to ensure that all our economies benefit. We have been active in the Euromed Process between the EU and our Arab neighbours, and which has set itself the ambitious aim of building a free trade area by the year 2010. Britain is determined to use its [EU] Presidency to help bring this aim to reality.[40]

Cook gave examples of the role of British companies in individual countries, including Jordan, Egypt and Saudi Arabia. He highlighted expanding links between Britain and the Gulf Cooperation Council (GCC) states – including links between their respective armed forces, police forces and civil societies. He noted the role of the British Council, 'doing everything from organising an Anglo-Arab women politicians' meeting in Egypt, to helping the Palestinian Authority train its civil service'.

Cook also remarked on the number of Arab students studying in Britain, including 11,000 from North Africa, and the presence of British students in the region. He said that the National Trust was working with Saudi counterparts on conservation issues, and that the Bank of England had been helping the UAE authorities combat money-laundering. He also emphasized that:

> The Islamic community in Britain is flourishing – there are over nine hundred mosques in Britain. There are now two Islamic schools supported by the government. There is far more that binds our two worlds than separates them. We face common problems, and we are working on common solutions.[41]

The two policy issues on which Cook elaborated at greatest length were Iraq and the Middle East peace process (discussed in subsequent chapters). He defended the British policy on sanctions on Iraq and explained that Britain would be using its presidency of the EU in 1998 to push for movement on the peace process.

The reform agenda

The promotion of democracy in the Middle East was on New Labour's agenda from the outset.[42] Even though, as Cook claimed, commercial links between Britain and the region were positive, at least from Britain's perspective, the sense prevailed that the region lagged behind global economic trends and that poor governance, lack of a vibrant civil society and minimal democracy were partly to blame.[43] The Euro-Mediterranean Partnership initiative, launched at Barcelona in 1995, was therefore one of the vehicles used by Cook, particularly during the British presidency of the EU in 1998, to push reform.

This initiative promised EU assistance to Arab partner countries around the Mediterranean as well as Israel, in pursuit of free trade, economic liberalization, political reform, security cooperation and cultural interchange.[44] Part of the agenda was to promote protection of human rights and steps towards transparency, accountability, more representative government and civil society. Most progress was made in the economic sphere, though the

Arab partner countries complained, with justification, that the Europeans maintained protection of their agricultural industries, thereby depriving them of a significant opportunity to boost their exports to Europe. Britain and other north European countries blamed aspects of the EU's Common Agricultural Policy and protectionism for this.

Arab governments proved reluctant to bow to EU pressure for political reform, but the British government searched for ways in which Britain and the EU could facilitate gradual change without creating a backlash. This effort was pursued beyond the Mediterranean countries. Significantly, whereas the previous Conservative government had preferred to speak about the virtues of 'good governance', under New Labour the word 'democracy' was allowed to enter the discourse – and under this umbrella the Foreign Office sought several ways to encourage greater accountability, due process and participation.

From a new funding programme for the promotion of human rights, diplomats dealing with the Middle East secured money to spend in Kuwait, Sudan, Egypt and Yemen. The British Council was active too, for example sponsoring a meeting of lawyers in Egypt on the subject of human rights. Under the umbrella of the EU–GCC Dialogue, which had its first 'political' meeting in London at the FCO in 1998, the subjects of good governance and human rights were included on the agenda.

For the EU, and Britain in particular, reform of the Palestinian Authority (PA) became something of an obsession. This resulted in part from questions about the use of taxpayers' money by the PA, prompted in turn by allegations by Palestinians themselves that President Yasser Arafat was facilitating corruption among his officials and security forces. After the second Intifada began in 2000 the US Congress wanted accountability for funding that could otherwise fall 'into the hands of terrorists', and first Israeli Prime Minister Ariel Sharon and then the Bush administration wanted political reform to enable them to sideline Arafat in the leadership (see Chapter 7). The British government (DFID and the FCO) funded and facilitated a number of discreet initiatives to assist PA reform that continued throughout Tony Blair's three terms in government. In the meantime, as a result of the Bush administration's plans for reforming the region after the invasion of Iraq, the whole issue of reform in the Middle East gained new significance (see below).

CHANGING GEAR AFTER 9/11

Following the attacks on the World Trade Center and the Pentagon in September 2001, Blair devoted much of his speech at the Labour Party conference a few weeks later to exploring the implications. He said the events of 11 September 'marked a turning point in history' and were a tragedy and an act of evil.[45] He cautioned: 'Let no one say this was a blow for Islam when the blood of innocent Muslims was shed along with those of the Christian, Jewish and other faiths around the world.' He also said there could be no compromise, no point of understanding with such terror: 'Just a choice: defeat it or be defeated by it.'

Turning to the actions that would be taken against 'the terrorist network of Osama bin Laden' and to cut off 'terrorist financing and end safe havens for terrorists' he declared:

> Here in this country and in other nations round the world, laws will be changed, not to deny basic liberties but to prevent their abuse and protect the most basic liberty of all: freedom from terror. New extradition laws will be introduced; new rules to ensure asylum is not a front for terrorist entry.

Blair also enumerated the instances where interventions had been necessary 'because conflicts rarely stay within national boundaries' and 'interdependence defines the new world we live in'. In this connection, he asserted, 'if we wanted to, we could breathe new life into the Middle East Peace Process and we must'.

On 4 October 2001 Tony Blair told the House of Commons he intended to put in the Commons Library a document detailing the case against al-Qaeda leader Osama bin Laden in connection with the 9/11 attacks. The document, Blair said:

> covers the history of Osama Bin Laden; his relations with the Taliban; what we know of the acts of terror he has committed; and some of what we know in respect of 11 September. I enter a major caveat, much of the evidence we have is intelligence and highly sensitive. It is not possible, without compromising people or security, to release precise details and fresh information [that] is daily coming in.[46]

In retrospect this document, based on intelligence, can be recognized as a portent of things to come. It is also noteworthy that at the time the US Embassy in London found it sufficiently useful to place on its own website.

As US action against al-Qaeda in Afghanistan loomed, the British, along with other NATO members, offered military, logistical and diplomatic support. The Americans duly availed themselves of this offer, while remaining firmly in charge. Nonetheless the likely cost of military action to ordinary Afghans and the fact that the undertaking was to involve toppling the Taliban regime exercised the minds of lawyers and human rights activists. British Muslims were drawn into the debate, not least because many had family connections in Pakistan, which became a launching point for the US campaign. This too was a portent of things to come.

43

Late in October 2001 the Minister for Europe Peter Hain defined the campaign – against a global network of terrorists – as a new kind of war in which 'there is no such place as abroad':

> The front line and the home front are interchangeable. The grievances that motivate Al Qaeda may have their roots in the Middle East; but their consequences reach right to your doorstep.[47]

Hain also noted that financial support for bin Laden and the perpetrators of 9/11 came from 'individuals made wealthy by the very forces of globalization that struck the World Trade Center'. While pursuing al-Qaeda on the one hand, he said, 'we should not forget the other essential part of our strategy', namely resolving key conflicts and especially that between Israel and the Palestinians.

Taking the fight to the Middle East

By this time Tony Blair had begun to raise his profile in the Middle East. In preparation for the invasion of Afghanistan, he telephoned the Iranian president to ask for his country's cooperation (see Chapter 6) and then despatched Foreign Secretary Jack Straw (who had replaced Robin Cook after the May 2001 elections) to Tehran. Blair himself embarked on two tours of the Middle East that autumn. Having adopted the cause of a two-state solution to the Israeli–Palestinian conflict (see Chapter 7), he was nonetheless assailed by complaints from Arab quarters about Western double standards on the implementation of international law, and raised doubts in Israel about his grasp of the issues.

On his first attempt to visit Saudi Arabia the ruling family, newly embattled as a result of the discovery that most of the perpetrators of 9/11 were Saudi nationals, was not ready to receive him. When he did go to Riyadh at the end of October he encountered strong condemnation of Israel and scepticism about the parameters of the peace process he wanted to revive. In Syria, according to the media:

> Mr Blair had twin objectives: one was to look for a way of weaning Syria away from its support for Hizbullah and other groups, and the other was to try to get Syria to re-enter talks with Israel on the return of the Golan Heights. He secured neither.[48]

Instead he was treated to a public rebuke by Syrian President Asad for his perspective on the conflict, with Asad defending the right of the Palestinians to resist occupation.[49]

In Israel Blair failed to persuade the government to abandon its policy of 'targeted killings' of Palestinian militants and reoccupying Palestinian towns evacuated as part of the Oslo process.[50] In the Gaza Strip the Palestinians were dismissive of his efforts to revive the peace process, but Blair issued a warning he was to repeat for several years, to the effect that Osama bin Laden and his ilk were seeking to set Muslims against Christians and divide the Arabs from 'the West', and that this way lay disaster.[51]

In 2002 Blair's foreign policy preoccupation was with US intentions for Iraq (see Chapter 5). While he did not draw a direct connection between the Iraqi regime and al-Qaeda, he did depict the Iraqi regime as a problem and not only because of its assumed possession of weapons of mass destruction. Despite claiming that the goal was the disarmament of Iraq and asserting that 'No-one wants military conflict', in September 2002 he told parliament:

> Of course there is no doubt that Iraq, the region and the world would be bet-ter off without Saddam. They deserve to be led by someone who can abide by international law, not a murderous dictator. Someone who can bring Iraq back into the international community where it belongs, not languishing as a pariah – someone who can make the country rich and successful, not impoverished by Saddam's personal greed. Someone who can lead a govern-ment more representative of the country as a whole, while maintaining ab-solutely Iraq's territorial integrity. We have no quarrel with the Iraqi people. Liberated from Saddam, they could make Iraq prosperous and a force for good in the Middle East.[52]

In his Labour Party Conference speech in 2002 Blair said that the world could go in one of two directions: 'Countries could become rivals in power or partners'. He reminded his audience that, for all the resentment of America, 'The basic values of America are our values too, British and European, and they are good values: democracy, freedom, tolerance, justice.'[53]

Strategy revisited

In early 2002 the Ministry of Defence produced *A New Chapter* for the *Strategic Defence Review*, outlining the anticipated role of the armed forces in contributing to the government's goal of eliminating terrorism 'as a force for change in international affairs'.[54] In this the MOD anticipated a multifaceted approach, in which military capability might be used to prevent, deter, coerce, disrupt and destroy the threat. Destruction would apply in cases where a military strike could destroy terrorist cells or facilities. Coercion was likely to mean applying pressure on regimes and states harbouring or supporting international terrorists.

Accordingly, the British government's response to 9/11 was multifaceted. Security forces were put on alert around Heathrow airport and the financial district of London in response to specific alerts; every household received a package of instructions on 'preparing for emergencies'; the police gained new powers of arrest and detention; financial transactions from around the world were henceforth scrutinized more closely; through intelligence cooperation with the Americans, e-mail and telephone communications were to be more comprehensively monitored for 'chatter' indicating possible terrorist plots.[55]

Some of these measures were felt by British Muslims more than others. In particular, there were reports that young men deemed to 'look' Muslim were more likely to be stopped for questioning than others who did not fit the profile. As was later revealed, Britain was also used as a staging post for some US flights to transport individuals to foreign locations where they could be interrogated under regimes less bound by human rights considerations than the United States.

Another effect of 9/11 and the subsequent focus on combating terrorism was to fuel the pre-existing debate in Britain on the rights and wrongs of overseas interventions. The argument that the United States had the right to retaliate against the perpetrators of the attacks of 11 September had many advocates, though some of the victims' families spoke out against military action likely to incur innocent casualties. Jurists and religious leaders joined the debate, deploying the arguments of 'Just War' theory, which calls for 'just cause', proportionate action and protection of innocents. Other elements, particularly in the Arab and Muslim world, actually questioned the certainty of the United States and other governments that al-Qaeda was to blame for 9/11.

Meanwhile, as of 9/11 it was No. 10 that took the lead on foreign policy formulation on strategic issues. The Foreign Office, somewhat overshadowed, nonetheless produced a new strategy document in December 2003. Its Foreword included a summary of the government's record:

> Since 1997 the Labour Government has helped to reshape Europe after the cold war. We have championed wider EU and NATO membership and confronted dictatorship in Kosovo. Outside Europe we have used our leading role in the UN, the EU and other international bodies to promote peace and security in Sierra Leone, East Timor, the Middle East and the sub-continent. We have joined military action to confront terrorism in Afghanistan and to enforce Security Council decisions in Iraq. Across the world we have worked to alleviate poverty and defend human rights.[56]

A three-page summary of the document's highlights listed Britain's strategic international priorities over the next five to ten years:

- a world safer from global terrorism and weapons of mass destruction;
- protection of the UK from illegal immigration, drug trafficking and other international crime;
- an international system based on the rule of law, which is better able to resolve disputes and prevent conflicts;
- an effective EU in a secure neighbourhood;
- promotion of UK economic interests in an open and expanding global economy;
- sustainable development, underpinned by democracy, good governance and human rights;
- security of UK and global energy supplies;
- security and good governance of the UK's Overseas Territories.

These were elaborated in the body of the document, which also emphasized the vital importance of working with others, in a multilateral framework, to achieve these goals. It thus envisaged working through the UN, EU, G8, NATO and the Commonwealth. In addition, high priority was to be given to engaging constructively with Islamic countries. Partnerships with *both* the EU and the United States were considered imperative and 'building a strong, global partnership between Europe and America is of paramount importance for the UK's – and the world's – prosperity and security'.

The restructuring of the Foreign Office (see Chapter 3) was a logical consequence of this strategy and designed to deliver on its goals. Performance of staff was to be judged on the basis of that delivery. This was very 'joined up' government, at least on foreign policy, in the conscious alignment of means and ends. Also, almost any policy lead on a specific issue likely to emerge from No. 10 under Tony Blair's leadership could be comfortably accommodated within the scope of the designated priorities.

Security and the reform agenda

After 9/11 the reform agenda, pursued by New Labour from the start, gained new prominence, in conjunction with enhanced cooperation on security issues between Western and Arab governments. The impetus on both counts came from Washington.

According to the Bush administration, the intervention in Iraq was supposed to serve the dual goals of democracy promotion and countering terrorism. Ahead of Bush's state visit to the UK in November 2003, US Secretary of State Condoleezza Rice explained:

> The alliance, the US-UK relationship right at the core of it … is actively engaged in making the world safer, with counter-terrorism and counter-

proliferation, but our great contribution to the world has always been we've cared about making the world better.[57]

Of Bush and Blair personally, she said: 'They are both leaders who are committed to the proposition that the spread of freedom is the key to a more secure world and to the ultimate defeat of terrorism'.[58]

The idea that Iraq was to be made the model for democratization in the Middle East triggered a new dynamic, with Washington pushing an initiative for 'The Broader Middle East' and the EU countering with the introduction of its New Neighbourhood Policy in the Mediterranean as a refinement of the Euro-Med Partnership. The British government, like the Bush administration and the European Commission, capitalized on the publication of *The Arab Human Development Report*, to which many promi-nent Arab intellectuals and experts had contributed, to make the case for reform more urgent and practically appealing. In April 2003 Jack Straw told a seminar for parliamentarians, organized by the FCO's new Directorate for Strategy and Innovation, that the message of that report needed to be taken more seriously, especially by Arab governments themselves.[59]

In July 2003, ministers signed off on a strategy paper setting up a special new unit to monitor Arab reform (see also Chapter 3) and 'develop UK thinking on how to deal with it', which led to the assignment of dedicated staff to the embassies in Bahrain and Cairo.[60] Addressing a meeting to launch the Foreign Policy Centre's 'Civility Programme on Middle East Reform', in March 2004, Jack Straw said:

> It is for the Arab world itself to decide how best it can pursue a process of reform, development and modernization. There is no template which fits each of the different countries in the region. The task for us in Britain and in the international community is to help to support it, drawing on our own experience of change – because we too have a vital interest in its success.[61]

Straw acknowledged and refuted fears that reform was incompatible with traditional values, Islam or religious observance generally. He noted that Britain's imperial past had 'left some sensitivities in parts of the Arab world', but said that this gave Britain both friends in and an understanding of the region. Referring to the Foreign Office's programme for engaging with the Islamic world, funded out of what was called the Global Opportunities Fund, he said the strategy was to form partnerships with Arab societies and institu-tions. Not for the first or last time, Straw also made reference, as had Robin Cook in 1998, to British Muslims, including in Straw's own constituency in the north of England, as a source of connection and understanding between the British and the people of the Middle East.

A selective reading of history

Straw's claim that Britain derived knowledge of the region from its imperial past echoes a view not uncommon among Arabs that the British 'understand' the Middle East better than the Americans. However, herein lies a key source of misunderstanding between Britain and many who dwell in the region.

It is impossible to understand the contemporary state system in the Middle East without reference to nineteenth- and especially early twentieth-century British and French imperial machinations in the region (see Chapter 1). The legacy lives on. Yet the British spent the last decades of the twentieth century casting off the psychological baggage of an empire they had almost completely dismantled by 1971. If Anthony Sampson and Ferdinand Mount were correct, by the end of the 1990s the British had retrieved their pre-imperial, trading-nation, 'freebooting' persona. However, as historian Derek Hopwood once remarked, when discussing British relations with the Middle East: 'Oppressed people remember their history while the oppressor forgets'.[62] Consequently, when New Labour entered the stage, committed to making Britain 'a force for good in the world' and then became party to the US invasion of Iraq, there were bound to be some misunderstandings.

The intention in the chapters that follow is to trace how Blair and New Labour grappled with the problems of the Middle East in an effort to bring order, stability, a measure of democracy, freedom from dictatorship in Iraq and statehood for the Palestinians. In so doing they ended up encountering the legacies of empire. Yet, as will be seen, they showed remarkable reluctance to grant that these legacies might actually shape and influence both the contemporary British condition and British relations with the Middle East.

3

New Labour:
New Policy-making Process

'In the end values and interests merge.... The spread of our values makes us safer.'
– Tony Blair (1999)[1]

According to the logic espoused by Tony Blair and his closest colleagues and advisers, the espousal and projection of a positive self-image, grounded in moral rectitude, could together make them 'a force for good' in the world. After Labour's election victory in May 1997, this logic was to be applied to the role of the party in government and the role of the country in the world.

This sense of mission and moral rectitude was not without precedent in British history. A similar outlook prevailed in the heyday of British imperial power in the nineteenth century when the Victorians saw Britain as both more advanced and more mature than rival powers, manifest in 'the bounding prosperity of their economy, and an enormous accession of a quality they called "freedom"'.[2] To a lesser extent the new mood in 1997 also bore some similarities to the reinvigoration of national pride championed in the 1980s by Margaret Thatcher. However, changes wrought by New Labour in the policy-making process were new and far-reaching.

'REBRANDING' BRITAIN

New Labour strategists consciously and enthusiastically adopted the concepts and language of business in their notion of policy (or product) development and marketing. In 1999 it was noted: 'After the election victory of New Labour, a change was pronounced: marketing techniques and corporate jargon were employed to mould the perception of Britain in the eyes of both domestic and foreign mass publics.'[3] According to Mark Leonard, who led a project called 'Re-Branding Britain' initiated by New Labour's first Foreign Secretary Robin Cook, globalization had blurred the distinction between domestic and global politics, and consequently:

the standards which we have [to] apply to our behaviour around the world also need to be reassessed and brought into line with the standards that we expect of ourselves at home, and hence reputation becomes a key component of a country's standing in the world ... 'who you are' is actually almost as important as 'what you do' in the late 1990s.[4]

According to Leonard, the 'brand' that had come to attach itself to Britain was both outmoded and unhelpful for the pursuit of British political and economic interests. If Britain could resolve its ambiguity about Europe and come to terms with its imperial past, then it could be more influential in the EU and could capitalize on its place in the Commonwealth to make that organization more dynamic. He proposed defining and agreeing 'a new set of stories that link the British past to its future and which take account of the changes in Britain today':

> ... such stories emphasise Britain's place as an importer and exporter of ideas, goods, as [a] hybrid nation which has got all sorts of cultures and sub-cultures that comprise it; our readiness to do business; our role as a 'silent revolutionary' in initiating all sorts of new forms of social organisations to suit new circumstances, and finally a country wedded to an ethos of fair play and support for the underdog.[5]

The message was very much about values, espousing them and projecting them. Also important was the messenger. Leonard himself was exemplary: a young man in his twenties, full of new ideas and motivated to make a difference, he was chosen to head the New Labour think tank – the Foreign Policy Centre, set up in 1998 with Tony Blair and Robin Cook on the board.

New Labour leadership

If Leonard gave expression to Labour's new voice, Tony Blair was its embodiment. Strong leadership was considered an important defining characteristic of New Labour, to distinguish it from the 'Old'. Lack of discipline and ideological disagreements among the Labour rank and file were considered partly responsible for past failures at the polls. Labour leader Neil Kinnock had begun a process carried forward by Tony Blair to reposition the party to appeal to the political mainstream, marginalize radicals and dissenters and enforce a strict adherence to the leadership line.

> The Blair project was joined to a cult of leadership. This was both a legacy of Thatcher – Blair expressed admiration for her conviction style and sense of purpose – and a reaction against a public perception that Labour lacked strong leadership ... Under Blair, shadow ministers were sometimes

presented with policy proposals over which they had little say. Dissenters, potential and actual, found themselves deprived of official party slots in the media.[6]

In transforming the Labour Party so that it would be identified with the aspirations of the majority of voters, Blair was key but not alone. Peter Mandelson, a close friend of Blair and twice a member of his cabinet, is credited with masterminding the 'rebranding'.[7] As he has said subsequently, his skill in operating behind the scenes gained him a reputation for scheming that would later, for a time, count against him in political life. Yet both in and out of government office he retained influence with the Prime Minister. His first Cabinet position was as Secretary of State for Trade and Industry, but he had to resign over a conflict of interest that he had failed to declare. Later he was made Secretary of State for Northern Ireland, but again had to resign over an alleged indiscretion of which he was later cleared.

For a brief period in New Labour's first term, Mandelson was slated for the post of foreign secretary, to replace Robin Cook. When he visited the Middle East in 2000–01, ostensibly in a private capacity,[8] he was received in Syria, Israel and Egypt as a friend of the Prime Minister with at least an informal role in British relations with the region. After his second resignation made a Cabinet reappointment politically infeasible at that time,[9] Mandelson retained an informal role as the Prime Minister's point man on certain aspects of foreign relations, though not directly involving the Middle East. After EU enlargement, in 2004 he was appointed as Britain's sole Commissioner (for Trade) in Brussels and was favoured by the new Commission President José Manuel Barroso with a place in his inner circle of 'reform-minded commissioners' to push through an agenda for economic restructuring.[10]

Gordon Brown was equally central to the repositioning of New Labour in the 1990s. Most importantly, as Chancellor of the Exchequer he managed the economy in such a way as to dispel fears in the financial and business community that New Labour would revert to old socialist ways on central government expansion and high taxation. On the contrary, Brown presided over the era of speculation and debt accumulation in the banking sector that was subsequently blamed for the financial crisis that overtook the economy in 2008.

Brown needs mention here for two other reasons. First, his stewardship at the Treasury made it possible for Blair to devote more time to foreign policy, especially in his second term, than might have been feasible otherwise. Second, Brown's ambition to take over the top job was an underlying theme of Blair's leadership and a recurring preoccupation of the British media. Whenever Blair appeared to be in trouble for his policy stances, not least on

Iraq, the assumption was that he was rendered more vulnerable to Brown's challenge. Thus, although their cooperation and rivalry were clearly not central factors in British policy toward the Middle East, they did influence the public's understanding of Blair's handling of the premiership.[11] Specifically, Blair's personal drive, motivation and leadership style were important to understanding policy content, presentation and implementation on the big issues of the era and, by extension, the consequences for the Middle East. (More will be said about the role of Foreign Secretaries Robin Cook and Jack Straw in due course.)

Blair himself had been central to the remaking of the Labour Party that made it electable again, after years in the political doldrums. What is more, winning once was absolutely not enough. The conduct of New Labour, once in office, was designed to assure the party and its leader the second term that had eluded their predecessors.[12] That required not just party but Cabinet discipline in the interests of projecting a clear and appealing message. As understood by Mark Leonard, the formula for finding the right message derived from embracing and projecting *the right values*. Tony Blair came across as both the embodiment of New Labour values and the most effective proponent of them.

As observed by Michael Portillo, a former Conservative Party minister and political commentator:

> He's the consummate politician, brilliant on presentation, he has a wonderful style. He has a real knack of putting his finger on what people are thinking about and what they want to hear. He has gained control of his party and offered leadership.[13]

The magic formula in 1997 was not that New Labour and its leader offered particularly new policies or ideas to the British electorate,[14] but rather that they came across as representing what most of the public wanted and liked, in a new and masterful way. Youth and vigour were also part of the image that worked in New Labour's favour. Blair was the youngest prime minister to take up the post since the early nineteenth century and the first in around 150 years to become a father while in office.

'Values and interests merge'

During his first term Blair's ability to please and charm led to some criticisms that he lacked depth or ideological commitment. It seems Blair himself considered it a virtue not to be ideological or caught up in the old left–right political polarization.[15] However, during the course of the Iraq crisis, when he was accused of having *too much* resolution and conviction, another side or depth to his character became apparent. In his biography, Philip Stephens describes him thus:

> ... the aftermath of 11 September and of the conflict in Iraq marked out Tony Blair as a different sort of leader. The gifted thespian had met the conviction politician, the nineteenth century Liberal and the twenty-first century pragmatist. His Manichaean outlook unsettled even some of his closest friends, but the willingness to gamble all distinguished him as someone in politics to change things. The paradox in the furore about Iraq's weapons programmes was that Blair would have dearly liked to frame the war in a different context: removing a dangerous tyrant was the more compelling cause.[16]

Stephens noted that Blair's Christian faith informed his sense of political mission, but unlike in American politics, overt Christianity is not considered appropriate in a British leader.[17] So Alastair Campbell, Blair's close confidant and the Director of Communications at No. 10 until 2003, ensured this did not feature too strongly in his public discourse or personal interviews with the media. Campbell's role went further: 'In Blair's projection of New Labour, presentation and policy had become inseparable, which meant that Campbell's writ ran well beyond that of a media adviser.'[18]

Blair's most powerful speeches, especially on matters of foreign policy, emphasized the importance of using power to make the world a better place. In a memorable address to the Economic Club of Chicago in April 1999, when he was attempting to galvanize US support for the deployment of NATO ground troops to Kosovo, Blair explained:

> No longer is our existence as states under threat. Now our actions are guided by a more subtle blend of mutual self interest and moral purpose in defending the values we cherish. In the end values and interests merge. If we can establish and spread the values of liberty, the rule of law, human rights and an open society then that is in our national interests too. The spread of our values makes us safer.[19]

In the same speech, Blair discussed the transformatory effects of globalization. He claimed 'we are all internationalists now' and called for changes to the rules of international trade and 'reconsideration of the role, workings and decision-making process of the United Nations, and in particular the UN Security Council'. He also posited a formula for military interventionism in pursuit of humanitarian goals. Given subsequent developments, it is also interesting to note that he singled out Saddam Hussein, alongside Serbian leader Slobodan Milosevic, for special censure.[20]

After 9/11 Blair used his speech to the Labour Party Conference on 2 October 2001 to appeal to audiences beyond Britain, and the event was broadcast on a number of media outlets around the world. He began with a call to action against the perpetrators of the attacks on New York and Washington, but going beyond that, he said that those who had lost family members deserved more than simple revenge:

> They want something better in memory of their loved ones. I believe their memorial can and should be greater than simple punishment of the guilty. It is that out of the shadow of this evil, should emerge lasting good: destruction of the machinery of terrorism wherever it is found; hope amongst all nations of a new beginning where we seek to resolve differences in a calm and ordered way; greater understanding between nations and between faiths; and above all justice and prosperity for the poor and dispossessed, so that people everywhere can see the chance of a better future through the hard work and creative power of the free citizen, not the violence and savagery of the fanatic.[21]

It is really no wonder that some American politicians and commentators thanked Tony Blair for framing the US war on terrorism in a more inspiring light than the Bush administration seemed able to do.

Aside from the rhetorical flourish, there were two aspects to Blair's worldview that contrasted with those of the Bush team. One was his belief in and emphasis on 'community' and international cooperation. The other was his more optimistic view of human nature. Philip Stephens defined it as the difference between a New Testament Christian outlook and an Old Testament one.[22] But whatever Blair's personal values, there were those, not least in the Middle East, who saw his rhetoric as no more than packaging for a hard-nosed, realist approach to the pursuit of British material interests. As will be discussed, such critics focused on policy outcomes, rather than intentions, and on their expectations of British policy, born of historical experience. In other words, New Labour's rebranding exercise could only go so far in reshaping perceptions of Britain, when actions belied the words.

Even so, the values espoused by Tony Blair and New Labour formed the core of policy – 'values and interests merge' – and were not just a presentational device. Yet what was also apparent and has given rise to scepticism was the relative lack of attention to detail in the Prime Minister's pronouncements on the new world order and how states should act. He excelled at the broadbrush approach to policy and left it to his ministers to translate this into more specific British policy positions – at the WTO, in the European Commission and the UN Security Council, or with respect to 'homeland security'. For instance, in signing off the 330-page draft European constitution in June 2004, the Prime Minister referred press questions on specific clauses and amendments to Jack Straw, correctly confident that the Foreign Secretary knew every one of them. Blair himself seemed unabashed that he did not.[23]

The New Labour agenda and Blair's leadership style had a palpable impact on the foreign policy-making process. The conventional mode was for the government of the day to set the overall direction and goals and for the Foreign Office to identify the interests at stake in specific areas and formulate policy options for ministers to choose from and the diplomats to pursue. According to John Coles (former Head of the British Diplomatic Service and Permanent Under-Secretary at the Foreign Office), the traditional procedure was either for policy advice to be passed up the chain of command in the Foreign Office, eventually to ministerial level, or in some cases for instructions to come from the top down. 'The guiding principle is that officials advise while ministers decide.'[24] If the situation demanded quick action, the Foreign Secretary might simply call a meeting, take advice verbally and decide on the spot. Even so, the expectation was that all those who needed to know would be informed, with opportunities for comment and advice to be taken into account, and the whole process would be recorded in writing.

Very often, several different government departments, such as the Ministry of Defence, the Department of Trade and the Treasury, would need to be involved in policy decisions. Obtaining agreement across departments takes time and may militate against 'bold thinking'.

> But its purpose is to make sure, so far as possible, that there is, at the end of the process, a policy which is endorsed by the government as a whole, not just an individual minister or department. Foreign policy is or should be the government's policy, not the policy of the Foreign Office or some other department. The present government's emphasis on the need for 'joined-up' policy makes the same point.[25]

In practice, the government of Tony Blair opted for more direction from No. 10 and the creation of various task forces, action teams and units around the Prime Minister to deliver 'joined-up' policy and chase implementation. Some sceptics also claimed that the aim was to counter the role of the Treasury in managing overall policy.[26]

A presidential and informal No. 10

In anticipation of a Labour victory in May 1997, a group of former civil servants met members of the Labour front bench for a series of meetings chaired by Professor Peter Hennessy. The purpose was to help prepare the prospective ministers for office, including how 'to get the best out of the Civil Service'. They discussed 'the emotional geography of office; the first few months; private office; special advisers; junior ministers; putting policy into practice; co-operation between departments; the Treasury – problems and some solutions; moving into No. 10; supporting the Prime Minister and strengthening the Centre; and cabinet committees'.[27] A consensus emerged among the former officials and advisers that 'the Centre, the system which supported the Prime Minister and No. 10, needed to be strengthened'. What was required was 'a strong sense of strategic direction to drive the Whitehall machine' as opposed to short-term political management, and No. 10 needed the resources to provide this.

Seven years later Peter Hennessy was to observe:

> Number 10 is operating a White House system but without having a White House. They are misusing the old system but they do not have a new one to replace it. It really is the worst of all possible worlds. … There's never been a worse time to be a permanent secretary or a cabinet minister … The normal weighting given to departments, to their top civil servants and their ministers has been greatly diminished by the power of the courtiers at Number 10 and the fact that policy is made on the hoof.[28]

These comments point to three charges levelled at Tony Blair's government over the intervening years. First was the lack of consultation and consensus-building across the spectrum of government. Blair's presidential style of leadership allowed for little, if any, discussion in Cabinet or across Whitehall. Ministries and thus the civil service were used simply for implementing policies decided upon and articulated, often with minimal attention to their input, by No. 10.[29]

The second charge was of insufficient record-keeping and formality. Policy decisions were very often reached in informal meetings or 'brainstormings' between the Prime Minister and his group of personal advisers and aides in No. 10. Such meetings were not usually minuted and only a few of the advisers had experience of traditional Whitehall practices. In other words, at the same time as being criticized for being too dictatorial, the government was also charged with being too informal in its decision-making. That said, a feast of internal e-mail correspondence was revealed in the course of the public inquiry chaired by Lord Hutton into the death of the former weapons inspector Dr David Kelly in summer 2003 (see Chapter 5). Alastair Campbell made his personal diary available. All the material was made public on the inquiry website and both the press and academic experts on the British political system gained new insights into the inner workings of the Blair government. The issue was not so much that there was no paper trail, just that formal records were not regularly kept and circulated.

The inquiry into intelligence failures on Iraq's weapons capabilities headed by the former Cabinet Secretary Lord Butler investigated the implications of this informality and concluded:

… we are concerned that the informality and circumscribed character of the Government's procedures which we saw in the context of policy-making towards Iraq risks reducing the scope for informed collective political judgement. Such risks are particularly significant in a field like the subject of our Review, where hard facts are inherently difficult to come by and the quality of judgement is accordingly all the more important.[30]

Butler's inquiry also discovered that 'excellent quality papers', written by civil servants to brief the Cabinet, were not discussed in Cabinet meetings, apparently because they were not circulated in advance or tabled for discussion.

The third and related charge was lack of accountability. Political appointees became more instrumental in decision-making, to the comparative exclusion of both elected politicians and professional civil servants. Whereas under John Major there were eight special advisers in No. 10, by 2002 Tony Blair had the benefit of twenty-seven.[31] The formal position of each in the chain of command, in so far as this existed, was probably less indicative of their influence than whether they had the Prime Minister's ear.[32] Some Whitehall civil servants have seen such access as at least a guarantee that these advisers spoke with some authority on the Prime Minister's behalf, but others feared that this was not always proven and that without rigorous record-keeping accountability was lost.[33]

The proliferation of policy advisers in the government system was not restricted to No. 10. They were appointed by ministers across Whitehall. It is therefore perhaps inevitable that some civil servants came to feel they were somehow not trusted. In any case there was cause for concern about civil service morale and hence performance. More significant, as noted by Peter Hennessy and mentioned in the Butler Review (on the use of intelligence in the prelude to the invasion of Iraq), was the concentration of power in No. 10 in such a way that those best equipped and experienced in policy execution were overtaken by policy advisers chosen for their political loyalties.[34]

The Blair government's defence was that the old ways were inappropriate to effective government in the high-tech era of round-the-clock decision-making and media pressure. However, after the release of the Butler Review in 2004 the government did announce that it would review procedures at No. 10 and revert to more systematic record-keeping. More tellingly, when Gordon Brown took over as prime minister he overhauled the system of decision-making by reinstating some formal procedures and re-emphasizing Cabinet responsibility and accountability to parliament. Even so, after a brief honeymoon period Brown was accused of all sorts of shortcomings.

Diplomacy and policy implementation

By the 1990s Britain's place in the world had changed dramatically since the days of empire. As Andrew Marr described it, whereas once the British 'happened to other people', now 'the world happens to Britain'.[35] To maximize what influence Britain still had therefore required working with others when possible. Diplomacy, the *raison d'être* of the Foreign Office, was obviously indispensable to pursuing a multilateralist foreign policy. Yet while Blair's government consistently advocated multilateralism, British diplomats faced difficulties harmonizing some policies with those of their foreign counterparts, especially other Europeans, on issues relating to the Middle East. This discrepancy (discussed further in Chapters 6 and 7) stemmed in part from Blair's desire to see Britain as the bridge between European and US positions on various issues as opposed to bridging policy differences inside Europe.

In any case, diplomats found themselves picking up the pieces when British policy had repercussions not at first envisaged by the team at No. 10. Up to a point this was ever the role of diplomats. Yet in so far as they no longer felt the same 'ownership' of policy, since they were not consulted or involved in its evolution, their task was discernibly more demanding and less rewarding than in the past.[36] (That said, evidently there were those whose careers in the diplomatic service flourished in the new atmosphere.)

Irrespective of New Labour's approach, globalization complicated the task of foreign policy-making and necessitated changes in the organization of the Foreign Office. According to John Coles, when he became a diplomat in 1960 the most prestigious departments in the Foreign Office were the geographical departments, those that dealt with specific areas of the world such as the Middle East or the Soviet Union:

> The great men (and they were nearly all men) were those who advised during the Arab–Israeli wars of 1967 and 1973 or who developed policy toward the Soviet world in the 1970s or who analysed events in China and their possible impact on Hong Kong. Today [2000], reflecting interdependence and multilateralism, the largest departments, where the most ambitious and able want to work, are the 'functional' departments, those that deal not with a geographical area, but with a subject or group of subjects, such as the two European Union departments dealing with external and internal EU affairs, the International Security Department, dealing among other things with NATO, and the United Nations Department.[37]

In a pamphlet entitled *The End of Foreign Policy?* Peter Hain, a cabinet minister who had held junior ministerial posts at the Foreign Office and the Department of the Environment, developed his views on what globalization might mean for traditional foreign policy-making. He foresaw the necessity for more global collective action by governments and NGOs to combat climate change, poverty, social exclusion, disease, drug abuse and terrorism. With respect to the Foreign Office, Hain suggested that as informational links to overseas posts improved, 'there would be a case for dismantling the geographically oriented departments' and using the overseas posts 'to support cross-cutting objectives in areas such as the environment, conflict prevention and human rights'.[38]

During Blair's first term some steps were taken to streamline British trade promotion across government departments. A body called British Trade International (BTI) was set up within the Department of Trade and Industry (DTI) to coordinate the activities of that department and the Foreign Office. The number of regional boards of leading business people appointed worldwide to advise on export policy and resource allocation was reduced to give emphasis to sectoral opportunities rather than geographic areas. Under this system the Middle East and Africa were lumped together as the responsibility of a single board, notwithstanding the concerns of some in the business sector who argued that the two areas were too dissimilar to warrant a common strategy.

Meanwhile, the role of the Prime Minister's personal adviser or representative on the Middle East peace process, Lord Levy, was informal and never very clear. He had been a fundraiser for both the British and the Israeli Labour parties and for a time his son Daniel worked for senior figures in the Israeli Labour Party, which was assumed to afford useful access. Certainly Levy was busiest on the Middle East front during Ehud Barak's time as Israeli prime minister (1999–2000), while his personal friendship with Tony Blair was considered his main asset thereafter.

When Blair formed his new Cabinet after the June 2001 election, Robin Cook, who by all accounts had grown to like his job as foreign secretary and expected to keep it, was moved to become Leader of the House of Commons. Jack Straw, who was selected to replace him, was apparently also taken by surprise. Some commentators interpreted this change as a bid by Blair to assert more control over foreign policy.[39] In any case, the move did appear to fit with expectations that joining the Eurozone would be a policy objective in Labour's second term. Straw was known to be more sceptical than Cook and could therefore make a more objective case for such a move if necessary. Peter Hain was given the number two job at the Foreign Office, with responsibility for Europe. Baroness Symons was appointed trade minister with offices, staff and responsibilities at both the DTI and the Foreign Office. This was intended to end confusion and conflict between the two ministries over responsibility for trade.[40]

With Hain concentrating on Europe, the remit for the rest of the world was divided up between three parliamentary secretaries. This meant that for a period there was no junior minister in the House of Commons with responsibility for the Middle East (among other regions). In fact, the task of representing the government in the region at a senior level was very often undertaken by Baroness Symons during the second Blair term. As the Iraq crisis unfolded, however, the Prime Minister took the lead and Jack Straw was prominent.

Inside No. 10, Blair had first one and then two senior diplomats on secondment to assist with foreign relations. One of the latter, Sir David Manning, had previously served as ambassador to Israel and went on to become British ambassador to Washington in 2004.[41] His remit at No. 10 included the Middle East. John Sawers progressed from being Blair's private secretary to become ambassador to Cairo. He then went as a special representative to Baghdad for a time, before heading the new Directorate General Political at the FCO. Robert Cooper headed the Cabinet's defence and overseas secretariat during Blair's first term and advised on post-Taliban Afghanistan for a while, before going to head the secretariat of the EU's High Representative Javier Solana.

More powerful than any of the serving diplomats on the No. 10 staff was Jonathan Powell, the chief of staff and a former diplomat. He was recruited in 1995 after Tony Blair became leader of New Labour, apparently as a result of their encounter in Washington, where Powell was serving at the time and briefed Blair and his colleagues on the first Clinton administration. During Blair's first term Powell, like Alastair Campbell, was given special powers that enabled him to instruct civil servants. When the Prime Minister reorganized the staff at No. 10 in 2001, Powell was given charge of one of the three new divisions (Policy and Government), alongside Campbell (Director, Communications and Strategy) and Lady (Sally) Morgan (Government and Political Relations). As a result Powell, a political appointee, wielded more authority than the principal private secretary, formerly the most senior staff member in No. 10.[42] Powell sought to keep out of the public eye as far as possible, in contrast to Campbell, who eventually left No. 10 in 2003. Campbell's replacement was not accorded the same powers, as a result of a decision to reframe the press liaison role that had come under scrutiny during the Hutton Inquiry.

In other words, Blair had a formal, an informal and a semi-formal network of personal confidants, including professional diplomats as well as political allies, whose influence on policy derived from their access to the Prime Minister. Thus there were different layers in the foreign policy-making process that could not be understood by simply examining the chain of command at the Foreign Office and its formal dealings with No. 10. Similarly, the formal structure by which the intelligence services were supposed to feed information to the political leadership, principally through the mechanism of the Joint Intelligence Committee (JIC), was complemented by more informal dealings.

Notoriously, the working relationship established between Alastair Campbell and John Scarlett, the Chairman of the JIC until 2004, may have resulted in a blurring of the lines between their respective responsibilities – as indicated in the Hutton Inquiry and Butler Review. Scarlett's responsibility was the supply of information and intelligence estimates based on that information, and Campbell's was presentation of government policy. One of the products of their combined efforts was of course the infamous dossier on Iraq's weapons of mass destruction released by the government in September 2002; Scarlett took formal 'ownership' and the Prime Minister wrote an introduction apparently drafted by Campbell. The result may serve as a testament to the confusion that can result from according as much importance to the *presentation* of the government's case as to the *substance*.

For approximately a year, from mid-2002 to mid-2003, Iraq was the primary focus of attention at No. 10 as well as the Foreign Office and Ministry of Defence. Once the die was cast and the occupation was under way, policy planners at the Foreign Office set about restructuring its operations, to focus resources on the government's preferred top priorities.[43] This involved enhancing the profile of 'strategic priority teams' as opposed to geographical departments. The five Directorates General – Defence and Intelligence, Political, Europe, Economics and Corporate – indicated the new 'functional' priorities envisaged by Peter Hain. Other sections dealt specifically with legal advice, finance, and strategy and information. Transatlantic relations, involving all the functional areas, were to be coordinated by a 'virtual team', operating across departments.

From 2004 the department dealing with the Middle East and North Africa was brought under the umbrella of the Directorate General Political, as were International Security and South Asia. Responsibility for the rest of Asia and Africa was placed under the umbrella of the Economics Directorate. Iraq, however, was allocated its own Regional Group reporting to the Directorate General Political. It was paralleled by a Regional Group for Russia (together with Central Asia and the Caucasus), eventually wound up in 2007. A Strategic Priority Group was also set up to manage a programme for 'Engagement with the Islamic World' in coordination with other Whitehall departments. A Human Rights, Democracy and Governance Group was created and produced a 'toolkit' on 'Promoting Democratic Principles and Values' in January 2007.[44]

End of an era

For much of the twentieth century the Foreign Office could be considered central to the formulation of British policy towards the Middle East, in its provision of advice to ministers. For several decades the Arabists, or Arabic-speaking diplomats, were the largest single contingent of area specialists in the Foreign Office and included many 'high flyers'. Their knowledge of local politics and personalities, informed by years of service in posts around the region, constituted a key resource for policy-makers. However, by the time New Labour came to power prestige had passed to other types of specialists in the Foreign Office, dealing with technical issues and related negotiations on international trade, finance and the internal market of the EU as well as Asia and the United States. In addition, the value of area expertise no longer rated highly in the calculations of No. 10.

The reputation of the Arabists also suffered from accusations of bias typified by those of the late Professor Elie Kedourie. In his essay 'The Chatham House Version',[45] Kedourie depicted a British establishment view of the Middle East that was overly indulgent of Arab sheikhs and monarchs, as well as anti-Zionist and anti-communist. Kedourie's other complaint was that purportedly independent academic analysis of Middle Eastern politics at the think tank Chatham House was actually carried out in conjunction with – and for a time under the roof of – the Foreign Office. From 1943 to 1946, Arnold Toynbee was simultaneously head of policy analysis at the Foreign Office and director of research at Chatham House.

That era has long since passed. However, the perception of a pro-Arab bias in the Foreign Office proved more long-lasting, especially in Israel, leading Tony Blair to make a deliberate effort to dispel this impression for good. Moreover, starting in the Thatcher years, such funding as the Foreign Office could previously disperse to academia or think tanks was much reduced in the name of introducing 'market forces' all round. Meanwhile, a number of new think tanks have sprung up in Britain reflecting contrasting perspectives from across the political spectrum. These have become associated with different political parties or positions, somewhat along the lines of the American model. As mentioned above, New Labour was directly involved in setting up the Foreign Policy Centre. The FCO's own internal research resources were also progressively cut back during the 1990s, though the diplomatic service remained a source of expertise and experience on the Middle East on which No. 10 did not draw consistently.

Under New Labour, 'establishment' thinking also shifted. Instead of reflecting a Foreign Office worldview and area expertise, policy was consciously framed to promote certain values. In a further shift from the past, from the late 1990s policy-making became concerned with responding to global pressures and priorities rather than regional imperatives. Thus policy towards the Middle East was not so much generated from the ground up but, rather, formulated from the top down. The goal was to maximize British leverage in key policy-making arenas such as the WTO, the G8, the UN Security Council, Washington and Brussels.

Until 9/11 and subsequent actions in Afghanistan and Iraq, the Middle East did not feature highly in New Labour's thinking. Yet those living in the region seem to have had little understanding of London's changed priorities. Instead, it was not uncommon to hear Arab officials and columnists state confidently that 'the British know the region' – and that therefore, whatever their policy was, it must be the product of considered analysis of the region itself and British interests therein.

In fact, New Labour came into power with no 'collective memory' on the Middle East. Indeed, Blair himself seems not to have known or cared much about Britain's historical role in the region. Thus in the late 1990s British policies towards the Middle East and elsewhere derived from other priorities – the effects of new global trends. As detailed in Chapter 2, when the Foreign Office published a strategy document spelling out the new priorities in December 2003, in the process it demonstrated how far British policy had moved from the heyday of the Arabists.

And by 2003, Britain was at war in Iraq. That inevitably increased the role of the MOD in Britain's dealings with the region. In fact, as discussed in Chapter 8, so important were Britain's defence commitments in Iraq and the Arab Gulf states throughout the 9/11 era that the MOD essentially took the lead, along with No. 10, in maintaining links with the Gulf rulers. The DTI and the private sector became almost as prominent in pursuing financial and commercial opportunities in the Arab Gulf states – the role of the FCO in the Gulf states was simply to facilitate such links.

CIVIL SOCIETY

The term 'civil society' has become part of the New Labour lexicon in government dealings with the Middle East and other regions (see Chapter 2). But in considering the mechanisms by which British policy was formulated, presented and implemented during the Blair era, a few words about Britain's *own* civil society actors are in order. Theories about the way the world works inform how policy-makers define their priorities and goals. Those theories are developed in depth by scholars, adopted by think tanks and discussed at length by commentators and columnists in the media. Their role in foreign policy-making should therefore be acknowledged.

The policy agenda and the media

The media have become increasingly instrumental in agenda setting, though not necessarily by design. Journalists themselves have been caught up in the events they seek to cover and have become suspicious in the face of government efforts to determine how a story is reported.

In the Middle East access for foreign journalists varies by country and according to the issues they are able to cover. Most Arab governments and Iran have frequently denied visas to journalists likely to report negatively on their domestic affairs. This has resulted in sometimes combative, sometimes compliant responses from the media. The practice of embedding journalists with military units that became commonplace during the invasion of Iraq has been criticized for compromising press freedom, though undoubtedly the fact that some journalists operating independently also became the object of kidnap attempts in Iraq much reduced their ability to operate there safely, if at all.

In Israel there is considerable press freedom and foreign journalists have enjoyed comparatively good access, though their exclusion from the Gaza Strip during the hostilities in December 2008 and January 2009 was a notable exception. Progressively, the foreign media themselves have become the object of scrutiny for their coverage of the whole Israeli–Palestinian conflict, as the protagonists seek to ensure their version of events receives favourable treatment.

Following the Israeli withdrawal from the Gaza Strip in 2005 and subsequent Palestinian factional fighting, foreign journalists and aid workers faced the danger of kidnap there too. After BBC Gaza correspondent Alan Johnston was captured and held for months by an alleged criminal gang in 2007, living in the area was deemed too unsafe for Western correspondents. Palestinian journalists working for outside news organizations have faced dangers too, in a few cases suffering injury or death as a result of Israeli army fire. In their own defence, the Israeli Defence Forces (IDF) have argued that the West Bank and Gaza are war zones and journalists operate at their peril. Yet when they were barred from entering Gaza in the war of 2008–09, journalists complained that the Israelis were not so much protecting them from harm as averting adverse media coverage of themselves.

British media attention to the Israeli–Palestinian conflict has been sustained in part by domestic interest. British Jews and Arabs are engaged because of family and ideological connections. The setting of the conflict, in the 'Holy Land', also generates a level of fascination and engagement not matched when it comes to stories about events in East Asia, Latin America or sub-Saharan Africa. The recent growth in the number and prominence of British Muslims, and the impact of the war in Kosovo in drawing attention to the fate of Muslims elsewhere, started to change public perceptions, even when Britain was not directly involved. As will be discussed, the 9/11 attacks and the invasion of Iraq proved a turning point for political consciousness about the Middle East for many Britons. In addition, the growing number of Britons migrating to the Arab Gulf states to capitalize on the economic and property booms in Dubai, Abu Dhabi, Bahrain and Qatar between 2003 and 2008 generated another set of connections between the British public and the region.

Meanwhile, satellite television has become big business in the Arab world and the Qatari government-owned satellite channel Al Jazeera has made its impact by covering regional news from an Arab perspective, in part as a deliberate attempt to counter Western dominance of the medium. The BBC has responded to the challenge by expanding its Arab-language service to include television as well as radio. In 2009 the BBC launched a Persian-language television channel – which was greeted with exceptional hostility and suspicion in Iran.

The net effect has been to make governments more conscious than ever of the power of the media, and New Labour was from the first determined to manage presentation of its policies in such a way that the government, not the media, would set the agenda. That was the task to which Alastair Campbell dedicated himself during his time at No. 10, with the result that the media became in turn more adversarial and determined to root out the 'story behind the story'. Blair's time in office witnessed an increase in the amount of media space devoted to discussion of his government's handling of the news. And the government has criticized the media for making news as opposed to reporting it.

Accountability and the public

In summer 2003 the BBC and No. 10 became locked in battle over the former's handling of a story about the British government's presentation of the case for war in Iraq. As the BBC subsequently admitted, Andrew Gilligan, one of its investigative reporters, should not have been allowed to accuse the government of 'probably knowing' its claims about Iraqi WMD were wrong – a charge of which the government was subsequently cleared in the Hutton Inquiry (as discussed in Chapter 5). However, the row would probably not have turned as acrimonious as it did, or led to the suicide of the weapons expert Dr David Kelly, who was exposed as the source behind Gilligan's allegation, had not the relationship between No. 10 and the media already become so confrontational.

In defence of the BBC at the time, it was suggested that it was in effect shouldering the role of the Opposition in parliament, whose task it normally is to question the government and force it to defend its case. Since the Conservative Party leadership had supported the war in Iraq it was not operating in formal Opposition mode on this issue. Also, Labour's parliamentary majority was so large, even in its second term, that only the combination of the Conservatives, other parties and a backbench revolt in the Labour Party itself could have threatened the government's position.

When the Hutton Inquiry found the government guilty of no wrong-doing, but charged the BBC Board of Governors and senior management with inadequate editorial oversight of news reporting and other faults, both the Chairman of the Board and the Director General resigned. Among press commentaries, some labelled Hutton's findings 'a whitewash'. The British public indicated sympathy for the BBC and the government, though cleared, reaped little benefit in public confidence.

Therefore, as will be discussed, British policy on the Iraq war gave rise to serious concerns and debate about the nature of British democracy. Yet public and media questioning of that policy did not translate into defeat at the polls for New Labour in 2005. The British electorate has not generally put foreign policy issues above domestic economic and social considerations in deciding how to vote at a general election, unless the former directly affect their livelihoods. That, at least, is the common assumption. However, a public opinion poll conducted for the *Financial Times* in August 2004 showed that the Iraq war had in fact shifted voters' priorities.[46]

An earlier poll, conducted in June 2001, asked respondents to rank various issues facing Britain in order of relative importance. The National Health Service came out top with 58 per cent, followed in descending order by education, Europe, race relations (14 per cent), the economy and unemployment (equal at 10 per cent), and last of all defence and foreign affairs (2 per cent). In August 2004, by contrast, defence and foreign affairs came out top with 38 per cent, followed in descending order by the National Health Service (34 per cent), race relations (30 per cent), crime (28 per cent), education, the economy, Europe, and at the bottom, unemployment with 7 per cent. While the government no doubt took note of this shift in priorities, it was at least partially saved by the fact that voters still preferred New Labour to the Conservatives at the time of elections in 2005, while the Liberal Democrats, who had opposed the Iraq war, trailed behind the Conservatives.

In fact, New Labour could claim that it had delivered on issues of greatest importance to the public in 2001, but that world events had subsequently overtaken domestic issues, irrespective of government policy. Labour could also argue that it had always said that globalization meant greater inter-dependence and less autonomy in economic, environmental and security concerns. To illustrate the point, when the August 2004 poll was undertaken, oil prices were approaching new highs, passing $40 per barrel (they subsequently trebled before plummeting again in 2008) and events in Iraq were seen as instrumental in the rise.

The role of NGOs

In his paper *The End of Foreign Policy?* quoted above, Peter Hain talked of the need for government to work with NGOs in meeting the challenges of globalization. As foreign secretary, Robin Cook had hoped to be responsive to the goals of human rights activists by giving an ethical dimension to foreign policy (see Chapter 2). Yet by 2004, crisis had overtaken the work of NGOs in both Afghanistan and Iraq, largely as a result of their association with Western government policies. Médecins sans Frontières felt compelled to end years of work in Afghanistan when its staff became the target of attacks by the local population. The problem, said the organization, was the result of the US armed forces telling villagers that aid would only be forthcoming if they revealed information about al-Qaeda and the Taliban.

Meanwhile, several NGOs deemed the situation in Iraq too insecure for them to operate there. The United Nations headquarters in Baghdad had been the object of a devastating attack in August 2003 and when a new team returned the following year they were obliged to operate under US protection, knowing that this could be counter-productive to their reputation and thus their ability to perform a useful role.

Since that time, humanitarian NGOs have faced difficulties in demonstrating their independence while accepting government funding to tackle humanitarian crises. Aid workers as well as journalists have risked attack and kidnap for ransom in conflict zones. Meanwhile, the British government, along with others, has looked to the non-governmental sector to increase its capacity to effect change in other parts of the world. The costs of humanitarian work, institution-building, reconstruction and development have increased as a consequence of the need to provide personal protection to those involved.

All these factors have increasingly featured in government calculations about the costs and benefits of foreign interventions, and the optimism once shown by New Labour had already begun to diminish before the financial crisis of 2008. On the home front, for several years at least, the British NGO sector burgeoned under New Labour, with a proliferation of think tanks and advocacy groups mobilizing members of the public in ways that the traditional political parties have become less able to do. As Tony Blair stepped down from office after ten years as prime minister, the Labour Party was losing members and in debt. Its rivals for power could not demonstrate significant grassroots support either.

Both the Conservatives and Labour will in future have to respond more effectively to new styles of political activism facilitated by the internet. The media have also been affected, with newspapers especially suffering from competition from bloggers and freelancers publishing on the web. In one respect, however, there has been a return to old practices since the end of the Blair era: under the leadership of David Miliband, the Foreign Office has regained a more prominent voice on foreign policy.

4

Britain's Role in the Peace Process: 1997–2001

This is the first of two chapters which explore Britain's role in the quest for peace between Israel and the Palestinians during the Blair years. Even before 9/11 and the invasion of Iraq, the British were committed to finding a resolution to the conflict. But that will require a concerted effort by all the main stakeholders, among whom Britain long ago ceased to play a decisive role. Since the 1970s, the United States has been the key peace-broker between the protagonists, and none of the other players expect to make peace without US involvement. Throughout his time in office Tony Blair operated on that assumption and sought to play 'a pivotal role' in harmonizing the positions of the United States and the European Union. Beyond that, he made several forays of his own which appear to have been designed to facilitate direct talks between the parties and to enhance the capacity of the Palestinians to meet Israeli and US stipulations for substantive engagement.

Britain's contribution to the Middle East peace process between 1997 and 2007 went through a series of phases, which corresponded with changes in the situation on the ground, in Washington and in the Prime Minister's reading of the opportunities and obstacles. From 1997 to May 1999, the Clinton administration was deeply engaged and the principal challenge was to keep the peace process on track in the face of recurring delays and obstacles during the premiership of Binyamin Netanyahu, who opposed the Oslo process and Palestinian statehood. During this period, as described below, New Labour characterized Britain as a player with 'unique influence and leverage', capable of coordinating Europe's policies with those of a US administration committed to peacemaking.

From mid-1999 the premiership of Ehud Barak seemed to give fresh impetus to peace hopes and opened up new possibilities for British diplomacy through access to Barak as well as the Clinton administration. However, the initial optimism waned as Israeli–Syrian negotiations collapsed and the Israeli–Palestinian summit at Camp David in July 2000 failed to deliver.

After the second Palestinian Intifada broke out in September that year, the Israeli peace camp collapsed too. Clinton strove in vain to clinch a deal before the Bush administration took over in Washington in January 2001 and Ariel Sharon became prime minister in Israel soon after. In the margins the British did what little they could to try to help keep peace hopes alive.

In the third discernible phase in Britain's contribution to peacemaking, from January 2001 to May 2003, the priority was to revive some sort of process. The new Bush administration was not interested, the Israelis and Palestinians were at war and then 9/11 transformed the global context. Thereafter the invasion of Afghanistan and then Iraq dominated attention. Even so the British kept up their refrain in Washington that something had to be done about the Israeli–Palestinian conflict.

In 2002 President Bush did finally break new ground by announcing support for a two-state solution, but it was another year before the so-called 'road map' for realizing that vision was launched in May 2003. This led to the next phase in British diplomacy on the peace front, which lasted until early 2006 and revolved around promoting the road map and keeping it on Washington's agenda. The British also exhorted the Palestinians to make greater efforts to meet Israeli demands on the security front and tried to turn Israel's 2005 withdrawal of Jewish settlers and 'disengagement' from Gaza into a moment of opportunity.

In January 2006 there was another dramatic shift in the context, when the Islamist movement Hamas won Palestinian legislative elections that had been backed by the US and monitored by the EU. For the next two years British and allied diplomacy was focused on adjusting to the Hamas victory.

This chapter deals with the first two phases of this story and Chapter 7 considers the situation from 2001, particularly in the context of 9/11 and the invasion of Iraq, which are the subjects of the intervening chapters.

KEEPING THE PROCESS ON TRACK: 1997–99

Before becoming prime minister, Tony Blair had not given any clear indication of his stance on the Arab–Israeli conflict, although journalist Ned Temko was to report years later that Blair had formed a personal aspiration to work for peace when, as Leader of the Opposition, he first went to Jerusalem to attend the funeral of Israeli Prime Minister Yitzhak Rabin, assassinated in 1995.[1] In any case, first indications of New Labour's thinking on the Middle East did not come from Tony Blair, but rather from the Foreign Office. Following his appointment in summer 1997, junior minister Derek Fatchett chose the countries involved in the peace process (Israel, the occupied Palestinian territory, Syria, Lebanon, Jordan and Egypt) for his first overseas trip. His pronouncements followed a time-honoured Foreign Office tradition of repeating the obligations of the parties under international law and calling for resolution of the conflict on the basis of the 'land for peace' formula.

However, apparently aiming to distinguish New Labour from the previous Conservative government, Fatchett proclaimed an intention to follow a 'principled approach rooted in ethics'.[2] In a speech to the British Society for Middle Eastern Studies (BRISMES) in July 1997, he said the 'principled approach' to the Middle East peace process would have two elements: 'respect for international legality' and 'impartiality'. He defined impartiality as speaking out when the parties to the Arab–Israeli conflict were deemed to be failing on their commitments.[3] On the face of it, this posture chimed with Foreign Secretary Robin Cook's announcement that British foreign policy would in future feature an 'ethical dimension' (see Chapter 2). From No. 10, however, came an insistence that the Foreign Office make efforts to disabuse the Israelis of their long-held impression that British diplomacy was more likely to favour the Arabs than Israel (see Chapter 3). The objective was to increase Britain's leverage with the Israelis to match its assumed influence among the Arabs.

Finding a niche

Tony Blair's first public foray into Middle East peacemaking was in November 1997, when he hosted talks in London between US Secretary of State Madeleine Albright and Israeli Prime Minister Binyamin Netanyahu. It was not a particularly fruitful encounter. Blair stressed the 'urgent need' to move forward on the steps outlined in the Israeli–Palestinian Interim Agreement or 'Oslo II' (of 1995) and Britain's 'great concerns' about the lack of significant progress.

For his part Netanyahu made it plain that he had no intention of facilitating the creation of a Palestinian state; would make no concessions on Jerusalem; and would bar the return of Palestinian refugees to the state of Israel. Even so, he advocated moving immediately to final status talks on Israeli–Palestinian relations, at the expense of the incremental Israeli troop redeployments envisaged in Oslo II. His stance was cause for frustration in Washington, since US efforts at the time were focused on effecting the implementation of phased redeployments. Amid the repeated delays and backtracking by Netanyahu, Israel forged ahead with settlement building in the West Bank, including the foundation of a new settlement called Har Homa at Jebel Abu Gneim, which would complete the encirclement of East Jerusalem by Jewish housing complexes.

Britain's assumption of the rotating EU presidency in January 1998 nonetheless appeared to offer New Labour an opportunity to inject new life into the peace process across the board. In the language of the Barcelona Declaration or Euro-Mediterranean Partnership Initiative launched by the EU and its Mediterranean 'partner' countries in November 1995,[4] Europe had the potential to be a leading 'partner' to the Middle East. A stronger British role in Europe and a new push for peace in the Middle East were thus mutually reinforcing goals. However, given Washington's very active engagement during the Clinton presidency, there seemed little that the British alone or the Europeans collectively could do except support US efforts. Had they broken ranks, as some in the EU contemplated, in order to protest against Israeli government policies, they could not have expected to change minds in the Israeli cabinet and would have irritated the Americans, to no useful purpose.[5]

Accordingly, in March 1998 Foreign Secretary Robin Cook launched a plan for the EU to reinvigorate the Middle East peace process through:

1. six immediate measures to restore confidence, including a substantial Israeli redeployment, the opening of the Gaza airport, and specific security commitments;
2. practical assistance from the EU, including help to boost the Palestinian economy and to fight terrorism;
3. renewed diplomatic activity and a strengthening of the European role, including forthcoming visits to the region by Mr Cook and the Prime Minister.[6]

Cook lamented the fact that the average Palestinian was 30 per cent poorer than when the peace process began, and noted that Europe was already engaged in intensive dialogue with the Israeli government designed to remove restrictions on the Palestinian economy. With a view to promoting the EU plan, Cook noted that the British Prime Minister had written to Clinton, Netanyahu and Palestinian President Yasser Arafat, stressing the importance Britain attached to reinvigorating the peace process.

For their part the Israelis were inclined to be suspicious of any initiatives emanating from the EU and took Washington much more seriously, counting on a more sympathetic hearing from the Americans. Seemingly sensitive to this dynamic, in his interactions with the Israelis Tony Blair concentrated on facilitating US diplomacy, leaving Robin Cook to represent the EU line. In their dealings with Netanyahu, Blair even appeared to play the role of 'good cop' to Cook's 'bad cop'. Thus, when Netanyahu came to London for talks with Albright in November 1997, it was Cook who emphasized the need to halt settlement expansion while Blair was less outspoken on the subject.

Shortly before Cook made his first trip to Israel in March 1998, Blair had a meeting with Netanyahu in London which could presumably have been used to prepare the ground, but tension followed. On 18 March Cook visited the site of Har Homa to publicly demonstrate EU objection to the settlement. Netanyahu reacted promptly, threatening to complain to Tony Blair personally and cancelling a scheduled dinner with the Foreign Secretary. The media made much of the incident, largely at the expense of Cook, who was later to call the episode a 'set-up' by Netanyahu.[7] After his return to London the Board of Deputies of British Jews cancelled an invitation for Cook to address them.

By April 1998 the Americans had brokered a compromise deal on the size and timing of the overdue second Israeli redeployment envisaged in 'Oslo II', though Netanyahu would not concede over a freeze on settlement building. He could count on the balance of opinion in the US Congress together with support from the Christian Right to counter pressure from the Executive, which left both the White House and the EU seemingly blocked on this key issue. Blair then made his first visit to Israel as prime minister, which coincided with Israel's fiftieth anniversary celebrations. He came flushed with the success of his peacemaking efforts in Northern Ireland. He advocated that both sides in the Israeli–Palestinian conflict make concessions for peace, but avoided specifics or causing affront by his choice of itinerary, making a visit to the Holocaust Memorial, Yad Vashem, a central feature of his trip.

Blair did secure Netanyahu's agreement to attend a conference in London, together with Arafat, the following month. However, just as Blair was about to make his way to Gaza to invite Arafat, Netanyahu publicly announced the London plan and revealed that it had been coordinated with the United States. The EU did not feature in this announcement – even though the event could logically have served as a concluding achievement of the British presidency. As it transpired, there was no conference, only 'talks' on 4–5 May 1998, with neither party talking directly to the other.

The outcome was a new US invitation to Arafat and Netanyahu to meet face to face in Washington, with the stipulation that they make progress on implementation of the agreed second Israeli redeployment. However, Netanyahu wanted this to be the last such redeployment, before moving directly to final status talks. In other words, he was not interested in the incremental process of handing over more land and authority to the Palestinians, which was the centrepiece of the Oslo process and intended to build confidence. Instead Netanyahu wanted to jump to the endgame – which for him would not and could not involve Palestinian statehood. He then ducked Washington's invitation, fixed for 11 May, in favour of more consultations with Albright on his next scheduled visit to Washington shortly thereafter.

Meanwhile, Israelis and Palestinians of all persuasions were asking if the peace process existed in anything but name.

With respect to the other front in the conflict – south Lebanon – Netanyahu continued to talk up his interpretation of UN Resolution 425 (which called for Israel's unconditional withdrawal from south Lebanon, which it had occupied since its invasion in 1982). Netanyahu demanded an enhanced UN presence and an Israel–Lebanon peace deal in return for Israeli withdrawal. For its part, the US State Department blamed Syria for hosting Palestinian rejectionist groups working against the peace process and called on Damascus to stop attacks on Israel by Hizbullah (see Chapter 6).

The end of New Labour's first stint in the EU presidency was marked by a conference of member states in Cardiff. The consensus on the Middle East was to continue to back the American line for reviving the peace process, but officials conveyed little optimism, predicting that Netanyahu would continue to drag out talks on the redeployment issue, conceivably until the expiry of the five-year Oslo interim period in May 1999. In an attempt to focus attention, France proposed an international conference, in two phases – first without the parties to the conflict and then including them; but the United States was not interested. According to Foreign Office officials at the time, given Washington's lack of interest, not to say opposition, there was no point in pressing the idea. The British were firmly of the view that without the United States no initiative could work.[8] If the British intention had been to coordinate between the EU and Washington, in fact what they achieved was a niche position as the principal European facilitator of US diplomacy.

Portents of 'the war on terror'

On 7 August 1998 the US embassies in Kenya and Tanzania were attacked by suicide bombers. A total of 263 people were killed, including 12 Americans, and 5,000 injured. The Saudi national Osama bin Laden, one-time champion of the US- and Saudi-backed resistance to the Soviet Union in Afghanistan, by forces known as the Mujahedin, was deemed responsible. Exiled from Saudi Arabia after falling out with the government over its stance in the 1991 Gulf war, bin Laden had decamped to Sudan and from there back to Afghanistan. On 20 August the Clinton administration took reprisals for the embassy bombings with missile attacks on sites they associated with terrorist activities in Sudan and Afghanistan. US Secretary of State Madeleine Albright opined that the 'war against terrorism' would be the 'war of the future'.

Albright and her team nonetheless persisted with their diplomacy on the Israeli–Palestinian front, finally succeeding in bringing Netanyahu and

Arafat face to face for the first time for nearly a year in September 1998. Subsequently closeting them both at a location near Wye River, Maryland, in October, the Americans eventually persuaded them to sign the Wye River Memorandum, which scheduled both the next Israeli troop redeployment in the West Bank and final status talks. The CIA was to become directly involved in Israeli–Palestinian security cooperation and CIA chief George Tenet deemed the Agency's role a facet of the war on terrorism. Yet no sooner was the deal done than Palestinian suicide bombers launched a murderous attack in Israel. This obliged Arafat to arrest some 300 members of Hamas while Netanyahu made implementation of the Wye Agreement dependent on fulfilment of Israeli security requirements.

Israeli redeployment did finally begin in late November. The Gaza airport was allowed to open on 24 November and the first 250 of 750 prospective Palestinian prisoner releases went ahead – although few of those could be considered 'political detainees'. There was a moment of optimism in mid-December when Clinton visited Gaza to witness the annulment of the PLO Charter, to demonstrate Palestinian acceptance of Israel. Even so, there were Palestinian demonstrations against the US President, prompted partly by the simultaneous bombing of Iraq by US and British forces, in the action dubbed Operation Desert Fox (see Chapter 5).

The death of King Hussein

Blair as well as Clinton were back in the region in early 1999, to pay tribute to King Hussein of Jordan, who died on 7 February. The funeral brought together heads of state from across the world as well as the region and the media watched carefully to see who might shake hands with whom. President Hafez al-Asad of Syria attended, notwithstanding the presence of Netanyahu; the Iraqi Vice President came; and Yasser Arafat, one-time foe of Hussein, attended too. Palestinians observed three days of mourning in the West Bank and Gaza. King Hussein had become Clinton's closest ally in the pursuit of the peace process after the assassination of Rabin, with whom Hussein had also formed a bond. The king had even struggled from his sickbed to help Clinton clinch the Wye River deal between Netanyahu and Arafat.

Tony Blair had not had occasion to become particularly close to Hussein, though the latter retained a house in England and was a frequent visitor to Britain. England was also where King Hussein had held many secret meetings with the Israelis over the years.[9] He had close connections with the British royal family and among the British soldiers and advisers who had served and supported Jordan over the years – some fighting with the Arab

Legion in the first Arab–Israeli war of 1948, others trained alongside Hussein himself at the Royal Military Academy Sandhurst. Hussein's family – many of them educated in England, including for a while his first son and successor Abdullah II – have continued to maintain close friendships in Britain (see also Chapter 6).

Yet as Jordan grew closer to the United States the British exercised less influence and leverage there. During the last years of King Hussein's reign, the New Labour government made no special efforts to nurture relations. Indeed, there were clear indications that Crown Prince Hassan, Hussein's brother, could not obtain the access at No. 10 or the Foreign Office that he wanted.[10] Conceivably the British already anticipated that Hussein would choose one of his sons to succeed him instead (which he did just before he died).[11] Whether they also foresaw that he would anoint his eldest son Abdullah, born to Hussein's British wife, seems less likely, since even Abdullah himself was not expecting it.

In any case, once Abdullah became king the influence of the Americans in Amman took on new dimensions. One was a higher level of interaction between the CIA and the Jordanian intelligence service, whose own operations became more pervasive. Another was the access to the royal court granted to the US Ambassador to Jordan, William Burns, whose appearances at the palace became so frequent observers joked about it.[12] Over time, as King Abdullah established his own style and stature, US involvement became simply routine, paving the way for coordination on intelligence and the training of the Iraqi armed forces after the invasion of Iraq. British relations with Jordan also gained new significance after 9/11 and the Iraq war, as discussed in Chapter 6.

Promises to the Palestinians

In terms of the prospects for Arab–Israeli peace in 1999, the big issue on the horizon was the 4 May milestone that would mark the end of the five years during which the Oslo process was supposed to deliver a final status agreement on borders, settlements, security arrangements, Jerusalem and refugees. Arafat had raised the stakes by threatening a unilateral declaration of independent statehood for Palestine on that date. The Israeli government countered with a more potent threat, warning that it would simply annex all the areas of the West Bank under direct Israeli control (at least 70 per cent, not counting those areas – around 20 per cent – under joint Israeli–Palestinian security control). Meanwhile, the US, Arab and European governments foresaw that the Palestinians would end up in an even worse situation, with a non-viable state and unable to exercise any real sovereignty.

However, Arafat needed to persuade his people that they had achieved something by going along with the Oslo process, which seemed so endless and unrewarding.

Concerns in Europe and the United States produced a coordinated plan to dissuade Arafat from making his declaration by coming closer than ever before to endorsing the goal of Palestinian statehood, provided the peace process continued. The Clinton administration was not prepared to say as much overtly – having long argued that direct agreement between the parties should determine the outcome. But the Europeans had already come much closer to foreseeing statehood as the logical expression of Palestinian self-determination, which they had supported since the Venice Declaration of 1980 (see Chapter 1). By tacit agreement, therefore, the EU took the lead. The EU's Berlin Declaration of 25 March 1999 provided the clearest ever endorsement of independent statehood for the Palestinians. It affirmed the 'continuing and unqualified Palestinian right to self-determination including the option of a state' and said that the EU 'looks forward to the early fulfilment of this right'.[13]

Clinton followed up with a private letter to Arafat and a statement on 26 April to the effect that the United States would work for the conclusion of final status talks within a year. This laid the ground for a new deadline in September 2000 and set the scene for the make-or-break diplomacy of that summer.

For immediate purposes, however, the combined US–EU strategy worked, and on 27 April the Palestine National Council decided against a unilateral declaration of independence. Britain's role in the drama was supportive of its EU partners, though not 'pivotal'. British diplomats did, however, join other Europeans in defying Israeli objections to maintaining contact with the Orient House – the office of Faisal Husseini, the key representative of the Palestinian Authority (PA) in East Jerusalem and the leading Palestinian voice opposing Israeli settlement expansion there.

BETTING ON BARAK: 1999–2000

On 17 May 1999 Israel's Labour Party triumphed in elections and Ehud Barak became the new prime minister. Netanyahu's parting shot, delivered while Barak was still forming his coalition, was a major bombing raid on Lebanon on 24–25 June, targeting bridges, power plants and phone links. The trigger was a rocket attack into Israel by Hizbullah, in retaliation for the injuring of a Lebanese woman by Israeli fire. Against this backdrop and to the dismay of Arafat and the PA, when Barak did take over he initially directed most of his attention to the Syrian–Lebanese negotiating track.

For Tony Blair, meanwhile, the advent of Barak's government represented an opportunity to make a difference. Blair's personal friend and fundraiser for the Labour Party Lord (Michael) Levy had connections with the Israeli Labour Party, including through his son, who worked for members of the party (as noted in Chapter 3). The appointment of Lord Levy as Blair's personal envoy on the peace process was made without publicity and only became apparent as he began a series of visits to the region, sounding out views in various capitals, notably Damascus. Between April 1999 and June 2000 he visited Bahrain, Egypt, Jordan, Lebanon, Oman, Qatar, Syria and Israel, where doors were opened to him on the basis of his access to both the British and the Israeli prime ministers.[14] Reportedly the Foreign Office was initially unenthusiastic. However, as ambassadors in the region became accommodated to this hands-on approach to foreign policy, they also facilitated Levy's shuttle diplomacy. He was given an office at the FCO and his role was acknowledged favourably by Robin Cook.

As it transpired, Levy's contribution to diplomacy carried little significance beyond Ehud Barak's period in office, and as far as the Palestinians were concerned Barak wasted valuable time reviving the Syrian negotiating track, ultimately without success, while Palestinian frustrations continued to mount. According to Afif Safieh, the head of the Palestinian General Delegation in London, Barak was 'a monumental disappointment', alienating his own colleagues as well as antagonizing his coalition partners.[15] At his first meeting with Arafat, Barak raised objections to the Wye Memorandum timetable for redeployments. With US and Egyptian mediation, at a summit in Sharm el-Sheikh on 5 September 1999 the parties finally agreed to a new timetable, giving Israel until January 2000 to implement the next redeployment and to negotiate a 'Framework Agreement on Permanent Status'. Final status talks resumed a week later, having lain dormant since they formally began in February 1996, but they initially focused more on process than on substance.

Meanwhile, Barak made a number of statements to various audiences, indicating that he envisaged no return of Palestinian refugees to within Israel; he considered the settlement of Maale Adumim part of 'Greater Jerusalem'; he would prioritize the Golan settlements for new investment; and key areas in the West Bank would be confiscated to enable road-building and settlement expansion. There was no indication of movement on the promised 'safe passage' between the Gaza Strip and the West Bank, or on prisoner releases. When tackled on the subject of settlements, Barak focused on the issue of the so-called 'illegal outposts', constructed without official Israeli sanction, thereby deflecting attention from the expansion of the main settlement blocks.

On the Syrian track, Damascus demanded that talks resume on the basis of where they had left off when Rabin was assassinated, but the Israelis disagreed with the Syrians on the content of what Rabin had actually offered and no document had been agreed. In addition to Lord Levy's informal shuttle diplomacy, the FCO took some steps to pave the way for peace in Damascus (noted in Chapter 6). These included facilitating visits by British academics with knowledge of Israel to enter into dialogue with Syrian academics, journalists and officials.[16] Meanwhile, both the US and the EU were keen to bolster and encourage Barak to make a fresh start after the period of stagnation in the peace process presided over by Netanyahu. Germany gave support to an idea proposed by Washington to enable Israel to become part of the 'European and others' group at the United Nations. However, on this the British were not supportive, arguing instead that Israeli inclusion should only be contemplated as a reward for actual progress.[17]

Talks about talks on the Syrian track eventually delivered a formal resumption of negotiations between Barak and Syrian Foreign Minister Farouk Shara in Washington on 15 December. President Clinton talked up the potential for a breakthrough and the improved prospects for regional peace. In the background Jordan announced the arrest of suspected supporters of Osama bin Laden, who were allegedly planning attacks on US and other targets in the region. Prior to this move, King Abdullah had already won praise from Washington by closing the Hamas office in Amman and exiling its leader Khaled Mishaal – who eventually established himself in Damascus.

The Israelis finally did implement the second phase of the second redeployment, though they unilaterally changed the timetable for the prospective third phase and issued confusing signals on the final status issues and Framework Agreement, suggesting there might need to be a further long-term interim arrangement. Clearly unhappy but determined, Arafat resorted to more public diplomacy. Even so, as became apparent when he appeared in London and held a joint press conference with Robin Cook, Arafat was increasingly rattled by charges of corruption in the PA and Palestinian security forces.

Discerning an opening for Britain to make a contribution, in connection with the shortcomings of the PA, several government departments (including DFID, the Treasury, the security services and the FCO) initiated projects to give technical assistance to the PA – advising and helping build capacity, for example, in its Negotiations Support Unit and Finance Ministry. Funds were also made available to British NGOs to work with their Palestinian counterparts on projects on civil society development, education and strategic planning. Through the EU, British taxpayers also contributed to 'people to people' exercises to promote dialogue between Israelis and Palestinians. British aid to the Palestinians totalled about £25 million in 2000.[18]

Surprises on the Syria–Lebanon front

In retrospect it is clear that the first half of Ehud Barak's premiership saw significant progress in the revival of the peace process on all tracks, helped along by Washington and the Europeans, including the British. By March 2000, however, the process was beginning to unravel.

Summoned by Clinton to a summit in Geneva on 26 March, President Asad of Syria and his aides were baffled and disappointed to discover that instead of the breakthrough they had been led to expect, they were presented with an Israeli offer they could not accept without losing face. The Israelis wanted to retain control of the northern shoreline of the Sea of Galilee. Washington and Israeli insiders subsequently lamented an opportunity lost, whether by mishandling, default or even design, as some alleged.[19] It was the end of the Israeli–Syrian negotiating track. When Bashar al-Asad succeeded as president, he lacked the stature and experience of his father and needed to consolidate his power; he was therefore not in a position to make concessions that his father had refused.

In the meantime, Barak delivered what proved to be his most significant legacy to regional relations in this period. In May 2000 Israel unilaterally evacuated its forces from southern Lebanon, ending 18 years of occupation. The UN subsequently pronounced the Israeli withdrawal complete, in compliance with Resolution 425. However, encouraged by Syria, the Lebanese claimed that the continued Israeli presence in a small area on the Lebanese–Syrian border known as Sheba Farms, captured by Israel along with the Golan Heights in 1967, meant that the withdrawal was incomplete. Hizbullah used the claim to continue its armed presence and attacks on Israelis in this vicinity. Nonetheless, the Israeli–Lebanese, or more accurately the Israeli–Hizbullah, dimension of the Arab–Israeli conflict remained relatively contained until a Hizbullah raid into Israel triggered the war of July–August 2006 (see Chapter 7).[20]

Palestinians saw the Israeli withdrawal from Lebanon as a victory for Hizbullah. Their leadership understood that they would be judged weak by comparison if they settled for less than a full withdrawal from the West Bank and Gaza Strip.[21] Violent clashes between Palestinians and Israeli forces erupted in the occupied Palestinian territory during May, heightening the tension and raising the stakes in advance of the make-or-break summit sought by Clinton and Barak and proposed by Clinton to Arafat in June. The Palestinian leader was reluctant, arguing that the ground was insufficiently prepared, but Clinton, in his last year of office, was running out of time and Barak's government was beginning to fall apart.

Collapse of the Palestinian track

From 11 to 25 July 2000 Arafat, Barak and their respective aides were closeted at Camp David, with Clinton and his officials shuttling between the parties 'floating' ideas and proposals in a vain attempt to reach agreement.

Much has been written about what went wrong at this Camp David summit.[22] In an apparent effort to rescue Barak from his Israeli critics, the Clinton administration praised Israeli readiness to compromise and lamented Palestinian inflexibility. Palestinians have since argued that Arafat erred in not handling the situation more diplomatically, rather than claiming triumph when he walked away in defiance. Some were certainly puzzled that he did not explain his side of the story and instead let his detractors monopolize the post-summit analysis.[23]

The Israeli claim that the Palestinians were offered the most they could hope for was disingenuous, given that they would be offered more in subsequent negotiations. Indeed, some have argued that if the proposals floated by Clinton in December 2000 – the so-called Clinton Parameters – had been on offer to the Palestinians at Camp David, the talks might have stood a better chance of success. As it was, according to Aaron David Miller, a veteran US diplomat involved in the process, the United States tended to concentrate too heavily on promoting positions the Israelis could agree to, at the expense of even-handedness.[24]

Immediately following Camp David, however, the perception that the Palestinians had turned down a golden opportunity gained credence, including in London. Reflecting on the situation in early September 2000, Foreign Office Minister Peter Hain reported that the British government had been extremely active behind the scenes, trying to avert a breakdown of the process. At the end of August Robin Cook had meetings with the acting Israeli Foreign Minister Shlomo Ben-Ami and Palestinian Foreign Representative Nabil Shaath. Hain himself visited Israel and the Palestinian Authority for discussions with Barak, Arafat and other key figures. Then Blair had long and detailed discussions with Barak, Arafat and Clinton, in the margins of the UN summit in New York, 'keeping very close to all the players with whom he has excellent relationships'.[25]

Britain, Hain claimed, had 'unique credibility' through being 'very close to the Palestinian leadership, close to this particular Israeli government', and 'relations between our Prime Minister and their Prime Minister are extremely good'.[26] Across the board, Hain reported, the British 'had a consistent message for the Palestinians that this is the best opportunity that they will get, if not ever then for a long time. That was the essence of the message we gave the Palestinians.'[27] Behind the message was Britain's desire 'to see an independent Palestinian state come out of the peace process'.

Barak did meet Arafat again after the Camp David débâcle, and Israeli and Palestinian negotiators, as well as US officials, continued to work on devising a deal. Barak, having lost his majority in the Knesset, preferred to switch focus again and called for a government of national unity to effect 'secular-civic' reform in Israel. This initiative proved short-lived; public faith in the peace process was about to run out on both sides.

The trigger for a new eruption of violence was Ariel Sharon's provocative visit to the Temple Mount – for Muslims Haram al-Sharif or Noble Sanctuary and site of the al-Aqsa mosque – on 28 September. Clashes between Palestinian demonstrators and Israeli police and security forces quickly turned ugly, setting off a chain reaction that turned into the second Palestinian Intifada (dubbed the al-Aqsa Intifada at the time). It proved much more bloody than the first uprising (1987–93), though just how far into reverse the peace process would go was not fully apparent until February 2001. By then Arafat had failed to capitalize effectively on Clinton's 'Parameters' and an angry and disillusioned Israeli electorate had voted Ariel Sharon their new prime minister.

The British were among those who weighed in to try to mediate an end to the violence in late 2000. In mid-October Robin Cook went to the region for a series of urgent meetings with President Mubarak of Egypt, President Bashar al-Asad of Syria, King Abdullah II of Jordan, Yasser Arafat and Ehud Barak. According to Peter Hain, Cook helped pave the way for the Sharm el-Sheikh summit of 17 October that called for a resumption of the status quo ante and a US-led investigation (which produced the Mitchell Report – see below).[28] However, commenting on the possibility that Britain might contribute more to the Middle East peace process, Hain offered the following appraisal:

> The American presidential transition may provide an opportunity for the European Union, and Britain in particular, to continue to engage in the peace process. We have a unique friendly relationship with the Palestinian people, the Israeli Government and their people, the Americans and the Arab world, and can perhaps play a more prominent role in the process than we have been able to do. If we are asked to do so, we shall, but we can do so only with the consent of the other parties involved, including the Americans who have been in the lead up to the present time.[29]

As it transpired, the US continued to pursue a resolution of the crisis until the very end of Clinton's second term in the White House. In the meantime, his successor, George W. Bush, was not confirmed as the winner in the November elections until December, following a decision by the US Supreme Court to resolve the dispute over voting returns in Florida. At the

UN, meanwhile, divisions emerged between EU members and the Americans over a resolution drawing attention to Israel's continued occupation of Palestinian territory. The EU also suffered a setback when the fourth Foreign Ministers' Conference of the Euro-Mediterranean Partnership Programme turned acrimonious and failed to agree a Charter for Peace and Stability that had been under discussion for many months. Refusing to attend in the presence of Israel, the Syrians and Lebanese boycotted the event; and in solidarity with the Palestinians, the North Africans ended the tentative contacts they had begun to develop with Israel. Skirmishes between Israelis and Hizbullah prompted UN Secretary-General Kofi Annan to make a new call for the deployment of the Lebanese armed forces to their side of the border, but to no avail. Hizbullah retained its predominance in the area.

Barak, who was due to go to the polls in February 2001, paid little attention to such machinations or the last-ditch peace negotiations at Taba between Israeli and Palestinian officials, who arrived at an outline agreement too late to salvage the process. George Bush was by then in the White House and Ariel Sharon was poised for a victory that he would use as a mandate to crack down on the Palestinians and isolate Arafat. The Palestinian response included an increasing number of suicide attacks on Israeli civilians, the horror of which began to erode the sympathy they had previously received for their mounting casualty rate under Israeli military measures.

Losing control

For Blair and the first New Labour government there was nothing to celebrate and much to fear as they watched the peace process unravel and the violence intensify in late 2000 and early 2001. Diplomatic contacts and coordination intensified across Europe and the Middle East, but there was no turning the tide of violence.

The Mitchell Report on the causes of the al-Aqsa Intifada – the result of an investigation by a committee chaired by US Senator George Mitchell – was published in April 2001. Promoting Mitchell's recommendations for returning the situation to the status quo ante became the centrepiece of British policy. Mitchell was also central to the efforts of the US State Department to halt the spiral of violence. Calls by British officials for an end to Israeli settlement-building more resembled US urgings than the emphasis on the illegality of the settlements made by EU officials in Brussels.[30] Yet harmonization of the positions of Kofi Annan, his representative Terje Roed Larsen, EU High Representative Javier Solana and Ambassador Miguel Moratinos (the EU's Special Representative for the Middle East Peace Process), the Jordanians and the Egyptians essentially substituted for the development of a forthright position on the actual needs of the situation on the ground. Thereafter, it became commonplace for British officials to focus more on maintaining a coordinated international approach and narrowing the gap between the positions of the protagonists than on the pursuit of a 'principled approach' for its own sake.

For his part, President Bush showed no interest in mimicking Clinton's active engagement and relied on the State Department and the CIA to intervene on the ground. Following a particularly bloody suicide bombing by Hamas at a Tel Aviv discotheque on 1 June, the combined efforts of German Foreign Minister Joschka Fischer and US Secretary of State Colin Powell persuaded Arafat to declare a ceasefire.[31] George Tenet was sent to oversee its implementation. Any notion of moving to the 'confidence-building measures' proposed by Mitchell depended on the effectiveness of these efforts. But neither these nor Arafat's own efforts deterred Sharon from his strategy of crushing the Palestinian resistance before contemplating peace moves. Meanwhile, attempts by France and Germany on the one hand and Arab leaders on the other to persuade the Bush administration to do more to stem the tide of violence met with a cool response.[32]

In Britain New Labour won a second term in the May 2001 elections, and Blair formed a new government – including a new Foreign Secretary, Jack Straw. While DFID's role gained in significance, that of the Foreign Office receded somewhat (see Chapter 3), in part because No. 10 was increasingly calling the shots on foreign policy, including on the Arab–Israeli conflict. After 9/11 Tony Blair became the driving force and face of British policy in the Middle East. The decision to join the invasion of Iraq, the subject of the next chapter, was the central factor in this shift.

5

The Road to War in Iraq

The purpose of this chapter is to explain what led Britain to join the United States in the invasion of Iraq in 2003. Neither blind loyalty to the 'special relationship' with the United States nor simple calculations about oil can serve as adequate explanations. Instead the story is more complex and interesting. It reveals much about Britain under New Labour and the leadership of Tony Blair and it forms the centrepiece of this account of Britain and the Middle East in the 9/11 era.

Blair was not bounced or manipulated into invading Iraq. The decision to make Britain a partner in the endeavour was his own, with varying degrees of support from his inner circle and most members of the Cabinet. The logic behind his decision, as pieced together below, is also fairly easy to discern. Crucially, it was in keeping with the interventionist approach to foreign policy that he espoused from the moment he attained office (discussed in Chapters 2 and 3). As Blair himself kept repeating, most notably after it turned out that Iraq no longer had a secret arsenal of weapons of mass destruction by 2003, for him 'it was the right thing to do'.

Blair can be, and has been, faulted on two main counts. One is that he was secretive about the information or lack of it on which he based his judgment – thereby pre-empting the debate in the Cabinet, parliament and the country that should have informed such a momentous decision. The second is that he gave minimal if any credence to relevant and available knowledge of the situation on the ground, in Iraq and the surrounding region, which should have been factored into planning for 'the day after' regime change in Baghdad.

As the Butler Inquiry was subsequently to find, the neglect of formal procedures in the way the Prime Minister arrived at key decisions (discussed in Chapter 3) was a cause for concern with respect to Iraq among other issues.[1] As the Butler Report also revealed, the government's conclusion in spring 2002 that stronger action than hitherto needed to be taken against Iraq was not based on any new intelligence.[2] On the eve of the invasion a year later, policy-makers and the intelligence community did not see fit to re-examine their own intelligence assessment on Iraqi weapons programmes in the light of new evidence.[3]

Crucially, the policy of containment that Blair inherited from the outgoing Conservative government in 1997 was *not sustainable* once the United States ceased to pursue it. However, in the absence of a coordinated multilateral approach to managing regime change, the odds were stacked against success.[4] It was a significant gamble to base a major policy decision on no more than a slim possibility that all the pieces would somehow fall into place once the invasion force entered Iraq, and to supplant judgment by the mantra 'failure is not an option'. The following sections explore these policy issues in more detail.

CONTAINMENT: RUNNING OUT OF STEAM

New Labour inherited a policy on Iraq that could not be easily redirected or abandoned. It derived from the ceasefire resolution (UN Security Council Resolution 687) that concluded the 1991 war to liberate Kuwait from Iraqi occupation, as outlined in Chapter 1. During the course of the 1990s the British had joined the Americans in a strategy designed to contain Iraq, in the name of regional security, so long as Saddam's regime remained in place.

Yet, as also indicated in Chapter 1, the British position rested on the conviction that UN inspections and the introduction of long-term monitoring arrangements would work. However, the so-called oil-for-food deal that underpinned containment was imperfect at best, increasingly open to abuse[5] and at worst counterproductive.[6] This was the situation facing New Labour when it picked up the reins in 1997.

New Labour's initial stance

Foreign Secretary Robin Cook had 'form' on Iraq, having led the Opposition attack on the Conservative government over revelations of its arms supplies to Saddam Hussein in the 1980s.[7] Other New Labour MPs, several of whom became cabinet ministers in 1997, also had a track record on Iraq, having condemned the poison gas attacks on Iraqi Kurds in 1988. Their stance included parliamentary motions to condemn the US and UK governments for supplying Baghdad with chemical products and to oppose export credits to Iraq. Ann Clwyd (who was subsequently appointed by Blair to champion human rights in Iraq after the 2003 invasion) had achieved prominence for her defence of the Kurdish cause. In sum, the arrival of New Labour in power seemed unlikely to hold out any benefits for Saddam Hussein. However, it was expected to be more receptive to the concerns of human rights organizations about the unintended consequences of the sanctions. While the majority of Iraqis suffered, the regime not only survived but thrived by manipulating the system.

In fact, the new government was clearly in a predicament. It had to find ways to relieve that suffering without letting up the pressure on Saddam Hussein. Reviewing the line adopted by the new government, Minister of State for the Armed Forces John Reid addressed an audience of Arab and British defence analysts in Abu Dhabi in April 1998 as follows:

> I recognize that sanctions have enabled Saddam to manipulate the truth and claim a propaganda victory in saying that our policies are leading to the deaths of innocent Iraqi children. Nothing could be further from the truth. The UK Government has no argument with the Iraqi people. You will know that we hosted a meeting ... to look at ways of improving the 'oil-for-food' scheme and ensuring that its revenues are spent on helping the Iraqi population who have suffered for too long under Saddam's brutal regime.[8]

For his part the Prime Minister did not give any indications of having developed a new strategy on Iraq during his first months in office, although '[a]s early as 1997 ... Blair was offering British participation in military action to clip Saddam's wings'.[9] In February 1998 Blair had his first meeting with Bill Clinton at the White House, at the end of which the President declared that 'if Saddam does not comply with the unanimous will of the international community, we must be prepared to act ... and we are.'[10] Blair announced the deployment of more British fighter planes to the Gulf, stating: 'If the inspectors are prevented from doing their work then we have to make sure, by the military means of which we are capable, that, in so far as possible, that capacity cease.'[11]

At this juncture the United States and Britain were not alone in their exasperation with Baghdad. Friction with UN weapons inspectors (UNSCOM) had become routine, but the Americans and British took the responsibility for ratcheting up the military pressure. The Australian Richard Butler had replaced the Swedish head of UNSCOM, Rolf Ekeus, in July 1997 and Butler's more abrasive style did not help defuse tensions. As these mounted in February 1998, UN Secretary-General Kofi Annan undertook a crisis mission to Baghdad and was successful in averting further escalation. However, all did not run smoothly between UNSCOM and the Iraqi authorities thereafter. Iraqi accusations that some of the inspectors were acting for US intelligence (which turned out to be true) heightened the tension.

President Clinton was under pressure over the Monica Lewinski affair and assailed by some outspoken Republicans over Iraq. Among the latter, Elliott Abrams, Richard Armitage, John Bolton, Zalmay Khalilzad, Richard Perle, Peter Rodman, Donald Rumsfeld and Paul Wolfowitz – all of whom later surfaced in and around the Bush administration – called for action to bring down Saddam Hussein.[12] In August 1998 the US embassies in Kenya and Tanzania were bombed and associates of Osama bin Laden were held responsible (see Chapter 4). In retaliation US forces attacked what were assumed to be his training camps in Afghanistan and a supposed chemical factory in Khartoum. In October confrontations between UNSCOM and the Iraqi authorities reached a new impasse. In the face of Washington's refusal to concede that sanctions would be eased once Baghdad fulfilled UN requirements, the Iraqi authorities ended their cooperation on 30 October.[13] The logic of US and UK policy hitherto implied that they would most likely have to carry through on threatened military action.

Presumably to prepare the ground at home, the Blair government compiled a short briefing note on 'Iraq's Weapons of Mass Destruction', presented to MPs on 12 November 1998. The message was clear and to be repeated in the months preceding the invasion of March 2003: the Iraqi regime could not be trusted and harboured the means to pose a threat to regional peace and security. This could not be tolerated. Bolstered by the Security Council's condemnation of Iraq's decision to end cooperation (Resolution 1205), the United States and Britain prepared for military action. They were then deflected by another attempt at last-ditch diplomacy by Kofi Annan. The UNSCOM inspectors, who had been withdrawn in anticipation of a showdown, returned to Baghdad but encountered new difficulties.

Having sight of a draft UNSCOM report by Butler citing instances of Iraqi intransigence, Clinton and Blair decided on action before the report was given to Kofi Annan or officially released.[14] The inspectors withdrew once more and on 16 December 1998 US and British forces launched Operation Desert Fox, targeting sites across Iraq thought likely to house weapons programmes or to otherwise pose a threat to the operation.

According to rumour, members of the Iraqi opposition had intimated to Washington that such a strike would trigger action against the regime in Baghdad.[15] This did not occur. Meanwhile, the bombing ended all possibility of UNSCOM returning to its work in Iraq. After the event British officials privately conceded that the whole episode had failed to resolve the impasse with UNSCOM and actually created new problems, since thereafter there were no means by which to gather intelligence on the ground about Iraq's weapons programmes. The regime was still in place, the suffering of the Iraqis was unrelieved and cohesion at the UN Security Council was unravelling.

Driven by this combination of factors, British diplomats devoted themselves to diplomacy at the UN. The result was Resolution 1284 of December 1999, which set the framework for a new inspection regime (UNMOVIC, the United Nations Monitoring, Verification and Inspection Commission which replaced UNSCOM) and thence conditional suspension of sanctions according to a set timetable.[16] The British had believed that they had brought the French on board for this initiative. They were to be disappointed when France chose to abstain rather than vote for the resolution, claiming the text was open to biased interpretations that could prevent progress towards the eventual lifting of sanctions.[17] The United States did vote in favour, but then took no interest in implementation of the resolution, seemingly because Washington had lost all faith in the UN-brokered inspections process anyway.[18]

The other measure sought by the British to overcome the disagreements on Iraq at the UN Security Council was a 'smart sanctions' regime that would substitute the ban on all imports except designated items with one that permitted all imports except specifically prohibited items. However, the effectiveness of this formula depended on the agreement of Iraq's neighbours to monitor all cargoes entering Iraq from their countries. Public opinion in the region was not conducive to this: smuggling was rife; Turkey and Jordan depended on trade with Iraq; and public opinion in Arab countries generally, together with some governments (such as that of the UAE), failed to identify with the US and UK line that Iraq still posed a serious danger.

Even so, the British government held to the line that the policy on Iraq had worked and with refinements could be sustained. Robin Cook defended the policy not only while he was at the Foreign Office but thereafter. He was not alone. Speaking on 11 September 2000, then Foreign Office Minister Peter Hain asserted:

> On Iraq, the policy of containing Saddam Hussein and containing the threat that he poses to his own people, especially the Kurds in the North and the Shia in the South, as well as to neighbours, has been successful. He has not invaded any countries in the last nine to ten years as he did previously and he has not been able to attack the Kurds with chemical weapons or other forms of attacks as he did previously.[19]

Hain went on to blame the Iraqi regime for failing to distribute the food and medicine available under the oil-for-food provisions. Blair himself made similar points in answer to a parliamentary question about the impact of sanctions on Iraqi children.

> We share concerns that the children of Iraq have suffered greatly, as have all Iraqis, at the hands of a ruthless dictator who cares nothing for their welfare. Unlike Saddam Hussein we are concerned at their plight. SCR1284 – a UK

initiative – has expanded the oil-for-food programme. This year alone it will provide more than $16 billion for the Iraqi people. In the face of this oil wealth, there is no reason for the Iraqi people to go short of food and medicine other than Saddam's own decision to deny them humanitarian relief.[20]

According to Carne Ross, who served on the UK delegation to the UN Security Council from 1998 to 2002, the British had evidence to substantiate their case, but tended to downplay concerns about the situation on the ground in Iraq, where the human suffering was 'of a quite appalling scale'.[21] The thrust of British policy during this period, and much of its diplomatic effort, were concentrated on winning the argument, particularly at the UN. The facts on the ground suggested a more strategic problem. Sanctions had not produced Iraqi cooperation on UN disarmament objectives; the population was becoming increasingly debilitated; a heinous regime was becoming more entrenched; and the ultimate, official UN goal of both disarming and rehabilitating Iraq remained elusive.

Viewed in these terms, the chain of events that led to Britain's support for military intervention in Iraq and the toppling of the regime can be understood as a bid to break out of a seeming dead-end.[22] Even though ministers were arguing in 2000 that Resolution 1284 and 'smart sanctions' offered a 'win-win for everybody',[23] given the configuration of factors at the UN, in Washington and in Iraq and the surrounding region, that approach lacked credibility. Thus it was that by March 2002 Peter Ricketts, the Political Director at the FCO, could suggest in confidence to the Foreign Secretary that a *real* win-win formula would be to force Baghdad into a corner whereby:

> either Saddam, against all odds, allows inspectors to operate freely, in which case we can hobble his WMD programmes, or he blocks/hinders, and we are on stronger ground for switching to other methods.[24]

However, some of the same factors that blighted the containment policy rendered the purported alternative of intervention even more problematic.

SLIDING TOWARDS WAR

For the duration of the first New Labour government, British policy on Iraq was thus devoted to making containment work. This meant maintaining sanctions but also trying to alleviate the suffering of ordinary Iraqis, and the subtext of British policy was about deflecting blame for that suffering away from the enforcers of containment and onto Saddam Hussein. In fact diplomacy at the United Nations effectively took precedence over attending to events on the ground and while the Americans spoke increasingly in terms of regime change, the British, in public at least, still maintained that reprieve was possible.

Alliance politics and 9/11

Following Operation Desert Fox, as the British gathered themselves for a year of 'painstaking diplomacy' at the UN, the US administration framed its policy as 'containment plus regime change'.[25] Washington kept up the pressure at the UN to enforce sanctions as strictly as possible in the name of depriving the Iraqi regime of cash. Congress passed the Iraq Liberation Act – providing $97 million in US surplus equipment and training for Iraqi opposition forces – and a special coordinator was appointed to try to reconcile the differences among the various Iraqi opposition groups. Meanwhile, there was no let-up in the enforcement of the no-fly zones, with regular bombing raids designed to erode Iraqi military capabilities and morale. From October 1999 the Clinton administration announced it would give 'non-combat' training to members of the Iraqi opposition.[26] The voices of those lobbying for more concerted action to effect regime change in Baghdad became more insistent.[27]

Speaking in November 2000, Tony Blair defended his commitment to an active foreign policy, inclusive of military engagement:

> Every time I have pursued a policy of military engagement since becoming Prime Minister I have faced strong opposition, interestingly not so much from the traditional left as from parts of the right. This was true over Iraq, where with America, we have stood firm against the most dangerous dictator in the world today.[28]

He went on to compare that stance with the interventions in Kosovo and Sierra Leone, in the name of defending both British interests and British values.

Yet Blair's resolve to deal with dictators still did not translate into any specific plan for Iraq and could not feasibly have done so, in the absence of a substantive US plan. American advocates of action against Saddam Hussein were countered in turn by more cautious elements, especially in the State Department, who found kindred spirits in the Foreign Office. In the same month that Blair was explaining his determination to confront dictators, the Foreign Office was exploring the possibility of easing sanctions. Peter Hain floated the idea that if Iraq began to cooperate there could be concessions on the issue of the no-fly zones[29] and Thomas Pickering, the US Under-Secretary of State for Political Affairs, talked about a more calibrated sanctions regime to recognize progress on disarmament.[30]

With the arrival of George W. Bush in the White House in 2001, the more hawkish voices surfaced within the administration. According to Paul O'Neill, the Treasury Secretary at the time, the new administration was committed to the removal of Saddam Hussein from 'day one'.[31] The confidential 'Iraq Options Paper' produced by the British Cabinet Office in March

2002 (obtained by the media in 2005) referred to 'US contingency planning prior to 11 September' (2001) which indicated that a ground campaign to topple Saddam Hussein would require 200,000–400,000 troops.[32] On 16 February 2001, US and British air forces attacked radar stations near Baghdad, and Reuters deduced that the action 'speaks volumes about the long term "special relationship" linking Washington and London, even when their leaders are strangers and come from opposite sides of the ideological fence'.[33] However, propensities, inclinations, contingency plans and even the aspirations of the neo-conservatives did not constitute a definite plan. They simply set the scene for thinking about Iraq after 11 September.

According to Tony Blair himself, the events of 11 September affected his estimation of the danger posed by Saddam Hussein.[34] Making the case for war in parliament in March 2003, Blair warned of the spectre of terrorists in possession of weapons of mass destruction and prepared to use them.[35] In addition:

> Blair was the most prescient among political leaders outside America in seeing at once that the attacks on New York and Washington on September 11, 2001 amounted to a geopolitical earthquake. He understood that the first attack on the US homeland since the British had sacked Washington nearly two centuries earlier would upend a global system that had survived the end of the cold war. Soon after the attacks I heard him remark that the first task for the rest of the world was to 'keep the US in the international system'. ... His role, as he saw it, was to get up close enough to Bush to bind the US into the multilateral system.[36]

Blair moved immediately to declare that Britain would stand 'shoulder to shoulder' with America and he headed to Washington, arriving for a meeting at the White House on 20 September.

Over dinner, reportedly, President Bush raised the subject of Iraq. That regime change in Iraq should be a top US objective after 9/11 had already been discussed within the administration, but action against al-Qaeda in Afghanistan was to take precedence.[37] Blair's reaction at the dinner, apparently, was to emphasize the importance of focusing on Afghanistan and avoid distractions, but he must have understood that Iraq would come up for consideration thereafter.[38] On his return to Britain, Blair and his government concentrated on making the case for intervention in Afghanistan; this included toppling the Taliban if they refused to deliver up Osama bin Laden and his al-Qaeda associates. In his address to the Labour Party Conference on 2 October, Blair made a stirring appeal for support for the United States in its hour of need, and on 4 October No. 10 published a brief on bin Laden, al-Qaeda and the reasons for assuming they were behind 9/11 (see Chapter 2).

The United States opened its Afghanistan campaign with air strikes on 8 October 2001. Although some 80 countries had made offers of help, only the British participated in the first wave of strikes.[39] Tony Blair busied himself with shuttle diplomacy and phone calls to leaders whose support or acquiescence was essential, including the Iranians (see Chapter 6). On a rapid tour through the Middle East at the end of October, taking in Syria, Saudi Arabia, Jordan, Israel and Gaza, he was greeted with Arab concerns about the war in Afghanistan, the effects of sanctions on Iraq and the plight of the Palestinians.[40]

On the home front Blair, the team at No. 10 and other Cabinet ministers worked to shore up British support for the action under way in Afghanistan.[41] Blair returned to the United States on 8 November 2001 and reportedly pressed the Americans to parallel their campaign against the Taliban and al-Qaeda with a rejuvenation of the Middle East peace process.[42] Seemingly his arguments did not fall on deaf ears: shortly afterwards Secretary of State Colin Powell appointed retired Marine Corps General Anthony Zinni to go as his personal emissary to the Middle East to mediate between the Israelis and Palestinians, though there was no appreciable progress as a result (see Chapter 7).[43]

Meanwhile, the possibility of further military action focusing on Iraq did not drop off the political agenda in Washington.[44] According to Bob Woodward, on 21 November President Bush asked Defense Secretary Donald Rumsfeld to draft plans for an invasion.[45] In Britain by contrast, mere mention of taking 'the war on terror' to Iraq after Afghanistan was met with a combination of incredulity and refutation. Pundits seemed to believe that Blair's influence in Washington would be used to caution against such a scheme.[46]

In an address to the Royal United Services Institute on 10 December 2001 Admiral Sir Michael Boyce, the Chief of the Defence Staff, outlined what he saw as the strategic choices for Britain following the *Strategic Defence Review* (see Chapter 4) and 11 September. He noted that Britain's understanding of the job remaining to be done in Afghanistan, where it had 4,500 troops in theatre at the time, differed somewhat from that of the Americans. He stated that:

We have to consider whether we wish to follow the United States' single-minded aim to finish Osama bin Ladin and *Al Qa'ida*; and/or to involve ourselves in creating the conditions for nation-building or reconstruction as well. ...

We will have to decide soon whether we make a commitment to a broader campaign (widening the war), or make a longer term commitment to

Afghanistan. Recent military success must be capitalised upon, so it is not a question of whether we will trap our hand in the mangle, but of which mangle we trap it in. My aim, incidentally, is not to get fixed in Afghanistan – but – if I have to address the causes of terrorism, I may have to.[47]

As early as December 2001, therefore, the British government was being reminded that choices would have to be made over where and for what purpose it had committed troops, and the importance of seeing through an operation once undertaken – if the war on terrorism was to be prosecuted successfully. As Boyce also stipulated, multilateralism was the key and to operate with allies meant working through institutional procedures and under international law.

Shifting the policy logic

By December 2001 the campaign to topple the Taliban and drive al-Qaeda members into hiding had made sufficient progress for speculation about Iraq to gain momentum, yet there was no official steer from Washington. Bush was cornered by the White House press corps one day in December and asked if Iraq fitted his definition of the enemy in the 'war on terror'. He replied in the affirmative. However, other events stole the limelight, including a flare-up of tensions in Kashmir. As 2001 drew to a close all the speculation around Whitehall indicated that British officials were telling their Washington counterparts 'anything but Iraq' for the next phase in the war on terror.[48] Blair was assumed to be using his unparalleled access in Washington to send the same message. In retrospect it is just as plausible that he was simply weighing the seriousness of US intentions.

In early January 2002, Iran came in for new opprobrium in Washington as a result of the *Karine-A* episode (see also Chapter 6), in which a ship intercepted by the Israelis in the Red Sea was revealed to be bearing arms (alleged to come from Iran) to the Palestinians. The fact that Yasser Arafat implausibly denied any knowledge of the shipment caused the Americans to despair of him completely as a potential peace partner for Israel. This suited Israeli Prime Minister Ariel Sharon very well (see Chapter 7). His strategy was to isolate Arafat and render him irrelevant. The Israelis had also made it their business after 9/11 to draw parallels between the dangers they faced from Palestinian suicide bombers and the experience of Americans at the hands of al-Qaeda. The *Karine-A* episode offered a perfect vindication for all those arguing that Israel was in the forefront of a wider battle against states armed with or seeking weapons of mass destruction and terrorism pursued in the name of Islam.

In Washington the neo-conservatives argued that 'rogue regimes' and terrorists were facets of a general malaise that America had helped to sustain through its traditional support for autocratic rulers, not least in Saudi Arabia – where fifteen of the nineteen perpetrators of 9/11 had originated. The remedy, according to the neo-con perspective, was the removal of dictators – and Iraq was the logical place to start. According to Max Boot:

> The debate about whether Saddam Hussein was implicated in the September 11 attacks misses the point ... it is not just a matter of justice to depose Saddam. It is a matter of self defence: he is currently working to acquire weapons of mass destruction that he or his confederates will unleash against America and our allies if given the chance. Once Afghanistan has been dealt with, America should turn its attention to Iraq.[49]

Boot anticipated that it would be relatively easy to depose Saddam Hussein and once that was achieved, he argued:

> we can impose an American-led, international regency in Baghdad, to go along with the one in Kabul. With American seriousness and credibility thus restored, we will enjoy fruitful cooperation from the region's many opportunists, who will show a newfound eagerness to be helpful in our larger task of rolling up the international terror network that threatens us.[50]

Along with the neo-conservatives another school of thought had the ear of the US President – the Christian Right. This constituency reinforced the moral tone that infused Bush's rhetoric. This tone was manifest in his State of the Union address of January 2002, in which he named Iran and Iraq, along with North Korea, as part of an 'axis of evil'. The effect in Europe and across the Middle East was electrifying. Bush's speech was received as a declaration of intent to take on all three states, unilaterally if need be, and Iraq was seen as the administration's most likely starting point.[51]

Against this background it would have been remiss of the British government not to take seriously Washington's thinking about Iraq. If the Americans went ahead with military action, they would be bound to request from Britain, at a minimum, use of its facilities on Diego Garcia and in Cyprus – which would require Britain to have a position on facilitating the action. Unless the UN Security Council ruled in favour of US-led military action, the legal case was dubious at best. That did not seem to deter the Americans, but (as pointed out by Boyce in his December speech) Britain could not afford such unilateralism. So it would either have to secure UN backing or try to dissuade Washington on practical grounds.

Conceivably, the British government could have turned down Washington's request for help. According to some American and British critics of the Iraq war, a firm refusal of support from Britain could have dissuaded Washington from an ill-conceived adventure. On this possibility, Robin Cook had the following to say:

> It would never occur to Tony Blair that there might be more respect for a Prime Minister who had the courage to say no to someone as powerful as the President of the US. He is programmed to respect power not rebel against it. ... I have no doubt that Tony Blair genuinely believed the world would be better without Saddam. I am certain that the real reason he went to war was that he found it easier to resist the public opinion of Britain than the request of the US President.[52]

In any case, the British were already in a bind. By their own acknowledgment the containment policy could not long be sustained in its existing form, since the Americans had become disenchanted with it and most others were undermining it.[53] Also, as Blair had discerned, the post-Cold War world order had been fundamentally changed as a result of 9/11 and he calculated that his role was now 'to keep the US in the international system'.[54] His strategy, no doubt reinforced by his own commitment to confront dictators, duly led him to tell George Bush that he supported the goal of regime change in Baghdad.[55] All that remained, therefore, was to rationalize the shift in British Iraq policy, obtain the necessary UN backing and ensure that regime change worked. 'Failure was not an option.'[56]

According to the US investigative journalist Seymour Hersh:

> In the early spring of 2002, the Bush Administration remained sharply divided about Iraq. There was widespread agreement that Saddam Hussein should be overthrown, but no agreement about how to get it done. The President had given his feuding agencies a deadline of April 15, 2002, to come up with a 'coagulated plan', as one senior State Department official put it, for ending the regime. The President was meeting that month with Tony Blair, the British prime minister, whose support for the Iraq operation was considered essential.[57]

For their part, senior British officials and advisers to the Prime Minister were also preparing the ground for that meeting. That preparation included compilation of the 'Iraq Options Paper', noted above, by the Overseas and Defence Secretariat of the Cabinet Office.[58] This outlined British policy goals, within the broad objectives 'of preserving peace and stability in the Gulf and ensuring energy security', as the 'reintegration of a law-abiding Iraq which does not possess WMD or threaten its neighbours, into the international community'. It asserted: 'Implicitly this cannot occur with Saddam in power.'[59]

The subsidiary objectives, according to the Iraq Options Paper, were:

- preserving the territorial integrity of Iraq;
- improving the humanitarian situation of the Iraqi people;
- protecting the Kurds in Northern Iraq;
- sustaining US/UK cooperation, including, if necessary, by moderating US policy; and
- maintaining the credibility and authority of the Security Council.[60]

Passing judgment on the policy of containment pursued since 1991, the paper deemed this to have been *partially successful*, but problems, such as Saddam Hussein's presumed pursuit of WMD, his brutality and the leakage in the sanctions regime, were acknowledged. The possibility of toughening containment was examined and deemed incapable of resolving the outstanding problems or achieving British objectives, *because* such an approach would offer 'little prospect of removing Saddam'. In other words, the Cabinet Office did not foresee achieving Britain's goals through sanctions and containment alone – only regime change in Baghdad could make that possible.

The paper then went on to note that the United States had 'lost confidence in containment' and 'some in government want Saddam removed'.[61] Three putative options for achieving regime change were examined, taking into consideration 'what sort of Iraq we want'. These were: (1) covert support to opposition groups; (2) an air campaign providing overt support to opposition groups leading to a coup or uprising; and (3) a ground campaign. These were not deemed mutually exclusive and options 1 and/or 2 could be precursors to 3. On logistical grounds it was thought a 'ground campaign is not feasible until autumn 2002'.[62] Having briefly examined legal considerations affecting the options and noted that there was no recent intelligence evidence of Iraqi complicity in international terrorism, the paper concluded:

> In sum, despite the considerable difficulties, the use of overriding force in a ground campaign is the only option that we can be confident will remove Saddam and bring Iraq back into the international community.[63]

To launch such a campaign 'would require a staged approach' including 'winding up the pressure'; careful military planning; coalition building; incentives for Iraqi and regional cooperation; tackling other regional issues; and 'sensitising the public'.[64]

Blair's task at his meetings with Bush in April 2002 was thus to use his unparalleled influence to impress upon the US President the importance of preparing the ground fully to ensure success. On his list of requirements were renewed US engagement in the Middle East peace process; the exhaustion of efforts via the UN inspections regime to rid Iraq of its WMD; concerted diplomatic efforts to build a coalition; and a strategy to prepare public opinion. Also, in view of Bush's 'axis of evil' speech, Jack Straw cautioned that the case had to be made for treating Iraq as the greatest and most imminent danger.[65] However, as subsequently emerged, when he did meet Bush, Blair gave his support in principle for military action to bring about regime change – though only his inner circle of advisers and Cabinet colleagues were aware of this at the time.[66]

Returning from his talks with Bush, Blair defended the case for interventionism:

> The moment for decision on how to act is not yet with us … But to allow WMD to be developed by a state like Iraq without let or hindrance would be grossly to ignore the lessons of September 11 and we will not do it. The message to Saddam is clear: he has to let the inspectors back in – anyone, any time, any place that the international community demands. If necessary the action should be military – and again, if necessary and justified, it should involve regime change.[67]

Preparing the ground

Over the ensuing months Blair was seeking to reassure everyone, including the rank and file of the Labour Party and some anxious ministers, that no decision had been made.[68] In the background, the government had worries that while the US government's military planning was proceeding apace, it lacked a political framework. 'In particular,' the Cabinet Office warned, 'little thought has been given to creating the political conditions for military action, or the aftermath and how to shape it.'[69] Reviewing the requirements outlined by Blair for UK support for military action against Iraq when he met Bush in April 2002, a Cabinet Office paper of July 2002 concluded that Blair's message would have to be reinforced, since:

> it is necessary to create the conditions in which we could legally support military action. Otherwise we face the real danger that the US will commit themselves to a course of action which we would find very difficult to support.[70]

At a meeting on 23 July 2002 between the Prime Minister, the Foreign and Defence Secretaries, intelligence and military chiefs and Blair's key advisers, a number of conclusions were reached, among them:

- We should work on the assumption that the UK would take part in military action. But we needed a fuller picture of US planning before we could take any firm decisions. CDS [Chief of the Defence Staff] should tell the US military that we were considering a range of options.

- The Prime Minister would revert on the question of whether funds could be spent in preparation for this operation.
- CDS would send the Prime Minister the background on the UN inspectors, and discreetly work up the ultimatum to Saddam. He would also send the Prime Minister advice on the positions of countries in the region, especially Turkey, and of the key EU member states.
- John Scarlett would send the Prime Minister a full intelligence update.
- We must not ignore the legal issues: the Attorney General would consider legal advice with FCO/MoD legal advisers.[71]

If the UK was to join a US operation British troops would have to start their own preparations and any deployment would attract public attention and potentially awkward questions about their expectations and intentions. Behind the scenes Blair and other British senior officials were working hard to enlist the Americans to the cause of multilateralism and proper forward planning. Yet anxiety seems to have mounted that their arguments were not really being heard in Washington, outside the State Department. Another concern was that Blair was sending different signals to different audiences and that Bush at least had the impression he was 'gung-ho for a war against Saddam Hussein'.[72]

Maintaining a public silence about their private concerns,[73] ministers resisted pressure for parliamentary debate until the autumn.[74] In the meantime a serious public debate surfaced in the British media. One of the opening shots came in the form of a letter to *The Times* on 29 July 2002 from Field Marshal Lord Bramall, the former Chief of the Defence Staff, who posited both a best-case and a worst-case scenario for the aftermath of a US intervention in Iraq. At worst, he wrote:

> Conflict in Iraq would produce, in that area, the very display of massive, dynamic, United States activity which provides one of the mainsprings of motivation of terrorist action in the region and indeed over a wider area. Far from calming things down, enhancing any peace process and advancing the 'war against terrorism', which could and should be conducted internationally by other means, it would make things infinitely worse.

Another senior figure in the British establishment, Sir Michael Quinlan, former Permanent Secretary at the Ministry of Defence, questioned the moral case for military action in the absence of compelling evidence to link Saddam Hussein to international terrorism and said that the WMD threat was better dealt with through deterrence.[75]

In due course the head of the Church of England, the Archbishop of Canterbury, joined the Catholic Church in refuting the justification for initiating war on moral grounds. Regional specialists contended that even if military victory were feasible in Iraq, the aftermath would pose a monumental problem of state-building. British neo-con sympathizers, as well as the Conservative leadership, countered that such views smacked of racism, since it implied that the Iraqis could not 'do democracy'. Encouraged by some Iraqi exiles, the pro-interventionists claimed that Iraq was ripe for liberation and democracy.[76]

Returning from his summer holiday, allegedly with his mind made up,[77] in early September Blair entered the fray with the warning that Saddam Hussein 'is without any question still trying to develop that chemical, biological, potentially nuclear capability and to allow him to do so without any let or hindrance … would be irresponsible … there is a real and existing threat that we have to deal with.'[78]

By mid-September he had ordered 20,000 British troops to be made ready for the possibility of action.[79] On 12 September Bush went to the United Nations, speaking the language of multilateralism and challenging the UN to confront the 'grave and gathering danger'.[80] A vital Blair requirement had been met. In further preparation of the ground, parliament was recalled for an emergency debate on 24 September. Fifty-three Labour MPs rebelled against the government line but failed to force a vote on military action.[81]

The same day No. 10 released the dossier on Iraq's Weapons of Mass Destruction[82] that would become the subject of much controversy the following summer and feature in both the Hutton Inquiry (2003) and the Butler Report (2004). The dossier, based on intelligence estimates and cleared by the Joint Intelligence Committee, became notorious because in May 2003, after the invasion of Iraq, the BBC journalist Andrew Gilligan alleged that Alastair Campbell had 'sexed up' the contents, and cited a senior intelligence source for his claim. His source was actually Dr David Kelly, a weapons inspector, who was subsequently exposed. Though he denied using the words attributed to him by Gilligan, Kelly apparently felt so damaged by the exposure that he committed suicide on 17 July 2003. The Hutton Inquiry was set up to examine what led to this distressing event and concluded that the government had not deliberately misled the public. The subsequent Butler Inquiry into the use of intelligence echoed this assessment, though Butler found that misjudgments had been made.[83]

Hutton's inquiry did reveal qualms at No. 10 about the weakness of the case presented in early drafts of the dossier[84] and Butler exposed the flimsiness of the evidence on which some of the claims in the dossier were based.[85] Butler's report also revealed that the government had failed to revise its estimate of the danger posed by Iraq, in the light of new evidence, in the run-up to the war.[86]

Among the assertions in the dossier, the one that drew press attention in September 2002 was the claim that Iraq could launch chemical weapons within 45 minutes of an order to do so. Repeated three times in the text, including in the Prime Minister's own introduction, this claim was later found to be attributable to only one, uncorroborated source and the government left unchallenged the assumption made in some newspapers that the weapons in question were strategic rather than battlefield armaments and could therefore threaten British forces in Cyprus. Thus the impression was given to the British public that Saddam Hussein's Iraq posed a direct threat to British nationals and interests. Indeed, Blair said in his introduction that Saddam Hussein was 'a current and serious threat' to the UK national interest. Curiously, ministers subsequently claimed that terminology did not mean Saddam posed an 'imminent' threat, which would have implied a case for pre-emption. The distinction no doubt rested on the government's conviction rather than proof, and after the invasion, when no evidence of WMD materialized, Blair would confidently claim that Saddam Hussein's hidden arsenal would be uncovered.[87]

In persuading Bush to take the Iraq issue directly to the UN, Tony Blair was working in tandem with US Secretary of State Colin Powell and against the inclinations of more hardline members of the administration, including the Vice President, Dick Cheney. UN members reacted favourably to Bush's speech, putting aside their reservations about his administration's apparent contempt for multilateralism (signalled in particular by the launch of the new US strategic doctrine in summer 2002, which spoke of pre-emptive military interventions in defence of US interests). Work began on devising a new UN approach to Iraq.

Led by Britain's ambassador to the UN Sir Jeremy Greenstock, the British applied themselves assiduously to drafting what became Resolution 1441, adopted unanimously by the members of the Security Council in November 2002. The achievement and the drawback of this measure was that all the members could read into it what they wanted. Those who saw it as a mechanism for avoiding war through renewed weapons inspections were later to find themselves at odds with those, notably in Washington, who saw it as smoothing the path to a multilateral endorsement for military action. For the British government the adoption of 1441 marked the formal end of containment[88] and parliament was invited to give the resolution its seal of approval, which it duly did.

The justification

Resolution 1441 did not threaten the use of force, only 'serious consequences' if Iraq failed to comply with its requirements. According to the British government's own legal advisers, it would be up to the UN Security Council to decide what to do in the event of Iraqi non-compliance or the chance discovery by UNMOVIC, led by Hans Blix, of hidden stockpiles of WMD. According to the government's legal experts, in advance of the adoption of Resolution 1441:

> A violation of Iraq's obligations which undermines the basis of the cease-fire in resolution 687 (1991) can revive the authorisation to use force in resolution 678 (1990). As the cease-fire was proclaimed by the Council in resolution 687 (1991), it is for the Council to assess whether any such breach of those obligations has occurred. The US have a rather different view: they maintain that the assessment of breach is for individual member States. We are not aware of any other State which supports this view.[89]

In effect and as argued by prominent lawyers since, Britain needed a further resolution, in addition to 1441, giving explicit endorsement for resort to force, in order to remain clearly within the law. For this to be forthcoming, the Security Council would have to find Iraq in breach of 1441. Between the return of the inspectors to Iraq on 27 November 2002 and early 2003, Blair and his government held their breath while the inspectors delivered ambiguous verdicts on Iraqi cooperation.

Meanwhile, the build-up of US forces in the Gulf was already extensive and posing a dilemma. Their presence enabled British politicians to argue that visible preparations for action served to turn up the heat in Baghdad and would help to persuade the regime to comply with UN demands. At the same time, all the speculation was that such forces could not be rotated in and out of the Gulf indefinitely while new inspections in Iraq took their course. Moreover, the local climate dictated military action before spring 2003 or its postponement to the following autumn. On 20 January the Secretary of Defence Geoff Hoon announced the deployment of 26,000 British troops to the Gulf. On 15 February around two million people came out on the streets of London and Glasgow to demonstrate against war, bringing together people from all walks of life, including many who had never marched or contemplated marching before. There were similar public demonstrations across Europe, the United States and elsewhere in the world.

British diplomacy went into high gear to lobby for another UN resolution to confront Saddam Hussein with an ultimatum and threaten the use of force. However, British pleading and arm-twisting by the United States failed to win support for this among the other permanent and non-permanent members. When Hans Blix reported back to the UN Security Council on 7 March 2003 he did not deliver a definitive judgment. Iraq had still not accounted for items unaccounted for since the early 1990s, but spot inspections had revealed no hidden arsenals and the Iraqis were, if grudgingly, more or less cooperating. By then Washington was losing patience, while France appeared determined to insist on more time for inspections. Jeremy Greenstock was charged with a last-ditch attempt to reconcile the conflicting positions.

But the Iraq crisis was always about more than Iraq's WMD. France was seeking to preserve multilateralism by obliging the US to bow to the UN, even though that could mean war eventually. Tony Blair was acting on the assumption that such a strategy was doomed since the United States would go it alone if the UN failed to be supportive. Hence he needed the other UN members to admit this reality and, by giving the US the cover of the UN, to preserve multilateralism that way. In the background, personal rivalry between the key protagonists was turning ugly. According to one account, the French President Jacques Chirac found Blair's ambitions to take a leading role in Europe and thence deliver Europe in the Atlantic alliance too much to stomach.[90] Blair reportedly feared that Chirac was hoping to use the crisis to humble the British Prime Minister. In any case, Chirac was enjoying unprecedented popularity at home for his country's stance at the UN. By contrast, Blair faced unprecedented criticism and unrest within his own party, as well as public resistance.[91]

Eventually, frantic British and US diplomacy at the UN failed to line up majority Security Council support for a new resolution. A remark by Chirac that he would veto such a resolution was blamed by a seething British leadership as the fatal blow.[92] But the case for war remained unsubstantiated.

Until early March the advice of the government's top lawyer, the Attorney General Lord Goldsmith, remained that a second resolution was needed to underpin the justification for war on the basis of a breach of 1441. His formal advice was not sought until the very last moment, but in a memo to the Prime Minister on 7 March Goldsmith stated: 'I accept that a reasonable case can be made that resolution 1441 is capable in principle of reviving the authorisation in 678 without a further resolution.'[93]

Yet he did warn that Britain could be taken to court if it acted on this basis and said that he remained 'of the opinion that the safest course would be to secure the adoption of a further resolution to authorise the use of force'. Chief of the Defence Staff Admiral Boyce needed a firmer basis than this to take the forces to war. On 12 March he apparently asked the Prime Minister for an unequivocal statement on the legality of war. Following communication between Blair and Goldsmith, such a confirmation was produced. But it was based on an assurance from the Prime Minister that was itself based on by then questionable intelligence.[94]

When he took his case for war to the House of Commons on 18 March 2003, Blair noted the repeated failures of the Iraqi government to give a full and final declaration of its activities and capabilities in respect of WMD. He said: 'Iraq has made some concessions to co-operation but no-one disputes it is not fully co-operating.' Also, 'Iraq continues to deny it has any WMD, though no serious intelligence service anywhere in the world believes them.'[95]

In the remainder of his speech the Prime Minister argued that the time had come for action in the interests of both disarming Iraq once and for all and upholding the credibility and effectiveness of the United Nations. He accused France of blighting efforts to agree a follow-up resolution to 1441, specifically endorsing military action, by announcing it would use its veto, and claimed:

> in a sense, any fair observer does not really dispute that Iraq is in breach and that 1441 implies action in such circumstance. The real problem is that, underneath, people dispute that Iraq is a threat; dispute the link between terrorism and WMD; dispute the whole basis of our assertion that the two together constitute a fundamental assault on our way of life.[96]

Blair also explained:

> I have never put our justification for action as regime change. We have to act within the terms set out in Resolution 1441. That is our legal base. But it is the reason, I say frankly, why if we do act we should do so with a clear conscience and strong heart.

He then itemized some of the oppressive characteristics of the Iraqi regime and cautioned those who would oppose taking the risks of war that by opting for inaction they would be choosing in effect to embolden Saddam Hussein and abandon the Iraqi people.

The Attorney General provided parliament with only a summary of his advice to the government and even the Cabinet was not aware of his equivocations. Elizabeth Wilmshurst, a deputy legal adviser at the Foreign Office, stated in her resignation letter of 18 March 2003 (which was not made public until March 2005):

> I regret that I cannot agree that it is lawful to use force against Iraq without a second Security Council resolution to revive the authorisation given in SCR 678. I do not need to set out my reasoning, you are aware of it ... I cannot in conscience go along with advice – within the office or to the public or parliament – which asserts the legitimacy of military action without such a resolution, particularly since an unlawful use of force on such a scale amounts to the crime of aggression.[97]

More prominent on 18 March 2003 was the resignation of Robin Cook as Leader of the House of Commons. He received a standing ovation for his resignation speech in the Commons. However, Blair's government won its mandate for war in the House of Commons, by a vote of 412 to 149. Eighty-four Labour MPs, one in five, joined Liberal Democrats, nationalists and some 15 Conservatives in voting against. A larger number of Labour members (139) had earlier voted for an amendment claiming the case for war was not yet made.

The Point of Departure[98]

Thus it was that Tony Blair and New Labour determined that Britain would join the US invasion of Iraq in 2003. The process by which the decision was made and upheld in parliament will be remembered as the single most important facet of Tony Blair's handling of foreign policy, overshadowing his initiatives on other issues. The implications of the decision for Britain's standing in the Middle East derive both from that decision and from its outcome. As of 2003, because it 'went along' with America on Iraq, Britain ceased to be regarded as a potential counterweight to or tempering influence on US policy in the Middle East.

6

Reaping the Whirlwind: The Fallout from the Invasion of Iraq for British Relations across the Middle East

I: INSIDE IRAQ

'Unlike the US and the UK, Iran invested better. They knew where to pump their money, into militias and political parties. If a war happens they can take over Basra without even sending their soldiers. They are fighting a war of attrition with the US and UK, bleeding them slowly.' – Iraqi Intelligence Officer in Basra (2007)[1]

The British decision to join the US invasion of Iraq in 2003 was reached in principle well before the government's case for war was put to parliament on the eve of the invasion. As the previous chapter has recounted, only a small group of decision-makers, not even the full Cabinet, were party to the deliberations which preceded this momentous step. The results were transformative both for the region and for British relations within it, but only in 2009 did the government of Gordon Brown yield to pressure to set up an inquiry into how the decision was reached.[2]

The government's reasoning was not exactly the same as that of the US administration, but, as Chapter 5 has shown, it was derivative of the US decision to launch an invasion aimed at regime change in Iraq. The British never claimed a direct link between al-Qaeda and the Iraqi government. That was a US imputation. The theory posited by Tony Blair was that a dangerous regime like that of Saddam Hussein could, if allowed to pursue its WMD programme, supply weapons to terrorists in the future. This served as a key British justification for toppling Saddam.

As it transpired, Iraq was not concealing WMD, and ousting the regime turned Iraq into a battleground that al-Qaeda hastened to exploit. Volunteers rushed to join the war on America and its allies, entering from across borders thrown open by the invasion. Refugees soon began to flee in the opposite direction, extending the Iraq war into a regional crisis of destabilizing proportions.

The principal beneficiary turned out to be Iran, whose leadership became more confident and belligerent in defying all diplomatic efforts to curtail both its nuclear power programme and its support for the Islamist movements Hizbullah in Lebanon and Hamas in the occupied Palestinian territory. Neither movement was an al-Qaeda affiliate and they did not share its radical Salafist ideology but they did use terrorist tactics and espoused bitter hatred towards Israel. As the leaders of Egypt and Jordan had warned, a Pandora's box had been opened and the forces unleashed posed a challenge to regional stability beyond the power of the United States to fully control, with or without British solidarity and assistance.

THE IRAQ WAR

On 19 March 2003 President Bush announced that hostilities had begun and the invasion of Iraq was launched. A plan to invade on two fronts, from Turkey and Kuwait, had to be shelved after the Turkish parliament surprised the US administration by refusing to facilitate the strategy. So, entering only from Kuwait, US ground forces pressed north towards Baghdad, encountering some fierce resistance along the way but no major set battles with Iraqi military formations. Iraqi Republican Guard forces went to ground and regular troops simply abandoned their uniforms (though not their weapons) and melted away.

Britain went to war alongside the United States on 20 March, fielding upwards of 25,000 troops. The only other country to commit forces in the field was Australia, which had around 2,000 special forces deployed to the western desert. Overflight rights, base facilities and logistical support were provided by a number of other countries, not least Kuwait, from which the British as well as the US ground assault was launched. While the Americans pressed ahead to Baghdad, British forces took up positions in and around Basra, in the centre of what became the British zone of occupation. As US forces arrived in central Baghdad, the symbolic toppling of a statue of Saddam Hussein on 9 April came to represent the moment his regime fell. But this was only the beginning.

Aboard a US aircraft carrier and with much fanfare, on 1 May 2003 Bush declared 'major combat operations' over. Allegedly the campaign had taken less time than anticipated. However, even though the predominantly Shia areas did not put up a fight and people came out to celebrate the fall of Saddam Hussein, there was little of the joyful welcome for their liberators that would have made good publicity for Bush and Blair.[3]

Back home, initial media coverage of the progress of the armed forces by reporters 'embedded' with US and British military units did make gripping television viewing and a Guardian/ICM opinion poll in April 2003 revealed that public approval of Blair's personal performance was positive, compared with a negative verdict in the weeks preceding the invasion.[4] Yet no sooner had the government seemingly emerged from its period of crisis over Iraq than news started to come in of widespread looting and destruction by crowds of Iraqis on the rampage in major cities. All the Iraqi ministries in Baghdad except for the oil ministry, which was under US guard, were gutted of furniture and fittings, vital records and technical equipment.[5]

The fact that the oil ministry escaped destruction fed perceptions across the region that America was only interested in Iraqi oil. The looting also presaged the breakdown of law and order, leaving ordinary Iraqis without basic security and in fear of kidnap, extortion and robbery. To make matters worse, the infrastructure of Iraq – electricity grids, water and sewerage systems and telecommunications – already in a dilapidated state when US and British forces arrived, went into a state of near collapse. Sabotage was rife and insurgents repeatedly attacked not only power lines but oil pipelines and installations, triggering a massive fuel shortage. In summer 2003 there were long, angry queues at petrol stations and the population had to endure the mounting summer heat without the relief of air conditioning or even electric fans.

Speaking at a news conference four months after Bush declared victory, the US Deputy Secretary of Defense Paul Wolfowitz admitted:

> Some important assumptions turned out to underestimate the problem. No significant Iraqi army units switched sides, meaning they were not available to help with security, while the police unexpectedly required complete overhaul. ... Worst of all, it was difficult to imagine before the war that the criminal gang of sadists and gangsters who have run Iraq for 35 years would continue fighting.[6]

It is astounding that he should have thought the Iraqi police force would be 'fit for purpose', if the country had been run by gangsters and sadists for over three decades. But apparently No. 10 was as surprised as the Americans over the extent of the problems encountered in Iraq.[7]

Occupation

Having toppled the regime the invading forces were legally responsible for the restoration of law and order. This troubled the British more than the Americans and it was the British representative at the UN, Sir Jeremy Greenstock, who ensured that the obligations of the occupiers were formalized through the adoption of UN Security Council Resolution 1483 on 22 May 2003. This

British contribution to upholding international law was neither understood nor welcomed in the region, however, where the opprobrium of occupation was considered a humiliation.

Washington's initial plan for running Iraq rested on the appointment of the retired General Jay Garner to head a so-called Office of Reconstruction and Humanitarian Aid (ORHA). He was answerable to the Pentagon, where the theory prevailed that once the regime in Baghdad was decapitated the pre-existing infrastructure would be there to help Garner run the country. He thought ninety days would be sufficient to organize reconstruction. Not content to rely on such optimistic theories, Blair sent Foreign Office Minister Mike O'Brien to Baghdad to report on the situation. He returned with a more cautious assessment.[8]

On O'Brien's advice, at the beginning of May Blair appointed John Sawers, a senior diplomat, as his special envoy to Baghdad to work with ORHA.[9] On 12 May Clare Short resigned as UK Minister for International Development, claiming Tony Blair had failed to heed her pleas to ensure a central role for the UN in the running and reconstruction of Iraq.

Among Short's concerns was the preference shown to US companies in the reconstruction. Not only was this poor public relations, feeding into Iraqi suspicions about US intentions and self-interest, but recourse to foreign companies deprived Iraqi firms of contracts and jobs. As was later acknowledged, Iraqis also stood a better chance than the foreigners of repairing the country's crippled infrastructure pending rebuilding.

Meanwhile, British companies began to complain that they could not compete with their US counterparts in the system established by the Americans for the allocation of contracts. However they had to concede that they were bound to pick up only the crumbs, since compared with a US pledge of $1.7 billion in reconstruction aid to Iraq following the invasion, Britain could commit only £240 million.[10] As for those Europeans who had opposed the war, they were almost entirely ruled out in the bidding process.

Almost as soon as Sawers arrived to take up his appointment at the beginning of June, Garner was replaced, ORHA disbanded and the so-called Coalition Provisional Authority (CPA) established under the retired diplomat Paul Bremer, who was directly appointed by President Bush. Valuable time had been lost in the transition and Bremer, apparently on official advice prompted by the Iraqi exile Ahmad Chalabi,[11] then made the fateful decision to disband the Iraqi armed forces and dismiss all but the most junior members of the Baath Party from the civil service. At a stroke he put tens of thousands of disgruntled Iraqi soldiers and competent bureaucrats out of a job. Undoubtedly a number of those disbanded from the army found their way into the insurgency, which gathered strength over the ensuing months.

Even though the United States was in charge, UN involvement might have provided a tempering influence on the occupation, but this possibility was diminished when the UN headquarters in Baghdad were blown up in August 2003. Among those killed in the blast was the much respected UN representative Sergio Vieira de Mello and many of his staff. Thereafter, UN Secretary-General Kofi Annan did not deem it safe to set up a similarly high-profile UN presence in Iraq.

US and British efforts to persuade other countries to commit troops to the counter-insurgency operation in Iraq and help restore order also fell short of aspirations. Several Muslim countries were encouraged to contribute on the grounds that this would counter the perception of a Western occupation. But they proved reluctant, without a UN peacekeeping mandate, which Washington was not inclined to seek.[12] Turkey professed a willingness to help, but the Iraqis themselves asserted that Turks would not be welcome. A number of European countries including Italy, the Netherlands, Denmark, Norway, Portugal, Lithuania and Romania, as well as New Zealand, were responsive to Tony Blair's request to provide soldiers alongside the 11,000 British forces still in place in southern Iraq as of July 2003, though between them they could only muster an additional 5,000 troops.[13] Poland offered as many again, but had to rely on its allies to pay the costs of deployment. Japan sent soldiers but under its constitution they could not engage in combat. Altogether the allied forces could not come close to the 150,000 US troops still in theatre.

At the start of 2004 the United States had around 130,000 military personnel in Iraq and by the end of that year the number was approximately 140,000.[14] Through rotation the number of US personnel dipped to 114,000 in March 2004, at which time there were estimated to be over 23,000 coalition personnel from 35 other countries deployed in Iraq. The largest non-American contingents came from Britain (8,000–10,000), South Korea (3,600), Italy (3,169), Poland (2,400–2,500), Ukraine (1,589) and the Netherlands (1,345).[15] Several countries chose not to renew their commitments after serving for several months in 2003–04 and by the end of 2004 there were no apparent options for reducing the burden on the US forces except by training Iraqis, as fast as possible, to take their place.

On the political front, Bremer appointed a 25-member Iraqi Governing Council (IGC) to work with the CPA. In doing so he highlighted the importance, as he saw it, of making sure that both Shia and Sunni Arabs as well as Kurds were represented, roughly in accordance with their assumed numbers in the total population. This became a pattern in US dealings with the Iraqis, resisted from some quarters – notably secular and Sunni Arab Iraqis – and embraced by others – in particular Iraqi Shia parties and their

Iranian supporters. Between autumn 2003 and the Iraqi elections of January 2005 the process of fragmentation accelerated.

British officials were among those who urged Bremer to put the Iraqis in charge as soon as possible to defuse the impression that the occupation would last indefinitely. However, the process by which Bremer decided to put this into effect simply compounded latent sectarianism and rewarded the Shia religious parties that emerged from hiding and exile in the wake of the invasion. On the basis of an agreement signed between the CPA and the IGC on 15 November 2003, extended negotiations finally produced a Transitional Administrative Law, concluded on 4 March 2004. This laid the ground for the handover of sovereign powers from the CPA to an 'Interim Iraqi Government' in July 2004.[16] The members of this body were selected at an assembly convened by the CPA, with UN input provided by Lakhdar Brahimi, the veteran diplomat who had performed a similar function in Afghanistan.[17]

Iraqis and others persisted in referring to 'the occupation' even after Bremer stepped down, the CPA was disbanded and the UN gave formal recognition to the new Iraqi administration. Behind the scenes the US Ambassador to Iraq still wielded considerable influence and a sizeable US civilian presence continued to operate inside the fortified centre of Baghdad, known as the Green Zone, under a security cordon impenetrable to ordinary Iraqis and divorced from the realities of life in the rest of the country. America's reputation was also seriously damaged by revelations of torture and sexual abuse of Iraqi detainees, perpetrated by US personnel at Abu Ghraib prison, which became public in April 2004.[18]

Democracy, populism, sectarianism and terrorism

For nearly four years opposition to the US and allied presence came principally from Sunni Arab and tribal quarters, some of it inspired by al-Qaeda. The Shia majority in Iraq were persuaded to facilitate the political process in large part by the urgings of the most influential Shia cleric, Grand Ayatollah Ali al-Sistani, who insisted that elections should determine the composition of the body tasked with devising a new constitution for the country. Consequently, elections were held in January 2005 under strict security enforced by US and allied troops. The turnout was 58 per cent. Portentously, most of the Sunni Arab minority population boycotted the process and the draft constitution concluded the following autumn enshrined the informal autonomy of the Kurdish north and marginalized the Sunni Arab minority.

The latter were persuaded to vote in the referendum on the draft constitution, but failed to win a majority in more than two provinces. They would have had to win three provinces to veto the draft. Even so, Sunni Arab Iraqis were again persuaded to go to the polls in the legislative elections of December 2005, on a promise that if they participated, the new government would revisit the terms of the constitution and recognize some of their concerns. As of 2009 the Iraqi factions and parties were still wrangling, although the Americans as well as the British made efforts to persuade the Shia-dominated coalition government to pursue a process of 'reconciliation' with the Sunni Arab minority. Eventually, in 2007 the Americans began to inject additional forces – the so-called 'Surge' – and arm Sunni Arab militiamen to turn on al-Qaeda fighters.

In the meantime, as of 2004 the situation was further complicated by the activities of Muqtada al-Sadr and his followers, the poorest and most alienated citizenry of Iraq, who responded to al-Sadr's populist nationalism. Affronted by the closing of a newspaper espousing his cause and the arrest of one of his aides, in early 2004 al-Sadr gathered his supporters for a show of strength in Najaf, daring the US forces to take him on at one of the most hallowed Shia sites honoured by Muslims generally. Ayatollah Sistani eventually intervened to avert a bloody denouement, apparently persuading al-Sadr to go along with the political process, but also preventing what would have been a hollow victory for the American forces had they pressed home their advantage.

The US strategy to crush resistance in Fallujah, in Anbar province, proved less flexible. Hostility in the town flared after American forces fired on a crowd of demonstrators, killing some civilians. The inhabitants wreaked vengeance on some US contractors, whom they captured and killed before parading their butchered bodies. In spring 2004 US forces attacked and besieged the town, threatening worse to come if the insurgents were not handed over. On that occasion a truce was brokered by the IGC, placing former Baathist officers in charge of Fallujah's security. Over the ensuing months the insurgents regrouped, among them various foreign volunteers to the cause, including, allegedly, the Jordanian Abu Musab al-Zarqawi. Trained in Afghanistan and variously described as a supporter and a rival of Osama bin Laden, Zarqawi was blamed for many atrocities and masterminding the radical Salafist component of the insurgency.

Fallujah and Zarqawi thus became the foci of US counter-insurgency strategy in late 2004. Following the US elections in early November, residents of Fallujah were warned to flee, though not all the young men of the town were able or willing to exit. The town was bombarded by air and ground forces and US tanks and armoured personnel carriers gradually retook the town, street by street. The operation wrecked Fallujah, rendering it unsuitable for the inhabitants to return until water supplies, sewage treatment facilities and electricity could be restored.[19] Then the insurgency flared in Mosul, a much larger town to the north, and rebel forces temporarily took over the security headquarters. The US forces did not consider it an option to deal with Mosul as they had with Fallujah, and if they had hoped to make an example of Fallujah the strategy had failed.

In the meantime Zarqawi slipped away, to resurface again as the architect of a spate of sectarian killings aimed at Shia Arabs that overtook Iraq in 2006. The trigger was a suicide bomb attack on the Askariya Mosque in Samarra, a Shia shrine, in February – the first in a wave of bombings of Shia shrines and neighbourhoods in Iraq's main cities that killed hundreds. The carnage was attributed to Zarqawi and al-Qaeda supporters determined to spread chaos and mayhem. The restraint that Ayatollah Sistani had urged on his followers dissolved and from spring 2006 reports of Shia militia death squads wreaking vengeance became commonplace. Only after many urban neighbourhoods had been segregated and the central government finally galvanized into action did the sectarian warfare abate, though Zarqawi was targeted and finally killed in a US air strike in June 2006.

BRITAIN'S PREDICAMENT

The involvement of British troops from the start of the invasion helped the Bush administration claim that the whole endeavour was a combined or multinational one, but it won the British government little leverage in the conduct of the war. There is anecdotal evidence that the British did not think highly of the US counter-insurgency strategy in the early days.[20] For a year or two the demeanour of British forces in and around Basra, where they patrolled on foot and dispensed with body armour when possible – in keeping with tactics refined in Northern Ireland and the Balkans – contrasted with some of the heavy-handed tactics of US armoured patrols in and around Baghdad.

However, as the Americans would point out, the British did not face the same level of hostility in the south as they encountered in the Sunni Arab heartland and Anbar province. Subsequently, the Americans would learn from their mistakes and devise new strategies, while the British troops began to lose control in and around Basra as they fell prey to an array of local opposition forces and crime rings, aided and abetted by Iranian operatives.

The sheer size of the US presence in Iraq, and its budget, dwarfed that of the British. Consequently, British officials sent to Baghdad were unable to do more than offer advice and suggestions to the Americans, but they could not prevail in the decision-making about how to run the counter-insurgency or the civilian administration. Crucially, without an effective Iraqi government to direct and defend the rule of law, local and regional leaders simply took matters into their own hands. In the British zone of responsibility a procession of diplomats, DFID personnel and private contractors were drafted in to run a makeshift regional administration and reconstruction effort under mounting security constraints.[21] Meanwhile, the Iranians became increasingly active in supporting rival Iraqi factions.

The British began to encounter more direct attacks as Shia militia groups and criminal gangs fought each other for control of resources, institutions and neighbourhoods. Revelations of British torture and brutality towards some Iraqis angered the locals and led the city council in Basra to refuse to deal with the British forces there for a period in early 2006.[22] The trend did not escape the notice of the Americans and some of the Bush administration's advisers were open in their criticism of the failure of British forces, as they saw it, to pursue more aggressively the various hostile elements, including militia allied to Iran.[23]

Some of these critics, from the Washington think tank the American Enterprise Institute, claimed authorship of the so-called 'Surge' strategy adopted by US forces to crush resistance in Iraq in 2007–08. Chastened by the Democratic Party victory in the mid-term Congressional elections of November 2006, attributed to growing public disaffection with the Iraq war, George Bush nonetheless refused to adopt the advice offered him by the bi-partisan Iraq Study Group[24] to prepare to exit Iraq. Instead he ordered the deployment of more troops to crack down on instability in Baghdad and thence beyond. He and the US Secretary of State Condoleezza Rice also became more insistent in their accusations that Iran bore responsibility for worsening the situation. In Iraq, US forces began arming and training Sunni Arab groups to take on foreign fighters affiliated with al-Qaeda. Disaffection with the radicals among Iraqis in Anbar generated a backlash against al-Qaeda upon which the Americans were able to capitalize.

The Iran connection

By 2007 British forces had begun to draw down troop numbers and hand over responsibility for security to local commanders, province by province. To pave the way, the British mounted Operation Sinbad to root out militia elements from the local institutions. Commenting on British strategy, a senior Iraqi general in the interior ministry in Basra told an Iraqi journalist working for the *Guardian*:

> The British came here as military tourists. They committed huge mistakes when they formed the security forces. They appointed militiamen as police officers and chose not to confront the militias. We have reached this point where the militias are a legitimate force in the street.[25]

The same journalist was one of a number who reported that Iran had become the main power-broker in southern Iraq, with connections right into the central government in Baghdad. That government, dominated by Shia parties with long-time connections to Iran, made formal agreements with the Iranians for reconstruction contracts and by 2007 were discussing cooperation on energy infrastructure development in Iraq.[26] The words of an Iraqi intelligence officer, cited above, were chilling and revealing:

> Unlike the US and the UK, Iran invested better. They knew where to pump their money, into militias and political parties. If a war happens they can take over Basra without even sending their soldiers. They are fighting a war of attrition with the US and UK, bleeding them slowly.[27]

It took a major US and Iraqi government offensive in 2008 to retrieve the situation in Basra, confront the criminal and rogue militia elements and restore a semblance of order.

Meanwhile, in May 2007 Washington decided to permit the US Ambassador to Iraq, Ryan Crocker, to talk directly to his Iranian counterpart, breaking a freeze on official dialogue that had endured since the Iranian Revolution in 1979. The subject of their conversation, hosted by the Iraqi government, was confined to the future of Iraq. Given the level of Iran's influence and involvement in the country, it appeared unlikely that the Americans could prevail without its cooperation. For whatever reason, the Iranians did not interfere in the 2008 operation to rescue the citizens of Basra from gang rule.

In the north of Iraq, where relative calm had prevailed since before the invasion, the prospect of more trouble then loomed. Having enjoyed virtual autonomy under Western protection since the mid-1990s, after the fall of Saddam Hussein the objective of the Kurdish leadership was to secure maximum autonomy in any future political system. As a result of their pressure, the Kurds gained an effective right of veto over the draft constitution. They also aspired to make Kirkuk their regional capital and intended to reverse the process by which Saddam Hussein had displaced them in favour of Arab Iraqis there. Thus no sooner had the Americans begun to reap the benefits of their 'Surge' strategy and recruitment of local Sunni Arab leaders to help counter al-Qaeda than Kurdish ambitions to control Kirkuk and its oil resources became a major obstacle to the passage of legislation needed to begin full-scale development of the Iraqi energy sector.[28]

Counting the costs

Blair's principal justification for the Iraq invasion – the danger posed by Iraq's WMD capabilities – was discredited relatively quickly. For months

Blair maintained that he still expected evidence of these to be uncovered, but the conclusion of David Kay, who went in as the post-war chief weapons inspector, was that on this 'we were almost all wrong'.[29] After extensive investigations, US inspectors reported that there were no Iraqi WMD remaining in the country.[30] The experts deduced that they must have been destroyed, both secretly and under UN supervision, in the 1990s. In the United States the CIA was held principally responsible for the intelligence failure and a thorough reordering of the agency was initiated.

The goal of turning Iraq into an exemplary democracy endured for longer. The transition from occupation to Iraqi sovereignty – followed by elections, a new constitution, a referendum and then further elections – was supposed to deliver that objective and provide the political basis for stabilizing the country and enabling economic reconstruction. Tony Blair and other members of the cabinet repeatedly pointed to the electoral milestones as symbols of a successful endeavour. Palpable disappointment only set in after the sectarian violence gained momentum in early 2006 and the political parties dithered over the formation of a coalition cabinet. By then Blair had resorted to explaining the invasion simply as 'the right thing to do' and asserting that the world was a better place without Saddam Hussein.

Yet even the manner of Saddam Hussein's ultimate demise – he was executed in December 2006 – gave little cause for satisfaction. His hanging was conducted hastily, on a Muslim holy day and against US urgings, by what was clearly a group of men from one of Iraq's Shia factions seeking personal revenge. Tried and found guilty of only one of the charges against him by an Iraqi court, he was executed before he could be held to account for other offences, including the gas attacks on the Kurds in 1988. Thus the episode did not speak well for the rule of law in post-Saddam Iraq.

Meanwhile, ordinary Iraqis could only find some measure of personal safety through affiliation with one or other of the warring militia, tribal groupings or criminal gangs. The police forces in the localities were infiltrated or run by sectarian militia, and were more or less a law unto themselves. Kidnappings for ransom became endemic. Iraqi academics and other professionals became assassination targets and those who could, fled Iraq. By 2007 there were at least a million Iraqi refugees in Jordan and the same number in Syria, and two million Iraqis were internally displaced. There was no let-up in sectarian violence until 'ethnic cleansing' had segregated whole neighbourhoods, the Americans had taken to arming some of the Sunni Arab resistance groups to tackle al-Qaeda, and the Iraqi security forces were finally galvanized to work alongside US forces to enforce their authority.

Using open sources, the Iraq Body Count recorded between 66,900 and 73,250 Iraqi civilian deaths by June 2007[31] and the medical journal *The Lancet* estimated nearly 655,000 Iraqi deaths as a consequence of war, 601,000 resulting from violence – the most common cause being gunfire.[32] The number of Iraqis seriously injured was assumed to be several times higher.

The day after Tony Blair stepped down from office on 27 June 2007, three British soldiers were killed and one seriously injured while supplying a base in Basra city. This brought the total number of fatalities of British military personnel in Iraq since the invasion to 156.[33] At this point the British military presence on the ground stood at 5,500.[34] Over 170 British military and civilian personnel were seriously or very seriously injured in Iraq between January 2003 and June 2007, and several hundred had had to be evacuated owing to illness.[35]

US military fatalities in Iraq between the invasion and 4 July 2007 exceeded 3,500 and the number of wounded exceeded 25,500.[36] Between May 2003 and early 2005 the US troop presence in Iraq averaged 140,000, with other coalition members, including the British, contributing a further 23,000.[37] By June 2007 the US presence stood at 157,000 with coalition support down to 11,524, including 5,500 British troops.[38] According to media reports, an estimated 126,000 American, Iraqi and other foreign nationals were working for the US government in Iraq by 2007, and some 1,000 private contractors had been killed and 13,000 injured since the invasion.[39]

By the time British forces finally wound up their operations in Iraq in 2009, the death toll of British soldiers killed in the campaign had reached 179. As to the total financial cost to Britain of its commitment in Iraq, a Treasury document released in 2009 under freedom of information rules revealed that officials advising the Chancellor Gordon Brown estimated in September 2002 that the cost of 'preparation, deployment and return' of UK troops from Iraq would be £2.5 billion.[40] At that point they thought that British forces would need to remain 'fully engaged' in Iraq for only six months. The actual deployment lasted six years and the total cost of British military operations in Iraq was £8.4 billion.[41]

II: AROUND THE REGION

The regional impact of the Iraq war was less dramatic but more insidious. Among the principal beneficiaries of regime change in Iraq and the ensuing chaos was Iran. Emboldened by America's travails in Iraq, not only did the Iranian leadership become more defiant about pursuing its nuclear ambitions, much to the consternation of Israel, the United States and the British, but the Iranian-backed Islamist movements Hamas and Hizbullah provoked war with Israel on the Gaza and Lebanese fronts – with bloody and inconclusive consequences (see Chapter 7).

It was in this context that Tony Blair gave a speech in Los Angeles in which he warned of 'an arc of extremism now stretching across the Middle East and touching, with increasing definition, countries far outside the region'.[42] In the face of this, he called for 'a complete renaissance' of foreign policy to combat 'reactionary Islam'.

Speaking to business leaders in Dubai in December 2006, Blair called for 'an arc of moderates' across the Middle East to combat Iran and Tehran-sponsored terrorism and extremism. In his speech he identified the autocratic Sunni Arab regimes of Egypt and Saudi Arabia as tolerant moderates, claiming, unconvincingly, that they were moving towards the kind of political reform he had previously advocated.[43] Yet more confusing was his identification of Tehran and the groups it supported – which included Hizbullah and Hamas, but also Shia factions represented in the elected government of Iraq – as the enemy. In so doing he complicated the British position in Iraq and obscured the threats posed by al-Qaeda, the Taliban and other anti-Shia and anti-Western radical Sunnis.

Blair's characterization of the regional situation was an oversimplification, but it was also an implicit acknowledgment of the destabilizing repercussions of the invasion of Iraq. The landscape had been transformed in ways apparently not foreseen or prepared for in British government calculations. The overall consequences for Britain and the region brought more problems than benefits.

BRITAIN AND IRAN: FROM RAPPROCHEMENT TO ANIMOSITY

At the time New Labour arrived in power in 1997 British relations with Iran were not warm. As discussed in Chapter 1, the Iranians retained a suspicion informed by their experiences of the British Empire, Britain's role in the toppling of Mossadeq in 1953 and its subsequent dealings with the Shah. During the 1980s the two countries maintained trade links and diplomatic relations, but differences between them meant that these were limited and British dealings with Tehran were handled through an interests section at the Swedish embassy. Rocked by the Iranian Revolution and the Iraq–Iran war in the 1980s, relations had plummeted after Ayatollah Khomeini issued a *fatwa* against British author Salman Rushdie for his book *The Satanic Verses*. Even after Khomeini's death British efforts to resolve the issue were unsuccessful. However, the election of Mohamed Khatami to the presidency of the Islamic Republic in 1997, coinciding with the election of the first New Labour government in Britain, heralded change.

Rapprochement

Khatami's readiness to promote trade and political interaction with Europe and his call for 'a dialogue among civilizations'[44] created a new atmosphere. The breakthrough on the *fatwa* issue came in the margins of the UN General Assembly in New York in September 1998. President Khatami made it known that Iran regarded the affair as 'completely finished' and the Foreign Minister Kamal Kharrazi told his British counterpart that:

> Iran has no intention, nor is it going to take any action whatsoever to threaten the life of the author of *The Satanic Verses*, or anybody associated with his work, nor will it encourage or assist anybody to do so.[45]

This was sufficient to put the matter to rest (though it would resurface at the end of Blair's premiership, when Rushdie was honoured with a knighthood). Britain and Iran moved to restore full diplomatic relations, though London and Tehran did not agree on the exchange of ambassadors until April 1999.[46]

British officials at the Foreign Office and the Export Credit Guarantee Department (ECGD) were also optimistic about the potential for a burgeoning economic relationship.[47] They depicted Iran as a country with a large population (approaching 70 million), a relatively high standard of living, a developed economic infrastructure and an entrepreneurial culture. On the downside, the state system was deemed to be overweening, corrupt and in need of painful reform – the main obstacle to which was assumed to be the *bonyads* or foundations, representing vested interests and reporting directly to the Supreme Leader Ali Khamenei.

Despite these concerns the British hoped to use an ECGD scheme designed to underwrite 'Good Projects in Difficult Markets' to facilitate British investment in Iran, starting with a project in Iran's special economic zone of Bandar Imam. Apparently the Iranians were impatient to see this materialize and were unimpressed by British explanations that it would take time because the availability of government credit guarantees had been severely reduced as a result of the near-collapse of the Asian tiger economies in the mid-1990s.

Iran's eagerness to recruit UK business support was part of a strategy to demonstrate to the Americans that all the major European economies and Japan were undeterred by US antipathy to the Islamic Republic or US sanctions. As Foreign Minister Kamal Kharrazi intimated on a visit to London in early 2000, Tehran saw Britain as closest of all the Europeans to the Americans and thus as a potential stepping stone on the way to dealing with the Americans.[48] Even if it never came to that, the Iranians wanted to deny the Americans the benefit of European solidarity.

In fact, for a while even Washington warmed to the opportunity afforded by Khatami's espousal of a reformist agenda in Iran. US Secretary of State Madeleine Albright made a couple of gestures designed to open a new chapter in US–Iranian relations.[49] These had been overshadowed by mutual hostility since the fall of the Shah and the detention of US diplomats as hostages in 1979–80 left an indelible impression. However, Albright's efforts elicited no reciprocal gestures from Tehran and the Americans concluded that Khatami was either unwilling or unable to effect the transformation of Iranian politics they were hoping for.

Britain did not despair so quickly of Khatami and persisted with efforts to develop relations. This required considerable patience and expert diplomacy on a number of occasions. Tehran was sensitive about the coverage of Iran by the BBC Persian Service. When the BBC gave attention to student demonstrations in Iran, the Iranian authorities complained of British interference in their affairs. They were also furious in 1999 when BBC domestic radio broadcast commentary by a supporter of the Mujahedin e-Khalq organization (MKO) – an enemy of the Iranian regime and at the time designated a terrorist organization by the British government. It turned out the BBC presenters on that occasion were unaware of the commentator's affiliation or at least its significance. These episodes had to be explained and tensions alleviated by diplomatic intervention. Similarly, the British Ambassador to Tehran Nick Brown was forced to apologize when *The Times* newspaper, to mark the turn of the millennium, republished a set of obituaries from the twentieth century that included one offensive to the memory of Ayatollah Khomeini.

The British were not alone in Europe in having to handle such moments of tension and unintended affront. A German national was accused of adultery with an Iranian woman. Italy suffered embarrassment when it was revealed that a talk by the author Salman Rushdie coincided with a visit there by President Khatami. And it emerged that Khatami could not attend official functions during a planned visit to France if alcohol was to be served. However, because of their history, Iranian suspicions of the British probably exceeded their distrust of other Europeans. For their part, the EU countries, Britain included, demonstrated a level of solidarity in their dealings with Iran that contrasted with their disagreements over Iraq. They even produced a joint negotiating stance over the nuclear issue in 2002, spearheaded by Britain, France and Germany – the EU3 (see below).

Jack Straw drew attention to this European solidarity over Iran on a number of occasions to refute claims that the British no longer had an independent foreign policy and to prove that they could on occasion disagree with the Americans when their judgments differed. At the same time, Britain apparently hoped to use its 'pivotal' position, as Blair called it, to mediate on transatlantic differences.

In demonstration of London's advantage over Washington in terms of access in Tehran, after 9/11 Tony Blair telephoned President Khatami personally to seek his cooperation in the impending US intervention in Afghanistan. This cooperation was forthcoming, to the evident satisfaction of Straw on the first of several visits to Tehran, during which he appeared to forge good relations with his Iranian counterpart and other officials, including those dealing with the nuclear issue. As discussed in Chapter 7, however, Straw's diplomatic forays in Iran had repercussions for British relations with Israel.

Deterioration

Iran's mediation with its contacts in Afghanistan, all opponents of the Taliban, was undoubtedly helpful to initial US operations there in 2001. However, after Washington realized that al-Qaeda fighters were escaping the country, some of them to Iran – where several were detained – the Bush administration became suspicious when these men were not then handed over to Saudi Arabia or other countries from which they apparently originated. As also noted in Chapters 5 and 7, in early 2002 the Israeli navy intercepted the *Karine-A* in the Red Sea – a vessel apparently carrying arms to the Palestinians, allegedly from Iran. In US eyes this was evidence of Iranian support for terrorism – one of the many charges levelled at Tehran by Washington. Almost immediately, in his January 2002 State of the Union Address, Bush designated Iran as part of an 'Axis of Evil' (along with Iraq and North Korea).

Coincidentally, the British had to weather another spat with the Iranians over their choice of a successor to Ambassador Nick Brown. Originally the British designated David Reddaway, a Persian linguist with an Iranian wife. The Iranian media spread the rumour that he was a spy. Officials meanwhile claimed to be affronted because Reddaway was more junior than their nominee to represent Iran in London, suggesting that the British did not value the relationship as highly as they did. The real explanation could be that they feared Reddaway was too able to discern what was going on in Iran. Another possibility was that the Iranians wanted to send a signal to the British that there could be penalties for standing 'shoulder to shoulder' with the Americans, especially in the face of US hostility towards Tehran. It took until September 2002 to resolve the issue of the ambassadors, when the British selected Richard Dalton, an experienced Arabist.[50]

By then opponents of the Iranian regime had managed to expose the existence of two nuclear facilities, at Natanz and near Arak, along with other facets of Iran's nuclear programme, which had been kept secret from the

International Atomic Energy Agency (IAEA). Even if these revelations did not render Iran in breach of the provisions of the Non-Proliferation Treaty (NPT) which allow signatories to develop civil nuclear programmes, the fact of concealment inevitably raised suspicions about Iranian intentions. Washington soon drew the conclusion that Iran intended to have a weapons capability. New and more intrusive inspections by the IAEA failed to reveal proof of this, but the suspicions remained and British as well as French intelligence hardened their positions.

Germany was Iran's leading trading partner in Europe and keen to see plans for an EU–Iranian Trade and Cooperation Agreement to enable European economic relations with Iran to expand. However, Germany was also an ardent defender of the NPT as the linchpin of the international counter-proliferation agenda. These factors were decisive in the inclusion of Germany, along with Britain and France – Europe's two nuclear powers – in the EU3 team that set about resolving the issue of Iranian commitment to the principles of the NPT. All three also had a track record in the tortuous business of diplomacy with Iran and were well placed to represent the EU as a whole.

The spadework was done by the foreign ministers of Britain, France and Germany, who embarked on a series of diplomatic missions designed to persuade the Iranians at least to sign the Additional Protocol of the NPT, thereby allowing the IAEA to undertake more intrusive inspections. By late 2003 they had secured Iran's informal agreement to do so and to suspend its uranium enrichment activities pending further negotiations.[51] Yet the Iranians' pride was at stake and their rhetoric expressed indignation that they should be made to forgo options available to other NPT signatories, not least Germany and Japan. They also pointed out that others in their region – Israel, India and Pakistan – were not even signatories of the NPT and had all become nuclear weapon states in defiance of the international community and suffered no serious strictures. (After 9/11 the United States dropped its erstwhile objections to Pakistan's bomb in the interests of securing its cooperation against al-Qaeda.)

The British asserted that the line they and the EU3 were pursuing was based on the need to find a formula by which Iran could demonstrate unequivocally that its nuclear programme was only peaceful. The suspension of uranium enrichment would serve such a purpose. On their side, however, the Iranians continued to argue in defence of their rights and good intentions and to explain that they did not feel able to trust any foreign supplier to honour their needs for enriched uranium. The EU3 approach was to try to find ways to reassure Iran that such supplies would be forthcoming provided it was fully open about its activities.

The Americans, by contrast, initially wanted Iran to abandon its nuclear ambitions altogether. The harsh criticism levelled at the Iranian regime by the Bush administration, especially after the invasion of Iraq, contributed to Iranian fears that Washington's real aim was regime change in Tehran as well as Baghdad. Consequently, even after Iran agreed to suspend its enrichment activities in late 2003, the EU3 proved unable to find a more lasting formula – since what Tehran wanted was a guarantee that America would not try to bring down the regime. EU3 diplomatic efforts continued but Iran resumed uranium enrichment. In 2006 the matter was referred to the UN Security Council, which adopted a resolution requiring Iran to cease uranium enrichment.[52]

For Washington, meanwhile, the enrichment issue became the central focus of relations with Iran. Eventually persuaded to give more leverage to EU diplomacy, Washington professed readiness to talk to the Iranians directly, but only provided they first suspend uranium enrichment. By then, however, Mahmoud Ahmadinejad had won the presidential election in Iran (in June 2005) and dramatically raised the temperature with his fierce rhetoric against Israel and denial of the Holocaust. He dismissed the idea that there could be any concessions from Iran on uranium enrichment and instead boasted about Iran's achievements in this respect.

As tensions mounted, along with fears of a direct US–Iranian clash in Iraq leading to a wider war, there was also speculation that the United States might resort to a pre-emptive strike on Iranian nuclear facilities. The Israelis asserted that they would not tolerate a nuclear-armed Iran – and Washington used similar rhetoric. Tony Blair maintained that he would not rule out the possibility of resort to force, in particular if Iran failed to comply with UN, EU and IAEA demands regarding its nuclear programme.

Meanwhile, as discussed above, Iran made the most of its connections among the Iraqi Shia to extend its influence with the Iraqi government and right across the centre and south of the country. Deployed around Basra in southern Iraq, where the Shia predominate, British troops were bound to be aware of Iranian comings and goings across the border. Even so, they said very little about it until the Americans began to complain about Iranian meddling in internal Iraqi affairs. By 2007 the British concurred with the Americans that the Iranians were the main source of weaponry reaching Iraqi groups attacking their forces.

In early 2007 members of the Iranian Revolutionary Guard Corps seized a group of British sailors and marines deployed in the headwaters of the Persian Gulf to counter smuggling. This incident, including staged appearances on Iranian television by the British servicemen and one servicewoman, was a source of humiliation for the British, even though diplomacy finally secured their release unharmed.[53] By May 2007 a former Iranian diplomat judged that British–Iranian relations had reached a new low point, 'not just zero, but below zero'.[54] That was the point at which Tony Blair left No. 10 Downing Street and it became Gordon Brown's problem to decide how Britain should react in the event of a US war with Iran. As it transpired, relations between Britain and Iran deteriorated further, with Britain taking more blame than the United States for alleged interference in Iran against the regime.[55]

BRITISH RELATIONS WITH SYRIA AND LIBYA

The repercussions from the invasion of Iraq, in the aftermath of 9/11, affected British relations across the Arab world as well as with Iran. The implications on the Arab–Israeli front are discussed in Chapter 7, and the effects on British relations with the Arab Gulf states in Chapter 8. But it is also worth singling out Syria and Libya here because they were both on America's list of 'rogue states' – along with Iraq and Iran – even prior to 9/11 and New Labour's assumption of power.[56]

During Blair's first term (1997–2001), it was one of Robin Cook's objectives as foreign secretary to explore the possibilities for diplomacy with the so-called 'rogue states'. While outreach to Iraq proved a non-starter (see Chapter 5), with Iran it was initially successful, as detailed above, but later foundered. With respect to Syria the results were mixed but largely disappointing before relations were overtaken by the repercussions from the invasion of Iraq. Thereafter Britain switched from encouraging internal reform to persuading Damascus to halt the flow of volunteers crossing the border into Iraq to join forces with locals fighting the occupation. With Libya, however, the outcome of diplomacy in the margins of the Iraq war delivered a significant breakthrough with respect to counter-proliferation.

Syria

Even before 9/11, New Labour thinking about Syria indicated awareness of that country's potential to play the 'spoiler' in regional politics. In November 1997 the Foreign Office Minister Derek Fatchett said:

> Secular Syria cooperates with Islamist Iran as a means of strengthening its bargaining position. Iran in consequence is making inroads in Lebanon through Hizbullah. Without Israel's occupation of Southern Lebanon, Hizbullah would lose its main raison d'être, and Iran its proxy. Surely the moral here is to work urgently on the Syrian track [of the Middle East peace process] along the lines on which the previous Israeli government was working and was making progress. Putting the Syrian track on hold is a

dangerous risk.[57]

However, at this point Washington was in the forefront of Middle East peacemaking and focused on the Israeli–Palestinian track. Syria was accused of giving succour to Hizbullah, Hamas and other 'rejectionist' groups (see Chapter 4). Iran was also accused of supplying money, training and arms to Hizbullah, Hamas and Islamic Jihad.[58] To add to the general picture of insecurity, in May 1998 France, Switzerland, Italy and Belgium all announced a crackdown on Islamist groups deemed to be plotting violence. The Algerian government warned of the increasing 'internationalization' of the phenomenon.

A subsequent revival of the Syrian–Israeli track foundered at a meeting convened by President Clinton with his Syrian counterpart Hafez al-Asad in 2000 (see Chapter 4) and shortly thereafter Asad died, to be succeeded by his comparatively inexperienced son Bashar al-Asad. Compared with his dour father, however, Bashar looked like a potential reformer and the Foreign Office saw an opportunity to encourage greater political freedom in Syria. To test the waters some British academics were encouraged to visit Damascus to talk to their Syrian counterparts and engage them in discussions about the possibilities of peace.[59] The Foreign Office also encouraged some discreet informal discussions with Syrian proponents of political reform.

Hopes of a 'Damascus Spring' proved short-lived, however. Most of the advocates of reform, several of whom had already served time in prison for voicing criticism of the old Asad regime, would eventually wind up in detention again. Meanwhile, after a seemingly shaky start, Bashar al-Asad was able to consolidate his position in power and became focused on economic but not political development in Syria, while also continuing his father's practice of interfering in Lebanese politics (see below and Chapter 7).

After 9/11 Tony Blair hoped to recruit President Asad's support for the new 'war on terror', but on this score the results also proved disappointing. As discussed in Chapter 7, when Blair visited Damascus in November 2001, Asad embarrassed him with a public rebuke for his stance on the Israeli–Palestinian conflict.[60] A year later, while on an official visit to London, the Syrian President denigrated British plans to host a conference on the Palestinian problem as 'irrelevant', assuming it would not address the core issue of occupation.[61] Asad warned the United States that even though it could easily win a war in Iraq, this would only widen the gap between the Arab region and the West, and terrorism would increase.[62]

In the wake of 9/11 Syrian intelligence did initially provide some assistance to the CIA in the pursuit and interrogation of al-Qaeda suspects, but Damascus wanted some political rewards, in the form of improved relations with Washington, that the Bush administration and neo-conservatives categorically refused to concede, especially after Syria opposed the invasion of Iraq.

Following the invasion, Britain was at one with the United States in pressuring Damascus to stop enabling Iraqi insurgents and foreign volunteers to operate across the Syrian-Iraqi border. British diplomats explained to their Syrian counterparts that once British forces were committed in Iraq the British government would inevitably be antagonized by Syrian support for their opponents. For their part the Syrians dissembled, hoping at the very least to gain some benefits for cooperation. They affected disbelief that there was no way of reaching an accommodation with the Americans given their shared antipathy to Islamist extremists and al-Qaeda in particular. From 2001 to 2004, therefore, the British explored the possibilities of mediating between Damascus and Washington, but with little to show for it.

Then the assassination of former Lebanese Prime Minister Rafiq Hariri in February 2005 triggered a new crisis in Syrian regional and international relations (see also Chapter 7). Many accused the Syrians of involvement in Hariri's murder, despite their denials, and Lebanese demonstrated in support of his legacy and against Syrian interference in the country. Hizbullah and the Maronite Leader General Aoun mounted counter-demonstrations. Hariri's friends and supporters – Saudi Arabia and France – united in pressuring Asad. Seizing the moment, Britain joined France and the United States in demanding, in accordance with UN Resolutions, the withdrawal of Syrian troops from Lebanon, where they had remained deployed since the end of the Lebanese civil war in 1990.

The Syrians had to give way and the troops were withdrawn, but thereafter Asad refused to cooperate with the special tribunal set up, with UN blessing, to investigate Hariri's death. As Washington pondered the best course of action to take with the Syrians, who continued to anger the Bush administration by supporting Hizbullah in Lebanon and Hamas on the Palestinian front, Tony Blair sent his foreign policy adviser Sir Nigel Sheinwald to Damascus to test the waters for diplomacy. His efforts revealed, apparently, that the one issue on which the Syrians remained most implacable was the Hariri inquiry. Some Lebanese concluded that the British might be preparing a deal to appease Damascus on this issue, in return for its cooperation on all other outstanding concerns and particularly Iraq.

However, no such deal materialized before Blair left office in June 2007 and Sheinwald headed to Washington as the new British ambassador. Thereafter Turkey moved into the role of mediator, exploring the possibilities of reviving Syrian–Israeli peace talks. With the advent of the Obama administration in Washington in 2009, meanwhile, Syria became the object of a new US diplomatic initiative to explore the possibilities of wooing Syria away from its alignment with Tehran, Hizbullah and Hamas. It looked as though the Syrians' obduracy had ultimately paid off.

Libya

British diplomacy with the Libyans was to prove more fruitful. When New Labour came to power Britain had outstanding concerns deriving not only from the Lockerbie bombing of 1988, but also from the shooting of a British police woman outside the Libyan People's Bureau in London in 1984. Since the bombing had targeted the US airliner Pan Am flight 103 over Lockerbie, resolution of that issue required satisfying US as well as British demands, but the British paved the way with a formula for trying the Libyan suspects and the reopening of diplomatic relations.

Thereafter, British and American intelligence agents conducted secret negotiations which led to Libya's renunciation of its WMD programmes at the end of 2003. At the time it was said that the US administration, and in particular John Bolton, in charge of counter-proliferation policy at the State Department, would have prevented the negotiations from going forward had the CIA not kept other Washington agencies in the dark until a deal was done. As it was, thereafter Washington tried to use Libya as an example to put pressure on others in the region, notably Syria and Iran. However, Damascus and Tehran considered the comparison beneath contempt and did not follow suit.

While Blair did not have a high profile during the initial stages of the rapprochement with Libya, he did mark its achievement with a visit in March 2004 to Tripoli, where he was received by Colonel Qadhafi. Just before leaving office in May 2007 Blair visited again to seal an arms sales agreement with Libya and celebrate BP's conclusion of a £450 million energy exploration deal. That deal signalled BP's return to Libya after an absence of three decades, following Qadhafi's nationalization of oil in the 1970s. Blair declared his meeting with Qadhafi 'positive and constructive' and shrugged off suggestions that the trip, along with one to Sierra Leone and another to South Africa, were about burnishing his personal legacy before finally stepping aside for Gordon Brown.[63]

Within a couple of days of Blair's departure from No. 10 the Scottish Criminal Cases Review Commission granted permission for Abdel Baset al-Megrahi – the one and only suspect convicted and jailed for the Lockerbie bombing – to make a new appeal on the grounds that there could have been a miscarriage of justice. Senior Libyan figures as well as some relatives of the victims of Lockerbie had remained suspicious that al-Megrahi was simply a scapegoat whose conviction enabled the case to be closed. Yet the issue resurfaced again in 2009 when a seriously ill al-Megrahi, having dropped his appeal, was permitted to return to Libya on compassionate grounds. The US administration was furious[64] and the British government was forced to deny allegations, fuelled by Colonel Qadhafi and his son Saif al-Islam, that it had played a role in arranging al-Megrahi's release in the interests of securing new British business deals in Libya.

Even so, British intelligence and the government could derive some satisfaction from successful intelligence work and diplomacy with Libya over the WMD issue. Meanwhile, the British could celebrate the conclusion of a valuable oil deal and the signing of other contracts with the Libyans at the expense of their commercial competitors.

COUNTERING TERRORISM: BRITISH RELATIONS WITH JORDAN AND EGYPT

British relations with Jordan and Egypt also saw changes in the wake of 9/11, but of a less contentious nature than those with Libya or Syria. Both Jordan and Egypt were already considered important allies in the quest for Israeli–Palestinian peace (as detailed in Chapters 4 and 7). They had also become important allies of the British as well as the Americans in terms of military cooperation and intelligence-sharing. After 9/11, the Egyptian government virtually said 'I told you so' to Washington and both President Mubarak of Egypt and King Abdullah II of Jordan issued public warnings of the dangers that would result from an invasion of Iraq. However, both governments extended their support to the United States and Britain as key partners in the 'war on terror'.

Jordan

After King Abdullah II ascended the throne of Jordan in 1999, he made a number of visits to Arab and Western capitals to seek debt forgiveness for Jordan and encourage new investment in the kingdom, promising political reform as well as economic restructuring. When Abdullah visited London in May 1999, Tony Blair expressed support for his aspirations for Jordan.[65] After 9/11, however, it was not only US and British priorities that shifted. Abdullah's did too, and Jordan introduced stiff new measures deemed necessary to combat terrorism. Amnesty International criticized the new provisions for violating human rights.[66]

The Jordanian intelligence services were already known for detaining and interrogating individuals suspected of terrorism, including Jordanian nationals who had returned to the kingdom after fighting with the Mujahedin against the Soviet Union in Afghanistan in the 1980s. Following the US invasion of Afghanistan in 2001, the affiliates and supporters of al-Qaeda dispersed, with some surfacing in the Middle East. The Jordanian authorities intensified their security and intelligence cooperation with the Americans in the identification and apprehension of such terrorist suspects.[67]

Meanwhile, by 2002 the possibility that the US would take 'the war on terror' to Iraq began to dawn on Middle East leaders and King Abdullah of Jordan warned that an invasion would open a Pandora's box. Received in London on a formal state visit in July 2002, Abdullah told the Prime Minister that the Middle East peace process would have to be rejuvenated before any action on Iraq could be taken.[68] Blair's spokesman declined to recognize a direct link.[69]

When the invasion did take place, Jordan soon became a refuge for Iraqis fleeing the fighting, as noted above. Their numbers swelled to around a million as the war progressed. Having already served as the conduit for such trade as was permitted with Iraq under UN sanctions in the 1990s, Jordanians doing business in Iraq after 2003 became the targets of robbery and violence. In August 2003 the Jordanian embassy in Baghdad was blown up by a car bomb, in an attack that killed 17 people and deterred the Jordanian government from expanding its presence there.

Public opinion in Jordan, already critical of US support for Israel, became overtly hostile to the United States – or at least US policy – in the context of the Iraq invasion. Britain was regarded with almost equal antipathy: respondents in a public opinion poll taken in 2004 described it variously as 'aggressive', 'repressive' and 'colonial'.[70] Asked about their overall perception of Britain, 55 per cent of Jordanians replied 'not positive at all'; 58 per cent had the same perception of the United States, but only 37 per cent viewed France negatively.[71] Some of the respondents did indicate, however, that they understood there were differences between the positions of the British government and those of the British public.

Sympathy for Arab militant groups using terror tactics, such as Hamas and Hizbullah, was also prevalent in Jordan. In the 2004 poll cited above, a majority of Jordanians viewed even al-Qaeda as a legitimate resistance organization.[72] However, when suicide bombers targeted three hotels in Amman in November 2005, killing 60 people, including members of a Palestinian wedding party, opinion in the kingdom shifted. Responsibility for the hotel attacks was later claimed by the Iraqi-based group led by the Jordanian national Abu Musab al-Zarqawi (see above), and support for the group eroded in Jordan. Security around public buildings and sites frequented by foreigners in Jordan was significantly increased.

Meanwhile, as subsequently emerged, Jordan had become a key 'hub' in the US secret renditions programme, allegedly receiving, detaining and torturing terrorism suspects picked up by the Americans and 'rendered' for interrogation in countries, including Jordan, where protection of human rights was not respected in 'the war on terror'.[73] Claims would eventually surface that the British, while not directly party to the US renditions programme, had nonetheless been complicit.[74]

One of the concerns of human rights lawyers and activists alleging this complicity was a Memorandum of Understanding signed by the British and Jordanian authorities in August 2005. This MOU 'purportedly guarantees, by the way of "diplomatic assurances", that certain individuals of Jordanian nationality would not be tortured or otherwise ill-treated if they should be forcibly removed to Jordan by the UK authorities'.[75] As of this writing, no one had been deported to Jordan on the basis of the MOU. However, when the MOU policy was challenged in court in 2007, the Special Immigration Appeals Commission, while acknowledging that torture in Jordan was a serious problem, 'relied on the British government's argument that the strength of ties between the two countries meant that Jordan would keep its word'.[76]

By its very existence, the MOU acknowledged the existence of torture in Jordan. In a curious twist to the story of British intelligence cooperation with Jordan, the MOU provided for independent monitoring of cases of individuals returned to Jordan under the agreement, which the Adaleh Centre for Human Rights Studies, a Jordanian non-governmental organization, subsequently agreed to undertake. As reported by Amnesty International, in 2006 Adaleh received funding amounting to £67,000 from the British government, apparently in relation to its monitoring.[77] The sending country, Britain, was to be informed of Adaleh's findings, but no provision was made for publishing its observations.

Alongside coordination on intelligence, British defence cooperation with Jordan increased after 9/11 and the invasion of Iraq. In addition to training at Sandhurst in the 1980s, King Abdullah II had served with the British 13th/18th Hussars (which later became part of the Light Dragoons) as a junior officer in the British army. In 2003 Abdullah was appointed Colonel in Chief of the Light Dragoons and paid his first visit back to the Light Dragoons as Colonel in Chief in 2004.[78] In the following years, the British armed forces conducted regular training exercises in Jordan and the British provided short-term training teams and advisory visits to assist the Jordanian Armed Forces.[79]

Jordan's role in the training of the reconstituted Iraqi armed and security forces expanded after 2005, as part of the US-led effort to reassert security in Iraq. While the country descended into near chaos, rendering it unsafe for international aid agencies and NGOs to operate from bases inside Iraq, these organizations operated out of Jordan. Private security firms, including those protecting British government personnel in Iraq, transited to and from the country via Jordan as well as Kuwait. In effect, Jordan became the mainstay, along with Kuwait, of US and allied operations in Iraq. Senior British military commanders as well as politicians made more frequent visits to the kingdom, to be received by their Jordanian counterparts.

In summary, it is clear that British–Jordanian relations were consolidated and strengthened after 9/11 and the invasion of Iraq. The central features of the relationship were military and intelligence cooperation, which also became priority concerns for the Jordanian authorities in the 9/11 era, as too for the United States and Britain in the Middle East in the context of 'the war on terror'. Even though both the British and the US governments eventually abandoned the terminology used by Bush and Blair for combating Islamist extremists and terrorism, they have not dismantled the apparatus for pursuing their security goals in the region, in which Jordan is a central player.

Egypt

The core elements underpinning British–Egyptian relations in the 1990s – trade, defence and intelligence cooperation, and a cordial, businesslike government-to-government rapport – did not change fundamentally as a result of 9/11. However, at the level of public opinion in Egypt, the British government came in for much criticism as a result of its support for the policies pursued by the Bush administration.

As noted in Chapters 4 and 7, the British government has consistently involved or consulted Egypt over the Middle East peace process. Tony and Cherie Blair chose Egypt as a holiday destination and were warmly received and protected from the media by the Egyptian leadership. British ambassadors to Egypt under New Labour have always been senior figures and rising stars in the foreign service, among them Sir John Sawers and Sir Derek Plumbly. The British Council has one of its largest operations in Egypt, in part because of the appetite of Egyptians for its English-language courses.

British trade with and investment in Egypt have been actively promoted by both governments and the balance of trade has been favourable to Britain over the years. In 1997 Egypt ranked fifth among Britain's trading partners in the Middle East, with UK imports from Egypt valued at $540 million and its exports to Egypt at $815 million. By 2004 UK imports totalled $933 million and exports to Egypt reached $1.184 billion – making Egypt Britain's fourth largest market in the Middle East, after the UAE ($4.1 billion), Saudi Arabia ($2.9 billion) and Israel ($2.5 billion).[80]

Bilateral military cooperation has brought members of the Egyptian armed forces to Britain on courses and exchanges. There have been regular joint exercises in Egypt, training at sea with the Egyptian navy and refuelling exercises between the forces. As stated by the FCO, 'Adventurous training, especially diving in the Red Sea, involves hundreds of British servicemen, officer cadets and University OTC [Officer Training Corps] students each year.'[81]

As in other Arab countries which were once part of the British Empire, in Egypt the United States has long since supplanted the United Kingdom as the most important military, diplomatic and economic presence. After making peace with Israel in 1979, Egypt became a leading recipient of US overseas aid (second only to Israel) that has averaged $2.1 billion per annum, inclusive of military assistance and equipment. In 1991 the Egyptians joined the US led-forces in the liberation of Kuwait, providing political weight to the Arab dimension of the coalition.

Thereafter, Egypt became the target of terrorist attacks, fuelled, as in Jordan, by fighters returning from the war against the Soviet Union in Afghanistan. The Egyptian government adopted a leading role in the struggle against militant Islamists that preceded George Bush's 'war on terror'. President Mubarak evinced no surprise at the 9/11 attacks but committed Egyptian intelligence to fighting the new war. However, like the Jordanians, the Egyptians were troubled by the line adopted by Washington in confronting Islamists, and Mubarak also warned that the invasion of Iraq could unleash a whirlwind and destabilize the region.

Washington's espousal of a reform agenda for the Arab world damaged US–Egyptian relations for a period – until the Hamas victory in the Palestinian elections of 2006 obliged the Americans to rethink the implications of democratization. In the interim, Mubarak came under US pressure to hold presidential and parliamentary elections in Egypt that would allow real competition between candidates. Elections did take place in 2005, but were so firmly managed by the regime that Egyptian reformists were disappointed. After making gains at the polls, the Muslim Brotherhood in Egypt was subjected to a new crackdown by the authorities. In the background the British also promoted reform, but proved less of an irritant to Mubarak, if for no other reason than that they were less influential than the Americans.

In any case, the British were more subtle in their approach. Also, Tony Blair was full of praise for Egyptian reform efforts and the British Embassy in Cairo adopted initiatives, such as training lawyers and journalists, which were not directly confrontational.[82] Among the Egyptian public, however, the British decision to join the invasion of Iraq was greeted with incomprehension and hostility. When the British Prime Minister toured the Middle East in autumn 2001 to drum up support for the war in Afghanistan, Egyptians bristled at his 'gung-ho' rhetoric and 'Britain's seeming eagerness to be part of the conflict'.[83]

[Blair] has suggested that Britain needs to do more PR in the Arab world. His personal efforts seem to have been a resounding failure. Why, people ask, is he rushing around with such zeal? Why does he look so pleased with himself? ... Spin will get you nowhere with people who have for a long time not trusted their governments – far less the governments of the west.[84]

When asked for their reaction to the invasion of Iraq, in a survey conducted in Egypt in 2004, nearly 70% of Egyptians said the use of force to overthrow Saddam Hussein 'was not justified at all'.[85] Asked about the outcome of the US-led operations in Iraq, Egyptians dismissed the idea that these would 'turn Iraq into a model for democracy in the region' or that they would 'provide Iraqis with a standard of living better than that under Saddam's regime'. Instead, they said the operations would 'pillage (loot, drain) the resources of Iraq' and would also 'enhance Israel's security'.[86] Jordanians, Syrians and Palestinians surveyed at the same time reached the same conclusions.[87]

With respect to Britain, a majority of Egyptians said they believed that relations between Egypt and Britain were good, but 54 per cent said their perception of Britain was 'not at all positive'.[88] Sixty-three percent of Egyptians had a similarly negative perception of the United States, while only 17 per cent were as negative about France.[89] Research undertaken by this author in Egypt in early 2006 revealed that among Egyptian intellectuals and columnists the prevailing view was that the British decision to join the US invasion of Iraq was based on a desire to please the Americans and join in the exploitation of Iraqi oil resources.

Overall the findings of this study demonstrate two trends. First, by standing 'shoulder to shoulder' with the United States after 9/11 and joining the invasion of Iraq, Britain incurred hostility derivatively, along with the Americans, as anti-Americanism rose across the Arab world. Second, through their close relations and coordination with Arab regimes, particularly those of Egypt and Jordan, the British won no plaudits among the populace. On the contrary, given public disillusionment with politicians and anger about corruption in high places, cooperation between the British and Arab governments has gained them both opprobrium.

7

Realpolitik and the Peace Process after 9/11

'By this year's end, we must have revived final status negotiations and they must have explicitly as their aims: an Israeli state free from terror, recognised by the Arab world and a viable Palestinian state based on the boundaries of 1967. For Britain to help shape this new world, Britain needs to be part of it.' – Tony Blair (2002)[1]

As discussed in Chapter 4, from 1997 to early 2001 Britain found a role in the Middle East peace process which combined support for US diplomacy, participation in EU initiatives and direct engagement with the contending parties. While constructive and practical, Britain's net contribution was nonetheless limited to what was possible within the broader context. Thus when the protagonists were responsive and the US engaged, the process gained momentum. Yet all too often fundamental differences between the parties over the ultimate objectives blocked agreement and undermined the process itself.

During the Clinton administration Washington provided a lead that Britain and other members of the EU were bound to follow. Some may have had reservations about the direction of travel, but none saw fit to question or oppose US diplomacy directly. They had no viable alternatives to offer anyway. Consequently, when the United States lost interest or despaired of the Palestinians, as it did after Bush replaced Clinton, the British, like others, gave priority to persuading Washington to re-engage. Then reviving some sort of peace process became an end in itself and the core issues of the conflict were subsumed in the competition for Washington's attention.

As will be seen in this chapter, 9/11 and the resulting shift in US thinking and priorities compounded this trend. Britain's position on the conflict also shifted – towards the US side of the US–European spectrum of opinion. In the 1980s and 1990s Britain was considered a bridge-builder *within* Europe, where Germany and the Netherlands were generally the most attentive to Israeli concerns, while France and Greece were usually the most supportive of Arab claims. From 2001, however, Britain was more likely to be found trying to straddle the divide between Washington's increasingly uncritical support for Israel and the continental European consensus on Israeli *and* Palestinian rights.

Yet Blair himself had become an advocate of Palestinian statehood. The problem he encountered in the Middle East was that his commitment to this goal was perceived as a device to sell his strategy on countering terrorism, which in turn involved support for US strategy. As in Europe so in the Arab world: he became so closely associated with US policy that his own ideas and theories on the Israeli–Palestinian conflict were not given credence. In Israel his problem was different. There only US thinking on the region mattered and to the extent that Blair was more supportive than Washington of Palestinian rights he would be listened to less.

COUNTER-TERRORISM AND PALESTINIAN STATEHOOD

As discussed in Chapter 4, the Middle East did not feature highly on Blair's initial list of priorities in his first term, so Robin Cook and his Foreign Office team were initially in the forefront of devising and articulating British policy towards the region. In time, as noted, Blair became more visible as an interlocutor with the Israelis and also played 'good cop' to Cook's 'bad cop' on sensitive issues. However, after Jack Straw replaced Cook at the beginning of Blair's second term in 2001, the role of the Foreign Office shifted from policy formulation to implementation and, as discussed in Chapter 3, the Foreign Secretary became more of a trouble-shooter and messenger than policy architect or innovator.

Straw's first visit to the Israeli–Palestinian battlefront came in late September 2001 on the back of a trip to Tehran, which Blair wanted him to undertake to coordinate with Iran on the anticipated US action against al-Qaeda in Afghanistan (see Chapter 6). Straw initially caused outrage in Israel by publishing an article in the Iranian press in which he said that 'one of the factors which helps breed terrorism is the anger which many people feel at events over the years in Palestine'.[2] Only Blair's personal intervention, with a phone call to his Israeli counterpart, prevented Israelis from boycotting Straw's visit. The episode looked like a replay of the time Blair had had to soothe Israeli Prime Minister Binyamin Netanyahu's ire over Robin Cook's visit to Har Homa in 1998 (see Chapter 4). However, there was to be no more 'good cop, bad cop' routine as the Prime Minister personally took the lead on British policy towards the Middle East.

Blair's diplomatic buffeting in the region

In autumn 2001 Blair embarked on a series of hectic trips to the region – principally to drum up support for the invasion of Afghanistan. Promotion of Palestinian statehood surfaced as one of the elements in his diplomacy. At a joint press conference with Yasser Arafat in October 2001, Blair stated very firmly that 'a viable Palestinian state as part of a negotiated and agreed settlement which guarantees peace and security for Israel is the objective'.[3]

In the government's strategy document on the US-led campaign in Afghanistan, resolution of the Arab–Israeli conflict was presented as vital for tackling the causes of terrorism. On a visit to Egypt in early October Blair said that he wanted to intensify Britain's diplomatic efforts, in concert with the United States, to revive the Middle East peace process.[4] When Blair went to Israel at the end of October, Sharon had just cancelled a trip to Washington on the grounds that the security situation required him to stay put. An Israeli government spokesman trailed Blair's visit as an opportunity to tell Sharon about a new initiative he had worked out with Bush.[5]

Whether because of or despite his coordination with Bush, however, Blair's trips to the Middle East in autumn 2001 did not garner much enthusiasm and caused him some embarrassing moments. On his first attempt to visit Saudi Arabia the ruling family were not ready to receive him (see Chapter 8). When he did go to Riyadh at the end of October he apparently encountered strong condemnation of Israel and scepticism about the parameters of the peace process he wanted to revive. In the first high-level British visit to Damascus since Syrian independence in the 1940s, Blair was treated to a public rebuke by the Syrian President for his perspective on the conflict. Asad defended the right of the Palestinians to resist occupation.[6] According to the *Guardian*:

> Mr Blair had twin objectives: one was to look for a way of weaning Syria away from its support for Hizbullah and other groups, and the other was to try to get Syria to re-enter talks with Israel on the return of the Golan Heights. He secured neither.[7]

In Israel Blair failed to persuade the government to abandon its policy of 'targeted killings' of Palestinian militants and reoccupying Palestinian towns evacuated as part of the Oslo process.[8] In the Gaza Strip the Palestinians were dismissive of his efforts to revive the peace process. One was reported as saying: 'It's all a political circus, a vicious circle. It's the annual Balfour Day ceremony and he's the first Prime Minister to come here since 1917.'[9] In fact John Major had gone to Gaza in 1995, but apparently that had left no lasting impression. During his own Gaza visit Blair issued a warning he was to repeat for several years, to the effect that Osama bin Laden and his followers were seeking to set Muslims against Christians and divide the Arabs from 'the West' and that this way led to disaster.[10] Peter Mandelson was to voice the same concern in an article for the *Observer* in November 2001 in which he called on the US President to show more resolve in seeking a solution.[11]

In the background there were some signs of an evolution in the US position, in favour of a twin-track strategy combining promotion of a two-state solution to the Israeli–Palestinian conflict with the pursuit of al-Qaeda.[12] However, by December 2001 the British press were reporting that Tony Blair had abandoned high-profile Middle East diplomacy, chastened by the reception he had received in the region. The Liberal Democrat foreign affairs spokesman Menzies Campbell said:

> Keen observers of the prime minister's language will have noticed that it has changed quite considerably from the earlier, almost fervent, commitment to a viable Palestinian state. The language has appeared to be modified after the US essentially gave Ariel Sharon the nod to proceed as he wished in relation to military action against the Palestinians.[13]

In the *Guardian* Paul Foot wrote a column entitled 'Tony Blair's very brief conversion', suggesting that the Prime Minister's support for a viable Palestinian state had evaporated.[14] More likely, he had not abandoned his goal, but had learnt at first hand the extent of the obstacles to be overcome and deduced that it would best serve his purpose to concentrate on persuading Washington to re-engage more energetically. Meanwhile, a new factor had come into play, namely US designs on Iraq.

COUNTER-TERRORISM AND THE ROAD TO BAGHDAD

In Israel members of the public equated the US experience on 9/11 with their own embattled situation in the face of suicide attacks on civilians, and the government emphasized this logic, portraying Israelis and Americans as sharing the same trench in the 'global war on terrorism'. Although no links were uncovered at this time between al-Qaeda and Palestinian militants and the Palestinian leadership was at pains to distance itself from the al-Qaeda agenda, Osama bin Laden claimed he championed the cause of the Palestinians against Israel and the United States.

In the circumstances it became increasingly difficult for Yasser Arafat to counter Sharon's depiction of him as a terrorist leader and obstacle to peace. So, while Europeans, including the British,[15] and some American officials continued to deal with the Palestinian President, the Israeli government adopted the line that it had no partner for peace and could not therefore be expected to consider negotiating. Then, in January 2002 came the *Karine-A* episode, when the Israelis intercepted a ship in the Red Sea carrying arms, allegedly from Iran to the Palestinians (noted in Chapter 6). Arafat denied all knowledge of the shipment, but the involvement of senior figures in his entourage discredited him. It was a decisive moment for US relations with Arafat from which he was never to recover.[16] US–Iranian relations were also about to plummet, as demonstrated in Bush's 'Axis of Evil' speech almost immediately after this incident.

Battle for the peace process

Throughout the run-up to the invasion of Iraq, Blair and his team at No. 10 did not give up on reviving the Middle East peace process. Unlike some in Washington they did not claim that the road to Jerusalem ran through Baghdad and that it would be best to sort out Iraq before turning to Palestine. Rather, the British advocated peacemaking on the Arab–Israeli front both as an end in itself and to facilitate addressing the Iraq issue.

In a briefing to the Prime Minister in March 2002, ahead of a meeting between Blair and Bush in Crawford, Texas, his foreign policy adviser David Manning noted 'the paramount importance of tackling Israel/Palestine'. Unless this was done, he said, 'we could find ourselves bombing Iraq and losing the Gulf'.[17] He concluded by suggesting that the Crawford meeting would give Blair 'the chance to push Bush on the Middle East': 'The Iraq factor means that there may never be a better opportunity to get this Administration to give sustained attention to reviving the Middle East Peace Process.'[18]

This assessment is questionable. According to former State Department official Dennis Ross, speaking to the BBC in a documentary aired in 2002, peacemaking in the Middle East was not a priority for the Bush administration – fighting the war on terror was. Washington's attitude towards Israel was defined by that priority and 'it's very difficult for the Bush administration to establish one standard for itself and then apply a different one to the Israelis'.[19] However, Colin Powell at least shared the British view that Arab allies of the Western powers needed some demonstration that Washington understood their anger and concern over developments in the occupied Palestinian territory.

In March, at Saudi instigation, Arab leaders meeting in Beirut produced an initiative of their own. Thereafter known as 'the Arab Initiative', this held out the prospect of Arab recognition of Israel in return for an end to occupation.[20] To Arafat's fury, Sharon prevented him from attending the Beirut summit – a move to which Jack Straw, among others, also objected. Straw said: 'We have made clear repeatedly that it is in no one's interests, least of all Israel's, that President Arafat be prevented from attending the summit'.[21] The Beirut initiative appeared to die a death at the time, although it was to be resuscitated in 2007.

The Israelis dismissed the Beirut initiative at its inception and kept Arafat under virtual house arrest thereafter. Following a resurgence of suicide attacks, Sharon then unleashed a full re-invasion of areas of the West Bank previously evacuated under the Oslo process. This was the backdrop to Blair's March 2002 *tête-à-tête* with President Bush, who used their joint press conference to call on Sharon 'to begin to withdraw without delay'.[22] To this injunction Sharon responded by simply 'expediting' the operation. Reporting back to parliament on the Middle East crisis after his visit, Blair said that both sides must see that violence was not and never would be the answer:

> The solution to this crisis will never be reached if it is seen purely as a security or military question. There *must* be a political process too. I believe the whole House will welcome President Bush's statement last week calling on the Israelis to withdraw from the Occupied Territories, and the Palestinian Authority to tackle terrorism. Without these basic minimum steps, and without a proper cease-fire with sticks, we cannot even begin to get a political process re-started.[23]

Shortly thereafter it was revealed that Britain, and also France and Germany, had informally imposed a halt on the export of weapon parts to Israel and wanted Israel to explain its use of British-made equipment during operations in the West Bank and Gaza.[24]

The perspectives of the Europeans and the Americans were beginning to show signs of significant divergence. In the United States Bush was constrained in any case by defenders of Israel. Meanwhile, EU members were aware that their leverage with Israel was bound to be limited, even as the administrative infrastructure and security apparatus of the PA came under attack by Israeli forces, eroding its ability to function as the provider of basic civic amenities or law and order.

Reflecting on the EU's role, Dennis Ross explained in the BBC documentary:

> The Israeli perception of a re-emergence of anti-Semitism in Europe is playing very, very negatively. I think it creates a sense that Israel is very much alone, it creates a sense that no matter what Israel does it will always be criticized….. So I think what you see in Israel right now is a public that is hunkering down, especially as it relates to Europe, and [it] pretty much has a siege mentality.

Thus, having hoped in the previous year at least to keep the PA ticking over pending a resumption of the peace process, in 2002 the EU settled for maintaining its survival. The EU's logic was that there must be a Palestinian partner in order for peace talks to resume and, however exasperating, Arafat was the elected Palestinian leader.[25]

At the end of April Jack Straw was instrumental in an initiative by Bush which obliged Sharon to end an Israeli siege of Arafat's headquarters in Ramallah, pending the latter's handing over to Israel six men accused of acts of terrorism. Britain and the United States provided monitors to oversee the detention of the men in a Palestinian jail in Jericho.[26] Yet the Palestinian Representative to the UK, Afif Safieh, was generally unimpressed by Britain's involvement, characterizing it as a country 'that wants to be halfway between the transatlantic privileged relationship with Washington yet an integral part of the European Union and its pillars'. He said that, as a result of this typically 'discreet diplomacy',

> the fact that Britain has not been assertive and vocal in its opinions of Israeli misbehaviour means today that [it] is perceived as a very hostile country to our legitimate aspirations. Opinion polls conducted by the British Council … in the Islamic and Arab countries show that the perception of Britain is very unfavourable.[27]

New twist: Bush's vision and the road map

In June 2002 Bush gave the first public endorsement by a US president of the goal of Palestinian statehood. It should have been a triumph for Blair's diplomacy, but it came with a crucial caveat – Bush required a change in the Palestinian leadership as a precondition for 'US support for the creation of a provisional state of Palestine'. In a speech he delivered in the Rose Garden of the White House on 24 June, Bush endorsed the vision of a 'two-state solution' but offered no timetable, made no call for Israeli withdrawal from areas reoccupied during the Intifada (contrary to the Mitchell recommendations – see Chapter 4) and made Palestinian independence dependent on Palestinians choosing a new leader, embracing democracy, confronting corruption and firmly rejecting terror.[28] Blair and Straw, like their counterparts in the rest of Europe and UN Secretary-General Kofi Annan, had hoped for something more promising, though they chose to temper their disappointment in public.[29]

A confidential Cabinet Office paper of 21 July 2002 noted:

> The Bush speech was at best a half step forward. We are using the Palestinian reform agenda to make progress, including a resumption of political negotiations. The Americans are talking of a ministerial conference in November or later. Real progress towards a viable Palestinian state is the best way to

undercut Palestinian extremists and reduce Arab antipathy to military action against Saddam Hussein.[30]

As this assessment indicates, British interest in a resolution of the Israeli–Palestinian conflict, through a two-state formula, was both an end in itself and a means to an end, in both the war on terror and the build-up to regime change in Iraq. The existence of mixed motives detracted somewhat from the appeal of the British line to the Palestinians. It also reinforced suspicions in Israel that it would be made to pay a price for the execution of the war on terror by others.

Britain was among several actors who decided to treat Bush's 'half step' as an opportunity. Through the vehicle of the Quartet (the UN, EU, US and Russia), they set out to develop a road map that would chart the path to the realization of Bush's two-state vision.[31]

At a press conference in New York on 17 September 2002, the members of the Quartet announced their outline plan, to proceed in three phases. The first (late 2002 to the first half of 2003) 'would focus on Palestinian security reform, Israeli withdrawal and support for Palestinian elections'. The second (2003) 'would focus on the creation of a Palestinian state with provisional borders and based on a new constitution as a way status to a permanent status settlement'. The third phase (2004–05) 'would envision Israeli–Palestinian negotiations aimed at a permanent status solution'.[32]

Between September and December 2002 the detailed plan was worked out through behind-the-scenes diplomacy. The Quartet statement of 17 September mooted the possibility of an international conference and Tony Blair took up the idea at the Labour Party Conference, declaring that by the year's end

> we must have revived final status negotiations and they must have explicitly as their aims: an Israeli state free from terror, recognised by the Arab world and a viable Palestinian state based on the boundaries of 1967. For Britain to help shape this new world, Britain needs to be part of it.[33]

The Israeli newspaper *Haaretz* responded with the suggestion that Blair was aiming to shore up support in the British Labour Party on the issue of Iraq. It noted that Sharon could not be expected to negotiate with Arafat and that President Bush was in less of a hurry to push negotiations than Blair.[34]

During the following months relations between Britain and Israel entered a thorny period. In November 2002 Iain Hook, a former British paratrooper employed by Crown Agents and DFID, was shot in the back by an Israeli military sniper while working with a UN mission on the reconstruction of the Palestinian refugee camp at Jenin in the West Bank. Jack Straw and Clare Short (the Minister for International Development) called for a formal inquiry, but received only verbal excuses for the occurrence from the Israelis.[35] In December Blair was not available for a meeting with Israeli Foreign Minister Binyamin Netanyahu in London, yet in early January he hosted Amran Mitzna, the leader of the Israeli Labour Party, at No. 10 ahead of Israeli elections later in the month.[36]

The palliative of Palestinian 'reform'

Sharon used the impending elections to persuade George Bush to delay release of the road map, which was finalized in December 2002. Blair tried to rescue the situation with a proposal to use the intervening period to focus on reform of the Palestinian Authority. Yet no sooner had he announced his intention to convene a conference on the subject – to be hosted by Straw and attended by members of the Quartet – than President Asad of Syria, on an official visit to London, declared the event 'irrelevant', since it would not address the core issue of occupation.[37] As noted in Chapter 6, Asad also used the opportunity of access in London to warn the United States that even though it could easily win a war in Iraq it would suffer considerably and terrorism would increase.[38]

Blair's plans meanwhile suffered a further blow, when on the eve of the conference a dual suicide bombing in Tel Aviv prompted Sharon to bar the Palestinian representatives from making the journey to London and they had to participate by video link.[39] Jack Straw told the audience, which included representatives from Egypt and Jordan but not Israel, that there could be no progress toward a final peace agreement until Israel withdrew from West Bank towns.[40] Following his victory in the Israeli elections, Sharon chose not to form a coalition with Mitzna on a platform for dealing with the Palestinians. Instead he began development of the unilateralist approach that would lead to the construction of Israel's security barrier (originally a Labour Party idea) in and around the West Bank and the withdrawal of settlements from Gaza.

Speaking to parliament shortly before the invasion of Iraq in 2003, Blair promised to continue his quest for Israeli–Palestinian peace. On the ground, there were two more shootings of British nationals in the occupied Palestinian territory: James Miller (a cameraman) and Tom Hurndall (a campaigner for the Palestinians). More ominously, on 30 April 2003 two British Muslims who had journeyed to Gaza conducted a suicide bombing in Tel Aviv. In retrospect, this last tragedy appears to have marked the end of a particularly cool period in British relations with Israel. In May Blair received Israeli Foreign Minister Silvan Shalom in London; *Haaretz* reported that Blair had told Shalom he 'remained a true friend of Israel', and that Britain and the United States now understood that peace would only be possible if the Arab world changed its attitude towards Israel.[41] Blair was also reported as saying that they would not allow Syria and Iran to sit on the fence about terrorism any more.

OUTMANOEUVRED ON THE ROAD MAP

The neo-conservative proponents of the invasion of Iraq championed the notion that regime change there would open the way for a remaking of the political order in the Middle East. Hostile regimes in Tehran and Damascus would find themselves next in the line of fire, or simply collapse under popular pressure for reform. Even Tony Blair, who kept the emphasis on the need to counter the threat posed by Iraq's alleged WMD programme, apparently believed that a moment of opportunity had been reached. In his speech to British heads of mission from across the Middle East, summoned to London in January 2003, Blair laid out the guiding principles of Britain's foreign policy in the twenty-first century. This included an initiative 'to reach out to the Muslim World' by: promoting the Middle East peace process; seeking 'greater democratic stability, liberty and human rights' in Muslim countries; and building understanding between Islam and other religious faiths.[42]

Launch of the road map

Those in the region who opposed the invasion of Iraq and feared the very changes promised were intimidated by the speed and initial success of the operation. The Syrian government, in particular, was unnerved and disposed to facilitate Iraqi opposition to the foreign intervention.[43] Israelis were pleased to see the Iraqi regime toppled but they wanted changes to the draft road map and even came up with an alternative plan for a peace deal on their terms.[44] Following the appointment of Mahmoud Abbas as Palestinian prime minister on 30 April the text of the road map was finally made public. Ahead of the formal launch in Aqaba on 4 June, a US–Arab summit was convened in Sharm el-Sheikh to demonstrate regional endorsement of the plan and usher in the new era of 'Pax Americana'.[45] It was a line-up of those Arab leaders who could expect to be part of the new order, though none of them would become enthusiastic proponents of Washington's reform agenda and Arab public opinion was generally cynical or hostile.

Meeting in Aqaba on 4 June, both Sharon and Abbas went along with the ceremonials, but neither inspired the confidence of the other or their detractors at home. Sharon made no haste to capitalize on the road map, which he allegedly disliked, and Abbas did not receive the support he needed from the Americans or the Europeans to bolster his position in relation to Arafat or Sharon. The British government clearly saw the dangers and remonstrated with the Israelis over their refusal to have any dealings with Arafat while leaving Abbas exposed. Blair, entertaining Sharon to dinner at No. 10 in July, apparently tried to impress upon him the need for movement on the road map.[46] However, unable to make any headway or resolve Palestinian in-fighting, on 6 September 2003 Abbas resigned. Thereafter the road map languished and with it Blair's prospects of effective peacemaking.[47]

Meanwhile, America's initial triumph in Iraq began to unravel. In August the bombing of the UN mission in Baghdad dashed hopes that the international body could be instrumental in rebuilding the country. More violence ensued and the 'Coalition Provisional Authority' led by Paul Bremer embarked on a programme of measures, including 'de-Baathification', dismissal of the Iraqi armed forces and radical economic liberalization that would unravel the Iraqi state infrastructure (see Chapter 6). A series of initiatives to promote regional economic and political reform were launched, to the consternation of Washington's Arab allies (see Chapter 2). However, these had to be tempered in the face of the growing instability in Iraq, regional uncertainty and increased fears of terrorism.

Blair loses credibility

From early 2004 Sharon concentrated on developing his unilateralist agenda for separation between the Israelis and Palestinians.[48] He also continued his policy of isolating Arafat. In February 2004 the Palestinian Prime Minister Ahmed Qureia accused Britain of facilitating the Israeli security agenda by pressuring the Palestinians to improve their internal security arrangements.[49] Foreign Office officials apparently urged the Palestinians to counter Hamas activism, promising that this would enable them to pressure Israel to follow its commitments to freeze settlement expansion and dismantle illegal outposts. But according to one report:

> Palestinian frustrations with Britain are underpinned by a belief that Mr Blair has backtracked on his declarations a year ago that resolving the conflict was as important to Middle East peace as removing Saddam Hussein from power.[50]

Already losing credibility with the Palestinians and unable to gain the ear of Ariel Sharon, Blair's strategy suffered an irreparable blow in April 2004 when George Bush endorsed Sharon's unilateral plan to evacuate Jewish settlements in the Gaza Strip. The problem was that in doing so Bush said

Israel could not be expected to withdraw fully to its 1967 borders with the West Bank and Gaza or grant Palestinian refugees the right of return to their original homes (in Israel).[51] This was to pre-judge the outcome of peace negotiations and undermined the thrust of the road map.[52]

Blair tried to put a brave face on this turn of events when he appeared alongside Bush at a press conference on the White House lawn two days later. Yet he was hard pressed to reconcile his commitment to the road map with Bush's defence of his new position. Blair chose to embrace Sharon's Gaza disengagement plan as a step on the way to the goal of Palestinian state-hood. Not all were convinced by his case. In Britain the *Guardian* columnist Jonathan Freedland wrote that Blair had been humiliated and within days a group of 52 former senior diplomats wrote an open letter to the British Prime Minister declaring his Middle East policy doomed.[53] The leader column in the *Financial Times* pronounced the diplomats' critique 'basically right' and warned Blair to 'listen to the experts'.[54]

As ever, Blair's accommodation to developments, while garnering criti-cism at home and antipathy from the Palestinians, won him no new leverage in Israel. When the International Court of Justice issued an opinion in July 2004 that the Israeli security barrier being constructed in and around the West Bank contravened international law, the British joined other members of the EU in voting for a UN General Assembly resolution calling for its dismantlement.[55] This put the British at odds with the Israelis, as did Foreign Office protestations at Israeli assassinations of Hamas leaders in the occupied Palestinian territory.

Even in Washington, the British line gained no traction. A report produced by DFID in consultation with the Foreign Office in July 2004 revealed alarm at the drift in US policy on the Middle East. The report warned:

> The role of the USA, the country with the most leverage over Israel, is key. Frustration with aspects of the Palestinian leadership, preoccupations in Iraq, presidential elections and security concerns for US citizens may risk US disengagement at the highest levels from the peace process when it is most likely to start collapsing.[56]

In August American officials were reportedly privately admitting that they had abandoned attempts to oblige Israel to cease settlement expansion.[57]

At the Labour Party Conference in Brighton in September 2004, Blair again pledged his commitment to the Middle East peace process, declaring that after November (presumably referring to the US elections), 'I will make its revival my personal priority'.[58] It was, he said, a necessary compo-nent of combating terrorism. Within two weeks of Bush's re-election in November Blair went to congratulate him and raised his plan to capitalize on the prospective Israeli disengagement from Gaza. He seemingly received only a lukewarm response but proceeded to Israel to discuss his plans for a new conference in London with Sharon and Mahmoud Abbas. Following Arafat's death in November 2004 Abbas was set to win election as the new Palestinian president.

Sharon was not interested in a peace conference and was only persuaded to enable the event to go ahead as a new exercise in galvanizing the Palestinians to reform their political, financial and security arrangements. When this emerged as the agenda, Palestinian Prime Minster Qureia was critical on the grounds that yet more pressure on the Palestinians was simply conceding to Israeli demands.[59] It took considerable effort on the part of officials at No. 10 and the FCO to persuade Abbas, duly elected Palestinian president in January 2005, to take a team to London for the early March meeting. Eventually, agreement to attend by members of the Quartet, including the new US Secretary of State Condoleezza Rice and EU foreign policy chief Javier Solana, along with various Arab government representatives, persuaded Abbas to come.[60]

Illusions of progress

While the draft communiqué of Blair's London conference had to be negotiated with the Israelis, the gathering did end up producing some more significant commitments than anticipated. Members of the 'international community' pledged to support a two-state solution, with a 'secure Israel' and 'viable Palestinian state'. A US-led international team was designated to help reform, train and advise the Palestinian security forces. (In January the formation of an elite 750-member police unit in Gaza, partly funded by the British, had been announced.) Abbas promised to amalgamate separate security forces into a single structure. The EU and the World Bank promised to help rebuild the shattered Palestinian economy and a donors' conference was scheduled for later in the month. The Quartet issued a statement to the effect that the future Palestinian state must not be split up into disjointed pieces.[61]

Blair hailed what he called a 'ripple of change' throughout the Middle East. He attributed 'huge significance' to the decision of President Mubarak of Egypt to hold multi-party presidential elections, and to the Palestinian presidential election and political reforms in the Arab Gulf states. The new (second-term) Bush administration in Washington also sounded optimistic about the prospects for reform in the Arab world and peace on the Israeli–Palestinian front. Meanwhile, Western reactions to the assassination of former Lebanese Prime Minister Rafiq Hariri on 14 February 2005 indicated a new determination to hold Syria to account (see Chapter 6). Blair used his London conference to warn the Syrian regime that it would have to change and Rice joined the French foreign minister in a statement calling for Lebanon to be free from outside interference.[62] As noted in Chapter 6, Damascus was obliged to remove Syrian military forces from Lebanon, in accordance with a UN resolution of 2004, co-sponsored by the US, France and Britain.

On the Palestinian front, however, the democracy agenda portended new challenges for the peacemakers. Hamas, which had been designated a terrorist organization by the EU two years previously, won control of several local councils in open elections. Much to Israeli irritation, British officials saw fit to deal directly with these elected councillors and Jack Straw defended the low-level contacts on the grounds that: 'We have a diplomatic job to do and our diplomats in the occupied territories see part of their job, and indeed their job is, to have contact with elected representatives.'[63] Yet Straw and others in the EU, including the new EU representative on the Middle East Marc Otte, also argued that they would not remove Hamas from the list of terrorist organizations unless and until its leadership had renounced violence and revoked its call for the elimination of Israel. At the same time they acknowledged the inherent contradiction in promoting democracy and then refusing to deal with elected officials.

Meanwhile, in May 2005 Blair had won a third election victory, albeit with a much reduced parliamentary majority for the Labour Party. The decision to take the country to war in Iraq and the unanticipated need to maintain a significant presence thereafter had not turned the British electorate against New Labour. Blair's efforts to keep the Middle East peace process alive and his claims that the Israeli withdrawal from Gaza offered a new beginning may have helped to assuage some of his critics. However, the British were about to have a rude awakening.

REALITY OVERTAKES IDEALISM

On 7 July 2005 four suicide bombers – 'home-grown' Islamist militants claiming to act out of anger at the war in Iraq and the plight of the Palestinians – blew themselves up in London, killing over fifty and injuring many more on underground trains and a bus. After '7/7' the politics of the Middle East and the debate about dealing with terrorists would take on new significance in Britain.

Blair and his cabinet had to find a policy response to the new danger facing the British public within the country. Determined not to allow his critics to claim a connection between his foreign policy – particularly his support of Bush over Iraq – and the alienation of British Muslims, Blair focused on redefining the goal of a multicultural society in Britain that would draw a line between what he dubbed the vast majority of 'moderate' Muslims and an extremist fringe (see Chapter 2). He characterized British foreign policy as upholding British values of tolerance and freedom in the face of extremists overseas, including in the Middle East.

In Israel Sharon was ready to implement his grand plan for protecting Israeli civilians. In August some 7,000 Jewish settlers were withdrawn from the Gaza Strip and Israeli troops redeployed to the periphery. It was a searing experience for the settlers and the soldiers sent to conduct their evacuation, completed over three weeks. When it subsequently emerged that this would not bring an end to Hamas attacks on Israelis and that the government of Mahmoud Abbas was unable to rein them in, many Israelis began to question whether the whole strategy had simply demonstrated weakness in the face of terrorism. It took a year for the full implications to materialize, when conflict escalated on the Gaza and Lebanese fronts simultaneously.

In the aftermath of the withdrawal from Gaza, Sharon launched Kadima, a new political party dedicated to unilateral separation from the Palestinians. He persuaded the veteran Labour leader Shimon Peres and other Labour figures to join him and some Likudniks in the new party, while Netanyahu stayed with the rump of Likud. It was a bold move by Sharon and an unprecedented development in Israeli politics for a party to take shape around the single issue of how to deal with the Palestinians. In December 2005, however, Sharon suffered a stroke and went into a coma, leaving his deputy Ehud Olmert to take over leadership of Kadima. Sharon's sudden exit from politics meant that such prospects as there might have been of turning Israel's Gaza disengagement into a rollback on the West Bank as well went into reverse.

Meanwhile, developments on the Palestinian political front indicated rising disillusionment with the Fatah faction of Mahmoud Abbas, partly over corruption, but also over its failure to deliver peace and an end to the Israeli occupation. The Gaza disengagement did not bring an end to Israeli military action against targets in Gaza or an easing of the economic situation there, while settlement expansion continued in the West Bank and the system of military checkpoints there meant internal movement was restricted and hazardous for Palestinians. Calls from Abbas and various international players, including the British, for the Israeli government to coordinate its separation strategy with the Palestinian leadership fell on deaf ears, leaving the latter powerless to deliver any benefits to the population.

Hamas comes to power

After 7/7 British officials appeared to shift their position on dealings with Hamas. Certainly they talked less of needing to deal with elected officials irrespective of their affiliations and gave more emphasis to the desirability of bolstering 'moderates'. The Americans were less subtle. In the run-up to the Palestinian parliamentary elections of January 2006 – the first in ten years – Washington actually disbursed money to Hamas opponents and gave vocal support to Fatah in a vain attempt to bolster its electoral prospects. The strategy backfired, and neither the Americans nor the Europeans were prepared for what ensued.

The January 2006 election, monitored and pronounced essentially free and fair by the EU and others, saw a high turnout of 77 per cent of Palestinian voters. 'Change and Reform' – the platform mounted by Hamas members and sympathizers – won less than an absolute majority of the votes cast (44 per cent), but secured 76 (56 per cent) of the 132 seats in the Palestinian legislature. Fatah members and supporters appeared devastated and angry – unable to reconcile themselves to the outcome. Many latched on to signals from Washington that Hamas could not rule without its support and would soon be brought down. They resisted Hamas invitations to form a unity government.

For the EU member states, including Britain, the Palestinian election outcome presented a profound dilemma. They had championed the goal of elections and yet, under their own laws, they could not continue to provide funding to a Palestinian Authority led by an organization that they had branded as a terrorist group. Under British anti-terrorist legislation of 2000, it was illegal to even provide a platform to members of such an organization. In the circumstances, British officials would not deal with the new PA leadership, restricting themselves instead to interacting only with Fatah leader President Mahmoud Abbas.

A hiatus followed the Palestinian elections, with Hamas holding off attacks against the Israelis while working out the composition of its cabinet, and the international donor community suspending direct contacts with the PA pending the articulation of a formal policy. The EU provided some emergency funding to the Palestinians in the interim. In March Ehud Olmert and his Kadima Party won a plurality of seats in the Israeli Knesset elections, yet the basis for the party's platform had been undermined. Given Israeli antipathy to dealing with Hamas, Olmert could not credibly advocate a rollback of Israeli forces (and settlements) in the West Bank, for fear this would simply embolden Hamas and increase the prospect of more violence on that front. Olmert would eventually say that unilateral separation would have to give way to a negotiated arrangement with Palestinians, but for that he would need a Palestinian partner other than Hamas.

In April, the EU member states agreed with the other members of the Quartet to suspend funding of the PA and dealing with its officials, except the presidency, pending a satisfactory response from the Hamas leadership to three principles or injunctions. These called on Hamas to renounce violence, honour agreements previously accepted by the Palestinian leadership and recognize Israel. Eventually a 'Temporary International Mechanism' (TIM) was devised to pay the salaries of essential services personnel such as doctors and teachers.[64] However, this was to somewhat undermine the position of the EU and Britain, in so far as the EU and hence the British became more intimately involved in the survival of the Palestinian human and humanitarian infrastructure, and thereby responsible for its continuance.

From conflict to war

While the international community opted for financial and political pressure on Hamas, the Israelis also tried military means to combat Palestinian militants, some of whom persisted with rocket attacks on Israelis from inside the Gaza Strip. On 9 June nine Palestinian civilians on a beach in Gaza were killed by what appeared to be an Israeli artillery shell and Hamas called off its ceasefire. On 25 June, having tunnelled their way under the Gaza border, Hamas fighters attacked an Israeli border post and took captive Corporal Gilad Shalit. They demanded the release of Palestinians in Israeli detention in return for his release. Hamas and Fatah then reached the first of what would be a number of agreements to work together, seemingly in the belief that Hamas could continue in power so long as Abbas fielded contacts with the Israelis and others who refused to deal with Hamas. Yet on 28 June Israeli forces launched an assault on the Gaza Strip aimed at securing the release of Shalit. They also rounded up and jailed Hamas members from the West Bank, including 38 elected members of the legislature.

As the conflict escalated on the Israeli–Palestinian front, on 12 July Hizbullah fighters in Lebanon crossed into Israel, killing eight Israeli soldiers and capturing two others (who, it emerged later, did not survive their injuries). This was the beginning of the 2006 Israel–Lebanon war.

In retaliation for the Hizbullah raid and in the name of securing the captured soldiers, Israel imposed a naval blockade on Lebanon and launched a series of devastating raids on the country's transport and energy infrastructure. Hizbullah responded with rocket attacks into Israel, some penetrating as far as Haifa, which continued for the duration of the nearly five-week war – a total of some 4,000 missiles. On 14 July, the United States issued a warning to Syria and Iran that they would be held accountable for Hizbullah's actions. After much wrangling, G8 members meeting in St Petersburg produced a call for Israel to exercise restraint and for Hizbullah and Hamas to cease their attacks and return the kidnapped soldiers.

Thereafter Israel accompanied its bombardment of Lebanon with a ground offensive. Hizbullah fighters put up such a determined resistance that Israelis and others were forced to acknowledge they had underestimated the strength and skill of the militia. A subsequent inquiry in Israel (the Winograd Inquiry) would hold Olmert and his ministers responsible for launching an ill-thought-out campaign for which they were badly prepared and which failed ultimately to defeat Hizbullah. Across the Arab world, public opinion rallied behind Hizbullah, comparing it favourably with their own leaderships, which had proved incapable of taking on Israel through either war or diplomacy. Hizbullah boasted that it was a better champion of the Arab cause than al-Qaeda or all the warring factions in Iraq responsible for killing fellow Muslims.

The Iranian leadership accused the United States, Israel and possibly Britain of wanting the war.[65] Syria, which had suffered the humiliation of being forced to withdraw its forces from Lebanon the previous year, joined in the broader Arab condemnation of Israel, while playing host to many Lebanese civilians fleeing the battlefield. Those Arab governments, notably the Saudis, that had hoped to box the Syrian regime into a corner, were wrong-footed and forced to echo public anger at the devastation of Lebanon and heavy toll of civilian casualties.

A turning point for Blair

In his response to the conflagration Blair fundamentally undermined his reputation in the region. In step with the Americans, but not with other Western leaders or the UN Secretary-General, he did not criticize the magnitude of the Israeli response to the Hizbullah provocation. He refused to call for an immediate ceasefire to protect Lebanese (and Israeli) civilians, even when urged to by Labour backbenchers several days into the conflict and as the fighting escalated.[66] Instead, at a press conference on 24 July he said that 'anybody with a sense of humanity' wanted the killing to stop, but that 'if it is going to stop it's going to have to stop on both sides and that's not going to happen unless we have a plan to make it happen.'[67] Consequently, the Prime Minister aligned himself with Washington, which effectively meant giving the Israelis a 'green light' to deal with Hizbullah before pressure for a ceasefire became irresistible.[68]

Coincidentally, Blair suffered a singular embarrassment when he was caught by chance on microphone exchanging words informally with Bush at the G8 summit. The manner in which Bush acknowledged Blair, ate while talking and barely looked him in the face, verged on humiliating. Blair was heard offering to go to the Middle East to assess the situation, ahead of Condoleezza Rice, to prepare the ground, saying 'obviously if she goes out she's got to succeed … whereas I can go out and just talk.'[69] The fact that Blair seemed to be asking for permission to make a trip to the region, and was turned down, dealt a new blow to his reputation.[70]

For her part, Rice made the astonishing claim that the war marked a moment of opportunity for the region. As became clear, the conflict did constitute a showdown between Israel, Washington and its allies on the one hand and radical revisionist forces, including Iran, Syria, Hizbullah and Hamas, on the other. But Rice was proved wrong in her assumption that the US agenda for the region would triumph. Blair and his vision would suffer by association. Offering a flavour of the sentiment in the Arab street, a senior Palestinian intellectual and civil society activist in Jerusalem commented: 'The mad, blind and stupid Israeli military elephant is joined with the donkey of Washington and the monkey of London – people are very very angry and bleeding'.[71]

On the home front Blair suffered two further setbacks when a Labour MP resigned his government job over the handling of the crisis and aides to Gordon Brown and Jack Straw backed demands for a recall of parliament. By this time Straw was Leader of the House of Commons, having been peremptorily replaced as foreign secretary by Margaret Beckett – who lacked foreign policy experience and was thrust into the maelstrom of war in the Middle East almost immediately. Blair did not yield to the pressure for parliament to be recalled and having initially delayed his departure, set off for a holiday in the Caribbean while the war still raged.

The repercussions

In early September 2006, with a UN-backed ceasefire finally in place between Israel and Lebanon but no resolution on the Israeli–Gaza front, Blair embarked on another trip to the region. Ahead of his arrival, hundreds of Palestinians signed a newspaper advertisement criticizing him for his policies and positions and telling him he would not be welcome in the area. Ismail Haniya, the Hamas Prime Minister of the PA, wrote a column in the *Guardian* newspaper, accusing 'the new generation of British politicians' of failing to 'break with the past and stand for truth and justice in the Middle East'.[72] He called on Blair 'to work for the end of [Israeli] occupation' and appealed to the sympathies of Labour MPs and the British public – who,

Palestinians had heard, were 'unhappy about what Blair's government has been doing to our people'. In Lebanon, Hizbullah leaders and a coalition of secular parties and a senior Shia cleric issued warnings that Blair would not be welcome in their country. There were protests when he arrived in Beirut.[73]

The day before he arrived in Israel Blair announced his decision to step down as prime minister within a year. Not surprisingly, when he emerged from his initial meeting with Olmert the following day to meet the press, Blair was assailed by British journalists with questions about his announcement. According to an Israeli report, Blair appeared worn out and uncharacteristically reticent and subdued.[74] However, Olmert used the occasion to say that he was willing to meet Palestinian President Abbas without preconditions, indicating that he was no longer wedded to a unilateralist approach. This and Blair's subsequent suggestion that the Quartet should be ready to deal with a Palestinian coalition government including Hamas, if the latter accepted its conditions, enabled him to pose as peacemaker again.[75] Theoretically at least, this position also indicated a contrast between Blair and those in Washington who preferred to hold out for a purely Fatah leadership and negotiating partner.

Regional commentators would subsequently dub the Olmert–Abbas dialogue a sop for would-be peacemakers.[76] Some Israelis claimed later that Olmert was generous and Abbas missed an opportunity. Blair himself seemed to shift positions when, later in 2006, he endorsed Abbas's threat to dissolve the PA cabinet and call for new elections. Technically, under the Palestinian 'Basic Law' or constitution, the President did not have the power to call elections outside the four-year term of the Palestinian Legislative Council. Consequently, when Abbas issued such a call in December 2006, Haniya rejected the move as an attempted coup.[77] Factional fighting ensued between Fatah and Hamas members. However, speaking at a joint press conference with Abbas in Ramallah on 18 December, Blair gave his support to Abbas's proposal.

That was to be Blair's last visit to the area as British prime minister. Pledging his support for 'people who want a genuine two-state solution', he said:

> I hope … that we will be in a position over these coming weeks to put together an initiative that allows us both to give that support, in particular for reconstruction and development, and to alleviate the suffering and plight of the Palestinian people.[78]

He proposed bypassing Hamas with a plan to funnel financial aid directly to security forces under the control of President Abbas.[79] The US administration undertook to do the same, though Abbas was reportedly embarrassed when plans to approach Congress for $86 million for this purpose were discussed openly.[80] Such preferential treatment, at the expense of Hamas, complicated Abbas's task of forging a unity government between the factions.

However, it is clear in retrospect that the United States did not want such efforts to succeed. When King Abdullah of Saudi Arabia mediated an agreement between Fatah and Hamas in Mecca in February 2007, according to which Hamas agreed to respect previously reached agreements and form a government of national unity, Washington was wrong-footed, displeased and unsupportive. The Saudi move paved the way for the re-launch of the Arab Initiative of 2002, at the Arab Summit in Riyadh in March 2007. This offered normalization of relations with Israel in return for an end to the Israeli occupation of Arab land, the formation of a Palestinian state along the 1967 borders, and 'a just solution' to the Palestinian refugee problem.[81] In contrast to their dismissive reaction to the initiative in 2002, Israelis indicated their interest in a comprehensive peace deal with Arab leaders.[82]

However, Israel continued its insistence that the boycott of Hamas leaders be maintained pending full satisfaction on the Quartet principles. In Britain, as well as other parts of Europe, various voices were raised in opposition to the freeze on contacts with Hamas. A report by the all-party International Development Committee of the British House of Commons, issued in January 2007, called for dialogue with Hamas to urge a change in its positions and warned that the economic boycott of the PA following the Hamas election victory had worsened conditions for the Palestinians and was driving them into the arms of Iran.[83]

It was fear of the increasing regional influence of Iran – in Iraq, Lebanon and the occupied Palestinian territory – that underlay the Saudi mediation between the Palestinians in Mecca and the re-launch of the Arab Initiative. Following the Mecca agreement, while preparing to receive Mahmoud Abbas in London, Tony Blair actually welcomed the prospect of a Palestinian unity government and said it should be possible to deal with 'the more sensible elements of Hamas'.[84] However, antipathy to Iranian and other 'extremist' influences only reinforced the US and Israeli determination to marginalize Hamas. Their support for Fatah factional forces, together with the continuation of the financial boycott, even after the formation of the Palestinian unity government, heightened tensions between the factions, which descended into violence once more.

The decisive showdown between Hamas and Fatah in Gaza came in June 2007. Accusing the Fatah-controlled security forces of working against the Hamas leadership, Hamas fighters stormed premises of the Fatah forces, killed scores and forced the remainder to flee the Gaza Strip or go into hiding. Street battles paralysed life in the crowded Gaza neighbourhoods and refugee camps for several days, causing casualties among the civilians and terrifying the populace. Abbas reacted by declaring a state of emergency and dissolving the unity government. He accused Haniya of orchestrating a *coup d'état*, while the Hamas leader countered that he had only pre-empted a Fatah coup. Within days Israel, the United States and EU leaders pledged their support for Abbas and his hastily appointed emergency administration, headed by the former Finance Minister Salam Fayad as the new prime minister.

With Gaza under Hamas rule and international isolation, and Palestinian areas of the West Bank more or less under the control of Abbas and his Fatah forces, speculation mounted that the United States and Israel intended to capitalize on the separation to bolster their preferred Palestinian interlocutors at the expense of Hamas and the citizens of Gaza. Olmert promised to release to Abbas half the tax receipts collected on Palestinian purchases over the past year and hitherto held by Israel as part of the boycott. He also said he would release some 250 prisoners from among the thousands in Israeli detention – mostly Fatah members and associates. But despite the urgings of Egypt and Jordan he did not propose renewed peace negotiations, pending a consolidation of Abbas's position.

BLAIR THE PEACE ENVOY

The Fatah–Hamas showdown formed the backdrop to the revelation that Tony Blair was to be appointed Quartet envoy, following his resignation as British prime minister on 27 June. Rumours of the impending appointment surfaced a week before his scheduled hand-over to Gordon Brown. The idea had apparently been hatched in Washington and was not formally put to the other members of the Quartet until it was already public. His brief, like that of the previous Quartet envoy James Wolfensohn, would be to focus on Palestinian governance, institution-building and economic development. In practice he was expected to seek a wider role. In any case, Wolfensohn and even Blair himself had said previously that movement on the political front would be essential to make the Palestinian economy viable.

As it transpired, Blair was not able to extend his brief. President Bush preferred that Condoleezza Rice handle the politics and diplomacy of the Middle East peace process and that Blair restrict himself to his allotted tasks. Bush spelled this out to all concerned, including directly to the Palestinian President. Bush also launched his own peace initiative at Annapolis in November 2007. For his part Blair was no doubt disappointed. He had hoped to inject some of the magic he had deployed to help make peace in

Northern Ireland and thereby bring the protagonists together in the Middle East. Instead he found himself bogged down in the minutiae of roadblocks, sewage disposal, settler roads, 'illegal outposts', travel permits and ID cards.

Across the Middle East, meanwhile, Blair's reputation was tainted by association with the US invasion of Iraq and handling of the Israel–Lebanon war in 2006. His appointment as Quartet envoy was thus interpreted in many Arab circles as a scheme to oblige the Palestinians to accept a deal that would prioritize Israeli and US needs. It can be assumed, however, that Blair himself wanted the opportunity because it would give him the chance to achieve a key personal goal that had eluded him during his later years as prime minister – to further the cause of 'moderation' against 'extremism' and reframe his legacy.

Sadly for Blair, the role of Quartet envoy was too restrictive to give him that chance. More to the point, however, if Bill Clinton could not resolve the conflict – with all the power of the US presidency and his personal charisma and determination, and before 9/11 and the invasions of Afghanistan and Iraq had transformed the context – it seemed far-fetched to expect it of Blair, the ex-prime minister of Britain.

Notwithstanding a revival of talks between Olmert and Abbas after the Annapolis conference, no agreement was reached between them. It took the arrival of Barack Obama in the White House to generate renewed hope for Israeli–Palestinian peace, but the re-emergence of Netanyahu at the helm in Israel in 2009 indicated that progress would be limited.

8

Still Flying the Flag: Britain and the Arab Gulf States

'It might be said that the Western powers left the region through the front door and came back in again through the window. The penetration of the West into our societies since 1970 has been immeasurably greater than it ever was in the past.' – Easa Saleh Al-Gurg (1998)[1]

British relations with the Arab Gulf states – Saudi Arabia, Kuwait, Bahrain, Qatar, the United Arab Emirates and Oman – date back to the eighteenth century. Yet whereas once their leaders accommodated to British imperial power and looked to the British for financial support and protection from their neighbours, latterly they have become rich or even exceedingly rich in their own right and primarily dependent on the United States for security.

Their wealth derives from their abundant reserves of oil and gas and investment of surplus revenues around the world. Saudi Arabia possesses some 25 per cent of the world's known oil reserves; Kuwait and the UAE each have about 10 per cent; and Qatar sits on one of the largest gas fields outside Russia. In Oman oil and gas reserves are less extensive and Bahrain has exhausted its modest oil resources and turned to banking as well as Saudi subsidies for revenue. But collectively these states, which together comprise the membership of the Gulf Cooperation Council, founded in 1980, are important as providers of energy to the world and their accumulated wealth makes them attractive to both investors and commercial contractors.

Security of access to energy, trade and investment opportunities have been the irresistible imperatives driving bilateral relations between Britain and each of the Arab Gulf states in recent decades. In all cases also, the United States has been a competitor for contracts as well as the leading provider of protection from encroachment by either of the two rival contenders for hegemony in the Persian Gulf, Iraq and Iran. While accommodating themselves to American dominance in the security sphere, since the 1970s the British have found a niche under the US umbrella, particularly in the arms market, where they have kept ahead of other European and even some US competitors in recent years.

In the circumstances, therefore, it was to be expected that, once in government, New Labour would adopt a policy towards the Arab Gulf states that featured commerce, investment, defence sales and security cooperation more highly than other considerations such as arms control or political reform. All the GCC states are ruled by leading local families who count on tribal and religious loyalties, patronage and vigorous policing to sustain them in power, though Kuwait has a vibrant elected parliament and each of the other states has some form of consultative assembly. Each relies on itinerant foreign labour to sustain its economy, but in all cases the British have preferred not to push overtly for the rights of workers or human rights generally in the face of resistance from the conservative rulers.

Stability and continuity, together with gradual 'modernization' in accordance with local traditions and preferences, have been the stated objectives of British policy for decades. Relations were jolted by 9/11; none of the Gulf rulers wanted to acknowledge the presence of al-Qaeda sympathizers in their own states until terrorist attacks there obliged them to do so. However, such attacks did then induce them to cooperate with the Americans as well as their old friends the British in countering the al-Qaeda threat.

The rise of Iranian regional influence following the chaotic aftermath of the invasion of Iraq also led the Gulf states to a fresh accommodation to the necessity of US defence arrangements on their soil. However, whereas the Saudis opted for a more modest US presence after 2001, the smaller states preferred to pin their future status on more extensive defence agreements with the United States.[2] Britain continued its role within this context, providing arms, training, security and intelligence coordination and economic engagement that capitalized on historical links and bound it more closely to the Gulf regimes.

The centrepiece of Britain's engagement with the Arab Gulf states is the ongoing defence contract between the British and Saudi governments known originally as Al Yamamah (the Dove), the first stage of which was agreed in 1985 by the then prime minister Margaret Thatcher and King Fahd. As discussed below, within a decade this deal had achieved the status of the largest single arms deal in history. Fronted by British Aerospace (latterly BAE Systems), it became the lifeline of that company and thence the mainstay of Britain's indigenous arms manufacturing capability.

The British Ministry of Defence and the armed forces have played a central role in the delivery of commitments under Al Yamamah and successor contracts.[3] Given the importance of this and other defence deals in the Arab Gulf states, together with military training contracts and joint exercises, the MoD has taken the lead in managing British relations with all of them. The role of the Foreign Office has been secondary and the Department for International Development has barely featured, given that development aid has not been extended to the oil-producer states (except Yemen) since their independence. Meanwhile, members of the British Royal Family and successive Prime Ministers have toured the Gulf states repeatedly in the interests of nurturing strong personal links with the Gulf rulers.

SHARED HISTORY

A brief overview of Britain's historical role in the area illustrates how instrumental it was in the evolution of the Gulf states and, equally, how much it underlies contemporary relations. Whereas elsewhere in the Middle East Britain enjoyed only a few decades of imperial hegemony before new leaderships came to power and gained legitimacy by opposing this imperialism, in the Gulf British support was crucial to the survival of the smaller sheikhdoms and emirates. All gained independence by agreement with Britain and thrived thereafter.

The Kingdom of Saudi Arabia was founded in the early twentieth century by Abd al-Aziz bin Abd al-Rahman Al Saud (Ibn Saud), who conquered his rivals in a series of battles that extended his control from Nejd in the centre of Arabia to the shores of the Persian Gulf in the east and the Red Sea in the west. Ibn Saud also acquired many wives, cementing relations with other leading families and establishing a dynasty.

The galvanizing force that inspired Ibn Saud and his tribal supporters was the puritan creed of Mohammed bin Abd al-Wahhab, who had also inspired Ibn Saud's forebears in the nineteenth century and with whose descendants he formed an alliance. The British, in the process of consolidating their position across the Middle East in the 1920s, decided to give their blessing to Ibn Saud's rise and came to an accommodation with him over the boundaries of his kingdom with Jordan, Iraq and Kuwait.[4] Over time, however, the Americans established themselves as the foremost allies of Ibn Saud. From the 1930s they took the lead in the development of the Saudi energy sector and infrastructure through the Arabian American Oil Company, (now Saudi) ARAMCO.[5]

Britain meanwhile prevented Ibn Saud from expanding his kingdom into the Arab sheikdoms along the Persian Gulf coast that would eventually become the independent states of Kuwait, Bahrain, Qatar, the UAE and Oman.[6] The British had long-standing commitments to the rulers – dating from the early 1800s in some cases. Their rule in India and interests further east drove them to impose maritime control in the Indian Ocean, the Persian Gulf and the Red Sea.

They also had a presence in Yemen that lasted from the late eighteenth century until they were ousted by local forces backed by Nasser's Egypt in the 1960s.

The Trucial System

The lower Gulf littoral of the Arabian Peninsula was identified as 'the pirate coast' in the early nineteenth century by mariners on their way to and from India and the Far East.[7] Two centuries later, the predations of pirates operating out of Somalia in the Indian Ocean suggest some interesting parallels.

In 1820 the British government pressed the leading Arab sheikhs of the lower Gulf coast into a General Treaty of Peace.[8] This established that: 'There shall be a cessation of plunder and piracy by land and sea on the part of the Arabs, who are parties to this contract for ever.'[9] Fifteen years later, a truce designed by Britain to reduce maritime warfare in the Gulf was also signed by the sheikhs. This was renewed annually until 1843, when it was made valid for ten years. In 1853 a Treaty of Peace in Perpetuity was concluded.[10] The signatories agreed not to retaliate against any breach of the treaty, but to inform the British authorities, who 'will forthwith take the necessary steps for obtaining reparation'. The British also guaranteed to oversee the maintenance of the peace and ensure its observance.

It was as a result of these early arrangements that the sheikhdoms of the lower Gulf coast became known as the Trucial States.[11] In 1887 the rulers of the Trucial States signed their first so-called 'Exclusive Agreement' with Britain. Confirmed and extended in 1892, this arrangement stipulated that the rulers agree: (a) 'on no account [to] enter into any agreement or correspondence with any Power other than the British Government'; (b) not to consent to the residence within their territory of the agent of any other government without the assent of Britain; and (c) not to 'cede, sell, mortgage or otherwise give for occupation' any part of their territory, except to the British government.[12] This treaty remained the basis of Britain's relations with the rulers of Abu Dhabi, Dubai, Ajman, Umm al-Qaiwain, Sharjah, Ras al-Khaimah and Fujairah (which entered the system in 1952) until Britain's departure and their formal independence in 1971.

In 1922 the rulers of the Trucial States undertook not to grant oil concessionary rights to 'foreigners except to the person appointed by the High British Government'.[13] Subsequently, when concessions were obtained from the rulers for exploration for oil the company concerned would also sign a

'Political Agreement' with Britain stipulating that the company would not conduct any negotiations with the Trucial Sheikhs without the presence, or at least knowledge, of British political representatives.[14]

Britain also concluded agreements with various rulers individually to obtain facilities for both civil and military air traffic. Landing rights were acquired for the Royal Air Force (RAF) at Dubai and Abu Dhabi in the early 1930s. Meanwhile, the Ruler of Sharjah signed an agreement in 1932 by which he was to provide Britain's Imperial Airways with land for an airstrip and a specially built rest house for its crew and passengers, in return for a monthly rent and personal subsidy. In 1949 Sharjah provided facilities for an RAF base.

Exclusive relationships

Arrangements made with Bahrain and Qatar followed a similar, though not identical, pattern to those with the Trucial States. Kuwait came late to the treaty system and was the first to leave it. British involvement in the Sultanate of Oman had a much longer history and followed a related but distinctive path. In official British terminology the Gulf sheikhdoms were designated 'protected states', neither Crown Colonies (like the port of Aden) nor Protectorates (like the Yemeni hinterland). In the words of one observer: 'No two territories were exposed to exactly the same form of British influence or control.'[15]

Bahrain signed the General Treaty in 1820 and in 1861 the ruler agreed 'to abstain from all maritime aggressions of every description' for as long as he received 'the support of the British government in the maintenance of the security of' his 'possessions against similar aggressions directed against them by the Chiefs and tribes of this Gulf'.[16] The islands of Bahrain were thus accorded a more explicit guarantee of protection than was the case with the Trucial States. In 1914 Bahrain agreed not to grant any oil concessions except to persons appointed by the British government.[17]

In 1868 *Qatar* signed an agreement to keep the maritime peace, but entered into none of the other arrangements until 1916, when the ruler signed a treaty by which he accepted all the agreements previously entered into by the Trucial States in return for British protection from aggression 'unless provoked by him or his subjects'.[18]

The history of *Oman* distinguished it from the sheikhdoms of the Gulf littoral as a Sultanate of much greater territorial proportions, with an extensive Indian Ocean seaboard and – until divested of them at British instigation in 1862 – territories in Africa.[19] Even though British treaties with the sultans of Oman effectively established British hegemony in critical respects, which endured into the 1960s, the Sultanate was afforded the formal courtesies of a sovereign state in the bilateral relationship.[20] The first bilateral agreement was signed with the Sultan of Muscat in 1798. Others followed and in 1891 the Sultan bound himself and his successors never to cede, sell, mortgage or otherwise give for occupation 'save to the British Government, the dominion of Muscat and Oman or any of their dependencies'.[21] In 1902 he pledged not to allow the exploitation of coal without Britain's permission and made the same pledge with respect to oil in 1923.

In 1951 Britain signed a Treaty of Friendship, Commerce and Navigation with Oman (replacing an earlier one of 1939). This provided for:

> 'freedom of commerce and navigation' ... and generally that in matters of commerce, shipping (other than coastal trade and inland navigation) and the exercise of trade, the nationals of one country shall enjoy in the territories of the other the same privileges as the latter's nationals for those of any other country. Acquisition of land is provided for on a 'most-favoured foreign country basis' ... Other articles cover the appointment of consuls, the rendering of assistance to ships and aircraft in distress, and, subject to certain qualifications, 'freedom of conscience and religious toleration and the free and public exercise of all forms of religion'.[22]

The relationship was accorded substance in respect of security concerns by an exchange of letters in 1958, whereby Britain undertook to provide assistance to the Sultan of Oman in the strengthening of his army and the establishment of an air force, and to assist with a civil development programme. This assistance included provision of funds and seconded officers to the armed forces, as well as aid and advisers for the development of roads, medical and educational facilities and an agricultural research programme.[23] The Sultan agreed to continue provision of facilities previously granted for civil aviation and the use of airfields at Salalah and Masirah to the RAF.

Kuwait, situated at the head of the Gulf waters, in the shadow of Ottoman rule in Mesopotamia and across the Shatt al-Arab waterway from Persia, attracted little direct attention from the British in the nineteenth century. In 1896 the Ruler of Kuwait himself applied for admission to the Trucial System and was turned down by Britain, which seemingly feared taking on some responsibility for Kuwait's independence from the Ottomans. However, another approach in 1899 led to a secret agreement with Britain along the lines of the Exclusive Agreement of 1892, but omitting clauses prohibiting agreement or correspondence with other foreign powers. In 1901 the Ruler of Kuwait requested British protection, which was not formally granted, but he did receive an assurance that the British government would 'prevent by force, if necessary, the landing of Turkish troops in Kuwait'.[24]

In 1913 Kuwait entered into an agreement on oil, pledging not to give a concession 'to anyone except a person appointed by the British government'.[25] Following the outbreak of war in 1914 the British government publicly announced that Kuwait was 'an independent Government under British Protection'.[26] This state of affairs persisted until 1961 when, again at the instigation of Kuwait, an exchange of letters between the British government and the Emir brought the 1899 agreement to a close.[27] Within months Kuwait became a member of the United Nations and the Arab League. A bilateral treaty was signed with Britain, whereby the latter promised to assist Kuwait 'if the latter request such assistance'.[28]

Letting go

Whereas Kuwait emerged from its protected status by choice, Bahrain, Qatar and the Trucial States were informed of their impending independence by the British government in the late 1960s. In the run-up to Britain's withdrawal from 'East of Suez' in 1971 (see Chapter 1), six of the Trucial Coast emirates opted to form the United Arab Emirates. Initially preferring to go its own way, Ras al-Khaimah joined the union in 1972. Bahrain and Qatar, having mooted joint statehood with their UAE neighbours, chose in the end to remain separate. All formalized the end of their special treaty relations with Britain in an exchange of letters and signed Treaties of Friendship with the British government.

Pax Britannica, the term adopted to describe the Treaty System by the Viceroy of India, Lord Curzon, in 1899,[29] was now formally at an end. As discussed in Chapter 1, in the 1960s Britain thought it should hold on in the Gulf in order to please the United States, which was preoccupied in Vietnam at the time. However, economic constraints obliged a cutback on overseas commitments, the Gulf included, even though some of the rulers offered to help pay for the British to remain.

This was a portent of things to come. As of the 1980s it was the Americans who adopted the role of protectors of the Arab Gulf states, with the latter covering some of the costs through defence deals. By the 1990s US forces were using and expanding the facilities previously provided to the British. Easa Al-Gurg, who witnessed the role of the British in the Gulf both before and after the wind-up of their empire, has written about his observations and experiences as a confidant of the Rulers of Dubai, intermediary with the British, banker with the British Bank of the Middle East, successful businessman and ambassador of the UAE to London from 1991. In his autobiography he notes that as of the 1970s Britain and the United States realized that they could achieve their objectives, notably securing access to the region's oil supplies and the manipulation of the wealth that accrued from them, by controlling the mechanisms of international trade.

> These mechanisms were, supremely, banking and the international move-
> ment and management of money and the control of large-scale business,
> especially the sale of arms and security systems.[30]

TRANSITION AND OPPORTUNITY

The withdrawal of Britain's military presence in 1971 left a vacuum that the Americans initially sought to fill by arming the Shah of Iran as their proxy policeman of Gulf security. Saudi Arabia was designated as the 'Twin Pillar' in the scheme. The fall of the Shah spelled the end of that strategy and the Soviet invasion of Afghanistan in 1979 prompted Washington to develop its own Rapid Reaction Force – the precursor of US Central Command (CENTCOM) – to intervene directly in defence of US interests. Assured access to Gulf oil supplies was Washington's central concern, and its first direct intervention came in 1986 when it answered Kuwait's call for protec-tion of oil tanker traffic in the context of the Iran–Iraq war.

In the meantime the British had regrouped, and though no longer the main providers of security in the Gulf they did not depart completely. As Easa Al-Gurg described it: 'We had to recognize that although the British presence was officially no more, the British themselves were still very much with us.'[31]

Having committed forces to Oman in the 1960s to help defeat southern secessionists and revolutionaries supported from Yemen (the Dhofar war), the British persisted until the war was won in 1975.[32] In the process they managed the deposition of Sultan Said bin Taimur in favour of his son Qaboos, a graduate of Sandhurst who, unlike his father, was committed to the modernization of Oman. The strategy for winning over the disaffected Dhofaris was a 'campaign for hearts and minds' that included digging new wells, tackling disease and generally improving living conditions for the impoverished population. The British counter-insurgency doctrine adopted in southern Oman at the time bears more than a passing resemblance to the British and US counter-insurgency strategies developed through trial and error in Afghanistan in the twenty-first century.

In 1971 the RAF base in the UAE was evacuated, but there and elsewhere British servicemen (loan service personnel) and contract officers were attached to the national armed forces to help with training and the integra-tion of new armaments.[33] In Bahrain, Ian Henderson, a British senior security official, stayed on to oversee internal policing and achieved a reputation for dealing harshly with any dissenters. The Sultan of Oman was also assisted by a coterie of British military and security advisers.[34] British intelligence personnel liaised directly with their counterparts in the Gulf. The British also provided military training teams to the Saudis, in particular to the Saudi National Guard, whose remit was internal and border security.

The British navy also maintained a presence in the Persian Gulf waters. As of 1980, when the Iran–Iraq war began and the safety of British and other merchant vessels in the area was endangered, a regular patrol was established.[35] Thereafter the Armilla Patrol became a fixture, flying the flag, conducting exercises, sometimes in conjunction with local forces, and making regular port visits and courtesy calls in the Gulf states.[36]

As noted above, another facet of Britain's response to new opportunities was in the banking sector. The early 1970s witnessed the first oil boom, facilitated by nationalization of energy production across the region and accelerated by the Arab oil boycott imposed on countries providing support to Israel in the 1973 Arab–Israeli war. The Arab Gulf states rapidly acquired surplus oil wealth and were seeking investment opportunities. Capitalizing on their long-standing presence in the Gulf,[37] British bankers moved quickly to ensure that London's banking houses would manage as much as possible of the surplus capital.[38]

British manufacturing and construction companies also capitalized on the oil boom, picking up lucrative contracts to develop the infrastructure and feed the consumer markets of the Gulf states. They faced fierce competition from other Europeans and the Americans in the new free-for-all that followed independence. In time the Japanese and Koreans entered the scene and local businessmen and the Gulf governments drove hard bargains, especially in Kuwait. However, those British companies with global operations and local connections fared well and set the pattern for lasting engagement through the second oil boom of 1979–80 and beyond.

Speaking in the House of Commons in March 1984, the Foreign Secretary Sir Geoffrey Howe gave the following statement on Britain's interests in the Gulf states:

> We no longer have direct responsibilities for their defence, but we continue to enjoy close and valuable political relations. In some cases these include treaties of friendship, with provision for consultation in time of need.

> Some 90,000 British nationals live and work in the area. There is substantial British involvement there, and the countries of the Gulf area are now among our most important overseas markets. In 1982 the states of the Gulf Cooperation Council accounted for almost £3 billion worth of British exports, so there are many reasons why the security of those states is important to us.[39]

AN ENDURING DEFENCE COOPERATION

As this account demonstrates, British relations with the Arab Gulf states transited relatively smoothly from the era of Pax Britannica and exclusive access to capitalize on market opportunity in the post-imperial era. Successive oil booms smoothed the transition on both sides.[40] By the time oil prices peaked in the 1980s a mosaic of relationships had been established in the financial, commercial and security spheres that endured through the less prosperous period that followed. Saudi Arabia faced the most significant problems in balancing the national budget in the 1980s and 1990s, but here as in the other Gulf states, local families and businessmen still had wealth to spend and invest.[41]

In the meantime security concerns in the Gulf mounted. As Western fears of Soviet designs on Gulf oil receded, the challenges posed by Iraq and Iran increased, causing the Americans to increase their engagement. Already estranged from Iran, when Iraq invaded Kuwait in August 1990 the United States also turned against Saddam Hussein with a vengeance. If any prompting were needed, Margaret Thatcher provided it, encouraging President George H. W. Bush to take on Baghdad in defence of Kuwait and the sovereign rights of independent states. King Fahd of Saudi Arabia was persuaded to allow deployment of a massive US and allied force (including GCC contingents) in his kingdom. 'Desert Storm' was launched in early 1991 and Kuwait was liberated within weeks, with a minimum of allied casualties. The British fielded the second largest contingent in the coalition. After the war most of the coalition troops returned home, but British forces joined the Americans in bolstering Kuwait's defences and enforcing 'no-fly zones' over Iraq that endured until the invasion of Iraq in 2003 (see Chapters 1 and 5).

In the background, British commitments to assisting the armed forces of the Gulf states were enhanced and arms sales were a central feature of British engagement. The Al Yamamah contract with Saudi Arabia was so big it became an overriding consideration in British–Saudi relations and in policy formulation more broadly.

Al Yamamah – the centrepiece

The involvement of British Aerospace in Saudi Arabia began in the 1960s when a contract to supply the Saudis with British Lightning aircraft was agreed. Originally handled by the RAF, in time delivery on the Lightning contract became the responsibility of British Aerospace (BAe). By the 1970s the company had also moved into technician and pilot training, a lucrative line of business, but dependent on a continuous supply of RAF-trained personnel from Britain available for service in the kingdom. Coordination between the company and the British military establishment was thus an early requirement of servicing Saudi needs.

Equally necessary was a level of coordination with the United States, whose presence and influence in Saudi Arabia were already extensive.[42] In fact, the Americans had reason to accept a British role in the Saudi defence sector. If there was to be competition, better the British than less friendly allies, let alone Warsaw Pact rivals. Also, US approval of British involvement signalled recognition in Washington that the British could serve as a useful second channel through which to supply defence equipment and training to the Saudis, not least because Congressional scrutiny periodically undercut Pentagon ambitions to arm the kingdom.

By the mid-1980s the Saudis had decided they wanted a comprehensive air defence system, to include the US Airborne Warning and Control System or AWACs. After a struggle between the US administration and Congress, with the American Israel Public Affairs Committee (AIPAC) lobbying against the sale,[43] the AWACs deal was finally approved, though American service personnel were to retain operational control of the system. The Saudis also wanted to purchase a deterrent strike capability and originally hoped to buy US F-15E strike aircraft. Facing more opposition in Congress and not wanting another public battle, the Saudis explored alternative British and French options.

In September 1985 the British won the Al Yamamah contract, clinched through the personal involvement of the prime minister. Under this and the subsequent Al Yamamah II contract of November 1988, the deal pledged Britain to supply the Saudis with 72 Tornado fighters and 50 Hawk jet trainers, helicopters, naval vessels, the construction of two airbases, associated equipment, spare parts, training and support services.[44] The value of the contract averaged £2 billion per annum over more than a decade.[45]

Several facets of this arms contract are worthy of note. It was a government-to-government deal obligating the British government to the Saudi rulers. In operational terms the MOD together with the Defence Export Services Organization, an MOD subsidiary, dealt directly with the Saudi Ministry of Defence and Aviation. BAe was designated the 'prime contractor'[46] responsible for the delivery of the equipment and training packages included in the contract. Rather than supplying the Saudis directly, it subcontracted other UK defence contractors to supply parts and other requirements of the deal.

Al Yamamah I and II were 'countertrade' deals.[47] Payment for the defence equipment, training and related elements was made largely in oil as opposed to cash. Consequently BP and Shell were bound into the arrangements; they were to receive some 500 barrels per day of Saudi crude (the amount was subsequently increased) to sell at market prices and then transfer the proceeds to an account overseen by the MOD and from which BAe and other contractors were then paid. When oil prices fell below a certain level, insufficient funds reached the MOD account to cover the agreed price of the equipment and services supplied, and the Saudi government had to be appealed to directly to make up the shortfall in cash – which proved tortuous when the Saudi national budget was in deficit.[48]

Thus the stakes were high not only for BAe but also for the British government. The fortunes of BAe, as the largest British company and mainstay of the British defence industry, were crucial to Britain's defence capability. When Al Yamamah II was finally agreed, the announcement literally saved the company from crisis, coming just in time to avoid closure of the Tornado production lines at BAe's Warton factory.[49]

In addition, the Saudis insisted on an offset component to the deal. As part of the first agreement of September 1985 the British government committed to use its best endeavours to encourage offset investment in the kingdom, and a formal offset agreement was signed in 1988. The initial target was set at £1 billion, or 25 per cent of the technical cost over ten years.[50] Over time BAe itself invested in and advised British companies starting up plants in Saudi Arabia. The majority were not in the defence sector but included pharmaceuticals and food processing.

From the Saudi perspective the investments in high-tech industries were valuable to the development of the Saudi economy overall. From the perspective of BAe and the British government a considerable effort was required to meet the targets – on which Saudi–British relations and the fortunes of BAe would flourish or founder. Success also meant more British nationals working in Saudi Arabia, whose security was to become an issue for New Labour.

MAINTAINING RELATIONSHIPS

On the eve of New Labour's arrival in power, British military exports to the GCC states were estimated at $3.5 billion, second only to those of the United States, whose defence sales in the same area were valued at just over $4 billion in 1996.[51] Military sales were only a small part of overall British exports to the region, according to the British Ambassador to the UAE speaking in November 1997, and trade was increasing by about 20 per cent annually.[52] The total value of British exports to the Middle East was $16 billion in 1997, of which the GCC states accounted for $11.4 billion (Saudi Arabia $6.2 billion, UAE $2.5 billion, Qatar $987 million, Kuwait $808 million, Oman $607 million, and Bahrain $259 million).[53] British imports from the region were valued at $5.6 billion in 1997, over half of which ($3 billion) came from the GCC (Saudi Arabia $1.6 billion, UAE $845 million, Kuwait $329 million, Oman $176 million, Bahrain $55 million and Qatar $26 million).[54]

The number of British nationals in the GCC was rising, particularly in the UAE where the British constituted the largest Western community and 500 British companies were operating.[55] In Saudi Arabia there were several thousand British personnel working for BAe (thereafter BAE Systems) and other contractors. According to John Reid, the Minister of State for the Armed Forces in Blair's first government:

> The United Kingdom's military presence in the region has also remained at a higher level than before and includes the Armilla vessels, the No-Fly Zone patrols [over southern Iraq], substantial numbers of personnel on loan service, regular exercise programmes and visits by specialist training teams. The UK military contribution to the western presence in the region underpins the United Kingdom's political commitment to security in the Gulf. It is a reflection of our broader responsibilities as a member of the Security Council.[56]

Reid's reference to the Security Council related specifically to Britain's role in pressuring Iraq under the UN resolutions and related sanctions regime that endured throughout the 1990s (see Chapters 1 and 5). This subject featured early in New Labour communications with Kuwait, including discussions between the Foreign Office Minister Derek Fatchett and Kuwait's Foreign Ministry Undersecretary Suleiman Majed Al-Shaheen shortly after Labour won the May 1997 election.[57] The Kuwaiti ambassador to London sent personal messages of congratulation to each of the 418 New Labour MPs, noting the strong bonds of friendship between Kuwait and Britain and paying tribute to Britain's role in freeing Kuwait from the Iraqi invaders.[58] There were also exchanges of messages between the Kuwaiti Crown Prince Sheikh Saad Al-Sabah and Tony Blair and between the Kuwaiti Foreign Minister and his British counterpart Robin Cook.

In early 1998 British ministers began a round of high-level visits to the GCC. Cook made his first visit to Riyadh in February, and Blair in April. The Defence Secretary George Robertson also visited Saudi Arabia and went to the UAE to sign an agreement bringing into force a defence accord concluded in 1996.[59] In each case the subject of the Israeli–Palestinian conflict was raised and the British were repeatedly urged to use their EU presidency to bring the whole weight of the EU to ensure action on the issue (see Chapter 4). Speaking at a joint UAE–British conference at the Royal United Services Institute in London, after his Gulf visit, Robertson acknowledged the importance of rejuvenating a peace process, confronting Saddam Hussein, and providing military and security assistance to the armed forces of the GCC states.[60]

In January 1999 Tony Blair made a one-day visit to Kuwait, shortly after the conclusion of the 'Desert Fox' operation over Iraq (see Chapter 5). He visited RAF Tornado pilots and crew based in Kuwait and in his official talks with the Kuwaiti government pledged that Iraq would not be allowed to violate UN sanctions.[61] Following his appointment as defence secretary in 1999, Geoff Hoon paid a visit to the GCC states (the first of a series in the region) to pledge support for Kuwait and Gulf security.

Thus the pattern of official interactions and business contacts continued to the end of the decade. When oil prices dipped dramatically in the late 1990s competition for contracts in the GCC became fiercer. In 1998 a dramatic downward slide in world oil prices eroded the value of oil transfers that financed the Al Yamamah contract. BAe shares fell as a result and a cash payment was required to redress the shortfall.[62] At the time there was some speculation that the cash crunch in Saudi Arabia might have a beneficial effect on the prospects for economic restructuring there. Without such restructuring, the potential for destabilization as a result of high youth unemployment and rapid population growth was considered cause for concern, and in due course internal security problems did surface.

In 2000–01 a series of unexplained bomb attacks in Riyadh targeting and injuring foreign nationals, several of them British, led to the arrest of some British and other expatriates, including some of the injured. The Saudi authorities claimed the bombs were the result of a feud within an illegal syndicate supplying alcohol to the expatriate community. It was subsequently revealed that the arrested men were subjected to torture and that false confessions were extracted.[63] At the time the British government was keen to handle the affair as discreetly as possible and the men's families were discouraged from campaigning openly for their release.

The whole episode and the continued detention of some of those concerned raised disconcerting questions about torture and travesties of justice in Saudi Arabia, and about how the British government dealt with the affair. Some of the men were only released in 2003 in a prisoner swap involving Saudi detainees in Guantánamo Bay, which was allegedly arranged in order to placate US allies at the time of the Iraq invasion.[64] Media coverage tended to underline the secretive, not to say shady aspects of British–Saudi relations and the precarious status of foreign nationals working in the kingdom. The way the Saudi authorities dealt with the issue was illustrative of their initial reluctance to come to terms with the presence of al-Qaeda terrorists in their midst.

9/11, IRAQ AND AL-QAEDA

The 9/11 attacks put Saudi Arabia in the spotlight. Fifteen of the 19 perpetrators were of Saudi origin. Yet when the news broke, there was initially no media coverage in Saudi Arabia. Stories then surfaced of Saudi nationals being hastily evacuated from the United States, even though there was a blanket ban on civil aviation in the immediate aftermath of the attacks.

The Saudis were not alone in their state of denial. Across the Arab world there was disbelief that Arabs and Muslims could have been responsible, though some saw fit to express satisfaction that the Americans had had their comeuppance for what was considered their cavalier approach to the Arab and Muslim world generally. Yet in Iran ordinary people came out in the streets in a spontaneous expression of sympathy for the Americans and other civilians killed in the attacks. The Iranian government also proved much more supportive of US action in Afghanistan and Iraq than most Arab governments. However, Washington was not inclined to capitalize on Iranian hostility to al-Qaeda, the Taliban and Saddam Hussein much beyond the invasion of Afghanistan (see Chapter 6).

Critics of the Saudis, in and around the Bush administration, turned on them after 9/11, seeing their autocracy and Wahhabi proselytizing as contributing factors in the rise of extremism and al-Qaeda.[65] These critics were among those who advocated the invasion of Iraq as the starting point for regime change across the region and who believed that there should subsequently be fundamental change in Saudi Arabia too (see Chapter 2).[66] However, they were also opposed to the clerics in Tehran and by January 2002 Washington was identifying Iran, not Saudi Arabia, as the major problem, along with al-Qaeda (see Chapter 6).

Even though Foreign Office officials saw the complexities beneath the surface, including the traditional Sunni–Shia divide that suffuses Arab–Iranian antipathy in the region, the government preferred to focus on a broader distinction between violent extremists on the one hand and mainstream, law-abiding and peaceable Muslims on the other. Islam was not the problem, Tony Blair declared – extremists were. The challenge was to persuade the Arabs to share that perspective.

Regrouping in Saudi Arabia

From the point of view of the Bush administration, not only did the United States have too much at stake in Saudi Arabia to afford a major falling-out, but also combating al-Qaeda would require Saudi cooperation. Consequently, efforts were made by both Washington and London to bring the Saudis on board for the counter-offensive. Washington did, however, see fit to remove its troop presence from the kingdom and instead made greater use of the bases and facilities available in the smaller Arab Gulf states. The British did the same.[67] Meanwhile, Washington's critics of the Saudi regime were persuaded to tone down their rhetoric,[68] though members of Congress and contenders for the presidency would later adopt the line that the United States should reduce its dependence on Saudi Arabia.[69]

In preparation for the invasion of Afghanistan in October 2001, Britain interceded with the Iranian government, capitalizing on the rapport it had managed to establish since 1997 (see Chapter 6). It was also well placed to provide military support, given that it already had forces deployed in Oman to conduct a major joint exercise with the Omani armed forces in early September 2001.[70] Elsewhere in the Gulf Tony Blair set about preparing the political ground.[71] (However, as noted in Chapters 6 and 7, he was not able to visit Saudi Arabia on the first of two trips, apparently because the Saudis were not sufficiently prepared to receive him.)

The Saudis were not supportive of the Afghan campaign, for fear of the fallout, and were even more fearful of the regional implications of the invasion of Iraq.[72] They were much more conscious than the US administration of the effect the overthrow of Saddam Hussein could have on Sunni–Shia and Arab–Iranian relations not only in Iraq but around the whole area. They were also not ready to face the reality of al-Qaeda terrorists and sympathizers within the kingdom itself, infiltrating even the internal security services.[73] In the face of a trillion-dollar lawsuit filed by relatives of the victims of 9/11 against prominent Saudis in 2002, an internal debate on the need to re-evaluate ties with the United States intensified.[74]

The turning point came when Saudi Arabia itself began to experience terrorist violence:

> The wave of attacks by al-Qaeda or al-Qaeda inspired local groups, which began in 2003, had a further jolting effect, fuelling vigorous debate on the root causes of religious extremism. The bombings, repeated discoveries of weapons caches and frequent shootouts between police and armed militants prompted even louder calls for change, with reformers arguing that extremism grew out of the closed nature of the political system.[75]

The violence and uncertainty affected Western expatriates there. Residential compounds and industrial sites where Westerners and other foreigners worked were among the terrorist targets. By mid-2004 more than sixty people of various nationalities had been killed and the exodus of expatriates gathered momentum. In June the British Embassy in Riyadh authorized the voluntary departure of non-essential staff and their families, and British Airways announced that flight crews would no longer stay overnight in Saudi Arabia because of the security problems.[76] In January 2005 the airline decided to axe flights to the kingdom altogether.[77] The total number of British expatriates working in Saudi Arabia fell from 30,000 in early 2004 to 20,000 a year later.

Testing times for BAE Systems

While others took flight, BAE Systems had no option but to endure the insecurity. The company's operations could not be curtailed without seriously damaging the defence system of the whole country. Furthermore, the reputation of BAE itself would have suffered irreparably and its fortunes depended on winning a successor contract to Al Yamamah. As Britain was by now at war in Iraq alongside the Americans and other allies, it was no time to be seen to renege on defence commitments, and Saudi Arabia was in itself part of the battlefield with al-Qaeda.

Disconcertingly for BAE Systems, it was in the midst of this most testing time that MOD police launched an inquiry into allegations of illegal gifts and payments to the Saudis by the company. In May 2004 MOD fraud squad detectives seized boxes of accounting documents allegedly detailing millions of pounds of payments to the Saudis and implicating top BAE executives.[78] Calls for action by members of parliament prompted the MOD to explain that 'any evidence of wrongdoing or improper behaviour should be passed to the MOD police or Serious Fraud Office' for investigation, with which the ministry would cooperate if required.[79]

The police action in 2004 proved to be the beginnings of a Serious Fraud Office (SFO) investigation that continued until December 2006. It was halted at that point by the director of the SFO, in response to pressure from inside the government, BAE Systems and the Saudis to call off the inquiry, on the grounds of 'national security'.[80] It was the Attorney General who announced the closure of the investigation and the Prime Minister declared his assessment that British national security interests were at stake.[81] It was argued in support of the SFO's decision that to proceed with the investigation would have caused the Saudis to suspend intelligence cooperation with Britain – in itself considered vital to combating al-Qaeda.[82] The Saudis themselves had attempted to end the SFO probe by calling off discussions with BAE about a new defence contract worth £10 billion.[83]

The whole saga of the investigation and its closure raised a number of concerns. Given that the case had not been proved either way by the time the investigation was called off, it left the impression that something was being concealed and that BAE practices, known to the MOD, were questionable on ethical if not strictly legal grounds. However, as the Attorney General said, there might not have been sufficient evidence of corruption to support a successful prosecution.[84]

The adequacy of British laws against corruption was also questioned, notwithstanding changes made in 2002. Also, the grounds on which the government intervened to halt the investigation raised questions about the definition of the national interest, and the accountability of the executive and prosecuting authorities. Lastly, the possibility that the Saudis had succeeded in pressuring the British government to intervene in the course of justice simply to avoid embarrassment to the Saudi regime, BAE Systems, British ministers and officialdom left a very sour taste.

In February 2007 it emerged that the SFO was reviewing a former investigation into alleged corruption involving defence companies and the Qatari government. That investigation, instigated by authorities in Jersey, was called off by Jersey's attorney general in 2002 on 'public interest grounds'.[85] The Qataris had actually cancelled potential arms deals because of the investigation and in 2001 the Emir refused to receive two British ministers, one of them the Defence Secretary Geoff Hoon.[86]

These concerns continued to rumble on and some NGOs went to court to prove that the decision to stop the SFO investigation of BAE was unlawful.[87] They succeeded, and the court decided that the SFO should not have surrendered to the contention that proceeding with the investigation would threaten national security. However, that judgment was overturned on appeal.[88] By then Gordon Brown had replaced Tony Blair as prime minister and the reputation of both was tainted by the government's handling of the whole issue. The exact roles of government officials and the intelligence service were also subject to suspicion. As emerged in the judgment of the Law Lords on the appeal, the role of the British Ambassador to Saudi Arabia Sir Sherard Cowper-Coles was singularly important.[89]

FORTUNES RESTORED

It was also Sir Sherard Cowper-Coles who pronounced favourably on the results of the new counter-terrorism strategy developed by the Saudis in response to their grim awakening in 2004–05. As described by the British Ambassador in March 2006:

> In our view and in that of the British authorities and the British security services, the anti-terrorism campaign here is a model campaign. The understanding here is that combating terrorism is carried out not only through security measures or the storming of a terrorist hide-out in a specific district of Riyadh. This is also about combating the *takfiri* ideology and combating the social, educational and economic circumstances behind terrorism.[90]

A report of the British House of Commons Foreign Affairs Committee (of 2006) concluded that the United Kingdom 'could usefully learn from Saudi Arabia's experience' in the field of counter-terrorism, particularly in pursuing long-term policies to tackle the causes of terrorism.[91] The same report also concluded that the human rights situation in Saudi Arabia gave cause for 'grave concern', but that the UK's relationship with Saudi Arabia was of 'critical and strategic importance'.[92]

As subsequently reported in the press, the Saudis' re-education programme for ex-militants applied only to relatively mild, *potential* miscreants; the government jailed those accused of 'having blood on their hands'.[93] According to a Human Rights Watch report of 2009, more than 9,000 people had been detained indefinitely since 2003 under the Saudi counter-terrorism programme.[94] In a press release, the organization claimed:

> The United States and United Kingdom closely cooperate with Saudi counter-terrorism officials, publicly praising their religious re-education program, but have not criticized either the indefinite detention of thousands of people or the flawed trials of 330 suspects in July [2009]. Several thousand of those detained under counterterrorism efforts remain in prison throughout the country.[95]

For their part, the authorities in Saudi Arabia began to regain their confidence after their rude awakening and the introduction of new counter-measures in 2006. The mood across the GCC generally was transformed by the economic boom fuelled by a progressive four-year rise in the price of oil. Whereas in 1998 oil had been at a rock-bottom $10 a barrel, by January 2008 the price was $100 a barrel and rising. The Arab Gulf states were reporting budget surpluses, in contrast to the deficits that had hindered investment and growth in the 1990s.[96]

This was the new oil bonanza, comparable to that of the 1970s, and even though war-torn Iraq and Iran under sanctions derived the benefits too, it was the GCC states that boomed. British–Saudi relations recovered dramatically. In 2007 the Saudi Ambassador to London told a Saudi news agency that UK exports to Saudi Arabia exceeded the previous year's $3.5 billion, adding that 'Saudi Arabia has been enjoying its unique status as the biggest trade partner of Britain in the Middle East [and that] Britain is the second biggest foreign investment partner in Saudi Arabia'.[97]

In September 2007 the Saudis announced that agreement had been reached on the purchase of 72 Eurofighter Typhoon warplanes at a cost of £4.3 billion, in a contract that could eventually total £20 billion.[98] BAE Systems had weathered the storm. In 2007 Britain even surpassed the United States in the value of its defence sales worldwide, with Saudi Arabia its biggest customer overall.[99]

Constancy rewarded

In 2007 the British government announced it was targeting the Gulf for trade development in all sectors, along with India and China. In May the Chief Executive of UK Trade and Investment (UKTI), Andrew Cahn, launched a new British specialist trade hub in Dubai to help UK companies do business in the region 'from Morocco to Iran'.[100] The choice of Dubai for the new hub was based partly on the presence of a record 100,000 British nationals living and working in the emirate, which was also a tourist destination for many more.

UK exports to the GCC totalled £10 billion in 2006[101] and the British had begun to establish a presence in the new growth sectors of education and medicine. British energy companies, banks, business consultants, broadcasters and publishers, as well as other service providers and franchises, were among those establishing or expanding their presence in the Gulf by 2006–07.

For their part the Arab Gulf states were becoming major players in the global capital markets. In addition to sovereign funds accrued over years of quiet and well-judged investments overseas by Kuwait, Saudi Arabia and Abu Dhabi, 'a new breed of sovereign wealth fund … led by a new generation of Gulf Arabs and investors who are willing to take up the mantle of global buy-out firms' had emerged.[102] The Qatar Investment Authority was a comparative newcomer:

> QIA's current assets under management, estimated at $40–$50bn, pale in comparison with estimates of $500bn–$1,000bn for the Abu Dhabi Investment Authority and Kuwait Investment Authority's $250bn – earned after decades of careful management of stocks and bonds and strategic investments in companies such as BP.[103]

In many respects, therefore, the Arab Gulf states had successfully weathered the fallout from 9/11: they could influence the fortunes of companies and countries around the world with their capital and investments, and they were attracting ever more inward investment from overseas. For the smaller states that had once been under the umbrella of the British Empire, this was a happy outcome indeed. For Britain, sharing in their prosperity and their defence arrangements was a reward for British constancy and persistence through times of turbulence and uncertainty.

Speaking to a group of business leaders in Dubai on 20 December 2006, Tony Blair opened with the following statement:

> First of all what I would like to do is explain how closely the histories of our two countries have been intertwined for 200 years and over that time no

country has had a deeper involvement here. A unique relationship of which we in the UK are intensely proud. This is a partnership too that has left us with a deep well of shared experience, respect and friendship. We know how the other thinks, reacts and dreams.[104]

In fact, the international banking crisis and global recession were just around the corner. The British banking sector and economy took a heavier toll than the Gulf economies,[105] though the building boom in the Gulf came to a halt, especially in Dubai.[106] Many British expatriates in the UAE were among those most directly affected by the sudden change in fortunes. However, such developments, including the global recession, are beyond the scope of this study.

In terms of British relations with the Arab Gulf states in the 9/11 era, the fundamentals that had come to characterize bilateral relations remained in place and, if anything, became more entrenched. Ultimately the security of the GCC states continued to rest on US protection, irrespective of Britain's role. Yet the British operated in tandem with the United States and were integrated into the defence arrangements of the Americans *and* the Gulf states. Equally, British economic, financial and security interests had become inextricably intertwined with those of the Arab Gulf states.

9

Conclusions

Three key questions were explored in this work. First, what was 'new' about New Labour and how did this affect the policy-making process and British policies in the Middle East from 1997 to 2001 – before 9/11? Second, what changed in British thinking as a result of 9/11? And, third, how did the British government's handling of the Iraq crisis and invasion alter its policies and role in the Middle East? As the summary below shows, the implications of the changes in the policy-making process introduced by New Labour before 9/11 had consequences for the handling of the Iraq crisis thereafter. Thus the answers to all three questions are interlinked.

NEW LABOUR'S POLICY APPROACH

The changes introduced in the policy-making process and priorities by New Labour after 1997 were partly to blame for the way the Iraq crisis was handled. Under New Labour decision-making was managed primarily by the team around the prime minister in No. 10, at the expense of cabinet and parliament. In the run-up to the invasion, attention focused on alliance politics and the United Nations as opposed to military contingencies, potential nation-building tasks, the situation in Iraq and dynamics in the Middle East.

In the end, explicit UN backing for military action in 2003 was not forthcoming, the Attorney General changed his guidance on the legality of the invasion at the last minute, and the Chief of the Defence Staff had to rely on this and Tony Blair's judgment that British forces could enter Iraq alongside the Americans without fear of prosecution. Questions about the legal underpinnings of the war have been in contention ever since.

Prior to the invasion, debate about the possibility was foreclosed in Britain, ostensibly to keep alive the fiction that war was not inevitable and could be averted if Saddam Hussein cooperated. Blair and his inner circle of ministers and advisers at No. 10 did not draw on all the available expertise on Iraq and the region to help plan for likely contingencies. Detailed papers prepared by civil servants, including in the Foreign Office and Ministry of Defence, were not tabled for discussion in cabinet, and debate in parliament was not permitted until the eve of war.

In addition, even before 9/11, Blair's government did not shape policy to respond to imperatives in the Middle East region itself, but instead it adopted goals and policies deemed most likely to present Britain as a 'force for good' in the world. Establishing a rapport with successive administrations in Washington was also a priority for Blair. Yet in the process, in the context of the Iraq crisis, his government lost leverage in Europe. As a result, he failed to achieve his other goal of playing a central role in the EU and acting as a bridge or pivot in the Atlantic alliance.

In retrospect the British did not serve the 'special relationship' as well as they might have done by speaking truth to power. If the United States was set on regime change in Baghdad with or without Britain's support, the latter would have served the alliance better by paying closer attention to the likely consequences on the ground and fallout in the region, and alerting Washington accordingly.

As argued in Chapter 5, Blair did not go along with the invasion simply to please Washington. He deemed it 'the right thing to do' for his own reasons, including a missionary zeal to topple dictators and, as mentioned above, to make Britain a 'force for good' in the world. Thus, when it became apparent, as of 9/11 if not before, that the Bush administration intended to transform Iraq and thence the Middle East, the Blair government saw a moment of opportunity and a chance to be part of a grand endeavour.

The British government was also inattentive to the implications of the way the decision-making process in Washington was managed by the vice president's office in favour of invasion. It was content to rely on Blair's rapport with President George Bush and his team's access to Secretary of State Colin Powell and US National Security Adviser Condoleezza Rice, but crucially neglected to counter the influence of Dick Cheney and his advisers in Washington.

As it transpired, Britain played junior partner in a US undertaking that was only possible because US power was unrivalled at the time. The net result of the invasion of Iraq was to hasten the end of US hegemony. More attention to realities in the region and more open debate about contingencies and prospects could have influenced the thinking in Washington. Even if the US neo-cons were not listening, Britain's reputation would have benefited in the long run from the adoption of a more cautious line, and it could have bought some more time for coalition-building both internationally and in the region. Instead, there was a rush to action. This was hubris, derived from a misplaced belief in US capability, with scant regard for the lessons of Britain's own history, experience and expertise.

9/11 WAS A TURNING POINT

Britain's approach to the Middle East changed after 9/11. Blair's announcement that Britain would stand 'shoulder to shoulder' with the United States in combating the threat posed by al-Qaeda and what it represented could be taken as an affirmation rather than a major change. However, that need not have meant unquestioning support when it came to Iraq and, as of 9/11, under Blair's leadership the government signed up for 'the war on terror' in a way that ended up dividing the Middle East between 'those who are with us' and 'those who are with the terrorists' – in effect 'those who are against America'. Largely as a result, the latter gained in strength and America lost friends and influence.

The appreciation of many Americans for British support after 9/11 could have been sustained without unquestioning British acceptance of Washington's lead thereafter. As it was, the consequences of the Iraq invasion led to disillusion in the United States itself. In electing Barack Obama their president in November 2008, US voters signalled their appetite for change. In Obama they also chose the candidate who had opposed the invasion and promised to end the US military presence there. Once he was elected, Obama quickly dropped the rhetoric of 'the war on terror'.

However, within a year of taking office, the Obama administration had begun to experience the consequences of the loss of US prestige and influence in the Middle East incurred during the Bush era. Obama's preferred timetable for withdrawal from Iraq was in jeopardy, owing to continued violence and disagreements between the Iraqis. Arab governments, including long-standing US allies Saudi Arabia and Egypt, resisted US pressure to offer inducements to Israel to take steps to facilitate the creation of a Palestinian state in the West Bank and Gaza. The Israeli government defied Washington's call for a complete freeze on 'settlement activity' in the occupied Palestinian territory as a prelude to renewing Israeli–Palestinian peace negotiations, and the Palestinian President threatened to resign and/or take the Palestinian case to the United Nations.

RELATED IMPLICATIONS

Britain's handling of the Iraq crisis and invasion placed it in a double bind. As a result of its complicity with the Bush administration, its reputation and influence in the region suffered by association. Yet thereafter there were no gains to be made by distancing British policy from that of the United States once Bush had gone. The government of Gordon Brown, through Foreign Secretary David Miliband in particular, renounced the rhetoric of the Blair era and 'the war on terror', and embraced the goals of the Obama administration. But by then the damage had been done.

The invasion certainly transformed Iraq, but at a cost of hundreds of thousands of casualties, sectarian warfare and a multiplication of terrorist activities and threats. British operations in and around Basra, while initially successful in keeping a semblance of order, were ultimately discredited for enabling local militias and their Iranian allies to infiltrate local government and security forces. Only the intervention of US and Iraqi government forces eventually restored central authority before the British withdrew.

The introduction of democracy in Iraq opened the way for Iraqi Shia parties to assume power, marginalizing those representing the Sunni Arab minority. While the latter were eventually persuaded to abandon their resistance to the US and allied troop presence and to make common cause with them against al-Qaeda, by 2009 they were still squabbling with the Shia-dominated government. The Iraqi Kurds meanwhile cemented their autonomous control of the north and quarrelled with the government over governance of Kirkuk.

While international attention focused on Iraq, opponents of the US and NATO forces in Afghanistan were able to regroup, and dissident elements in Pakistan gathered strength. Given the strong links between significant numbers of British citizens of Asian origin and Pakistan, the stability of that country is of even greater consequence for Britain than that of Iraq. Meanwhile, in the background of the Iraq and Afghan wars, the failure to resolve the Israeli–Palestinian conflict despite British efforts has served to inflame anti-Western sentiment among Muslims everywhere.

At the regional level the changes wrought in Iraq contributed to the extension of Iranian influence, to the consternation of the Sunni Arab regimes allied to the United States and Britain. The election of President Ahmadinejad in 2006 saw the revival of revolutionary fervour in Tehran and increased obduracy over the question of Iran's uranium enrichment programme. Conceivably, had the Bush administration been prepared to join the Europeans in negotiations with Iran over this issue without preconditions, more progress might have been made. By the time Obama took office and initiated direct talks the hardliners in Tehran were locked in a power struggle with their rivals within the ruling elite and there was even less possibility of establishing a working relationship with the Iranian leadership.

Meanwhile, the fallout from the war in Iraq and increased Iranian influence emboldened other players in the region opposed to the United States,

Britain and Israel. These included Hizbullah in Lebanon and the Palestinian Hamas movement. Confrontation between their forces and the Israelis erupted into war on the Gaza and Lebanese fronts in 2006 and with Gaza in 2008–09. Tony Blair's response to the Lebanon war of 2006 incurred animosity in the region and unease within his own cabinet and party. In step with the Americans, but not with other European leaders or the UN Secretary-General, he did not criticize the magnitude of the Israeli response to the Hizbullah provocation. He refused to call for an immediate ceasefire to protect Lebanese (and Israeli) civilians, arguing instead that there was no point until 'we have a plan to make it happen'. Consequently, the Prime Minister aligned himself with Washington, which effectively meant giving the Israelis a 'green light' to deal with Hizbullah before pressure for a cease-fire became irresistible.

With respect to the Israeli–Palestinian conflict, Blair became an advocate of a 'two-state' solution before the Bush administration adopted that goal. He made repeated attempts to facilitate direct negotiations between the parties and give assistance to US mediation efforts as and when he saw an opportunity. He also urged the Bush administration to become more engaged, when Washington's attention was elsewhere. However, he proved less influential in Washington than successive Israeli leaders. British efforts to help the Palestinian Authority reform its institutions and build a more effective security apparatus, in conjunction with the EU and latterly the Americans, made some progress but failed to deliver an end to the occupation.

Following 9/11 and the declaration of the 'war on terror', there was an intensification of British intelligence and security cooperation with Arab allies, notably Egypt, Jordan and Saudi Arabia. The support of Jordan and Kuwait was vital to the prosecution of the war in Iraq. British commercial relations with the UAE positively flourished during the period of prosperity that preceded the financial crisis of 2007–08. Meanwhile, the convoluted story of relations with Saudi Arabia – at the centre of which was the Al Yamamah and related defence deals – was a perfect demonstration of the intricacies of British relations in the Middle East for British security in the 9/11 era. Blair's government may therefore be judged correct to have safeguarded those relations by ending the Serious Fraud Office investigation into the dealings of BAE Systems in Saudi Arabia, yet in doing so it revealed the extent to which Britain had become bound to the Saudi regime.

It is worth recalling one of Blair's most graphic depictions of the extent of the dangers facing Britain and its regional allies from a speech he made in Los Angeles in August 2006. He warned of 'an arc of extremism now stretching across the Middle East and touching, with increasing definition, countries far outside the region'. He called for 'a complete renaissance' of foreign policy to combat 'reactionary Islam'. But even though the instability and animosity he discerned were real and present, this was a sweeping generalization that conflated disparate and competing elements across the region. The events described here show that the unravelling of the regional order was as much a result of the strategy adopted by Washington and supported by Britain in the wake of the 9/11 attacks as it was attributable to the forces behind those attacks.

After Blair left office there was indeed a 'renaissance' of British as well as US foreign policy, but not quite in the way he seems to have envisaged. In January 2009 David Miliband said the use of the term 'war on terror' had been a mistake and might have caused 'more harm than good'. In May he said it was time to stop depicting Muslims as either moderates or extremists and called instead for 'a coalition of consent' between the West and the Muslim world.

A line has been drawn under the New Labour project to remake the Middle East, in partnership with the Bush administration, in the wake of 9/11. The task for British government will be to repair Britain's reputation in the Middle East while also cooperating with a very different dispensation in Washington which has lost the power to keep its regional allies, let alone its opponents, in line.

Notes

INTRODUCTION

1 For present purposes the Middle East is defined as the eastern Arab world or Mashreq, together with Israel and Iran and including Egypt and, in one section of this book, Libya. The Maghreb states of Morocco, Algeria and Tunisia are not included, and Sudan, Somalia and Yemen are mentioned only in the margins. When the term Levant is used it is to refer to the countries of the Eastern Mediterranean, including Jordan. Throughout the book the designation Persian Gulf or Gulf is used (not the Arabian Gulf), but the Arab littoral states – Kuwait, Bahrain, Qatar, Saudi Arabia, the United Arab Emirates (UAE) and Oman – are referred to collectively as the Arab Gulf states and/or the Gulf Cooperation Council (GCC) states.

2 Elizabeth Monroe, *Britain's Moment in the Middle East, 1914-71*, 2nd edition (London: Chatto & Windus, 1981).

3 As this book went to print, the official Iraq Inquiry chaired by Sir John Chilcot had just begun taking evidence. The personal recollections of the first senior officials to appear before the inquiry essentially substantiate the account presented in this book. Based on material available in the public domain as well as insights gleaned by the author during the period in question, the book is not intended to second-guess the findings of the inquiry, but rather to provide useful context.

I HISTORICAL BACKGROUND: STAGES IN THE RELATIONSHIP

1 Albert Hourani, 'The Decline of the West in the Middle East', *International Affairs*, Vol. 29, January 1953, p. 33.

2 Brigadier Stephen Longrigg, 'The Decline of the West in the Middle East: An Alternative View', *International Affairs*, Vol. 29, July 1953, p. 331.

3 See Wm. Roger Louis, *Ends of British Imperialism: The Scramble for Empire, Suez and Decolonization* (London: I.B. Tauris, 2006), in particular Essay 17, with Ronald Robinson, 'The Imperialism of Decolonization', pp. 451–502.

4 See, for example, Ralf Dahrendorf, *On Britain* (London: BBC, 1982); E.J. Hobsbawm, *Industry and Empire: The Pelican Economic History of Britain,* Vol. 3 (Baltimore, MD: Penguin, 1969); Bernard Porter, *Britain, Europe and the World 1850–1986: Delusions of Grandeur,* 2nd edn (London: Allen & Unwin, 1987); Keith Robbins, *The Eclipse of a Great Power: Modern Britain, 1870-1992,* 2nd edn (Harlow, Essex: Pearson Education Ltd, 1994).

5 Porter, *Britain, Europe and the World*, p. 16.

6 Dahrendorf, *On Britain*, p. 20.

7 Michael Edelstein, 'Foreign Investment, Accumulation and Empire, 1860–1914', in Roderick Floud and Paul Johnson, eds, *The Cambridge Economic History of Modern Britain*, Vol. II (Cambridge: CUP, 2004), p. 191.

8 Porter, *Britain, Europe and the World*, p. 11.

9 Ibid., p. 41.

10 Among those who boarded British vessels and attacked the crewmen in the late eighteenth and early nineteenth centuries were residents of Ras al-Khaimah and Sharjah, who acted in the name of Wahhabi Islam, and to this day the UAE rejects the characterization of these men as pirates.

11 Ali Ansari, *Confronting Iran* (London: Hurst, 2006).

12 Keith Kyle, *Suez* (London: Weidenfeld and Nicolson, 1991), p.13.

13 Porter, *Britain, Europe and the World*, p. 40.

14 Lord Curzon to Secretary of State for India, Despatch No. 175 of 21 September 1899, India Office, Foreign Department, *Political and Secret Proceedings*.

15 India Office, *Summary of the Principal Events of the Viceroyalty of Lord Curzon*.

16 Daniel Yergin, *The Prize: The Epic Quest for Oil, Money and Power* (London: Simon & Schuster, 1993), p. 161.

17 Ibid., p. 163.

18 Edelstein, 'Foreign Investment, Accumulation and Empire', p. 209.

19 Hobsbawm, *Industry and Empire*, p. 152.

20 Alan Booth, *The British Economy in the Twentieth Century* (Basingstoke: Palgrave, 2001), pp. 55–8.

21 Hobsbawm, *Industry and Empire*, p. 152.

22 Booth, *The British Economy in the Twentieth Century*, p. 4.

23 Hobsbawm, *Industry and Empire*, p. 153.

24 Elizabeth Monroe, *Britain's Moment in the Middle East, 1914–71* (London: Chatto & Windus, 1981).

25 FCO, Foreign Policy Document No. 36, 'Jordan and Palestine 1914–1920'.

26 This section draws on an earlier account by the author; see Rosemary Hollis, 'Great Britain', in Bernard Reich, ed., *The Powers in the Middle East: The Ultimate Strategic Arena* (New York: Praeger, 1987), pp. 182–4.

27 Britain, it said, 'was prepared to recognise and support the independence of the Arabs', subject to three exceptions: in the coastal areas 'lying to the West of the districts of Damascus, Homs, Hama and Aleppo'; in the regions affected by 'our existing treaties with the Arab chiefs' (the Gulf littoral); and in regions in which 'the interests of our ally France' limited Britain's freedom to act alone. The word translated as 'district' in the first of these exceptions was *vilayet*, which could also be translated as 'province' – with somewhat different connotations.

28 For the texts of the Sykes-Picot Agreement (1916) and the McMahon Letter (1915) see Walter Laqueur and Barry Rubin, eds, *The Israel–Arab Reader: Documentary History of the Middle East Conflict* (New York: Penguin, 1984), pp. 12–17.

29 For a succinct analysis of the genesis of the Balfour Declaration see D.K. Fieldhouse, *Western Imperialism in the Middle East 1914–1958* (Oxford: Oxford University Press, 2006).

30 John Norton Moore, ed., *The Arab–Israeli Conflict: Readings and Documents*, sponsored by the American Society of International Law (Princeton, NJ: Princeton University Press, 1977), p. 879.

31 See M.E. Yapp, *The Making of the Modern Middle East 1792–1923* (Harlow, Essex: Longman, 1987), Chapter 6.

32 Quoted in Ann Williams, *Britain and France in the Middle East and North Africa, 1914–67* (New York and London: Macmillan, 1968), p. 42.

33 See Toby Dodge, *Inventing Iraq* (New York: Columbia University Press, 2003), Chapter 2.

34 On the Mandate for Palestine, see Norton Moore, *The Arab–Israeli Conflict*, pp. 892–901.

35 Clive Leatherdale, *Britain and Saudi Arabia, 1925–1939: The Imperial Oasis* (London: Frank Cass, 1983), p. 62.

36 See Dodge, *Inventing Iraq*, pp. 10–11.

37 Ibid., Chapter 2.

38 Louis, *Ends of British Imperialism*; and Albert Hourani, *A History of the Arab Peoples* (London: Faber & Faber, 1991), pp. 320–32.

39 Hourani, *A History of the Arab Peoples*, p. 324.

40 Kyle, *Suez*, p. 15.

41 Hourani, *A History of the Arab Peoples*, p. 320.

42 Louis, *Ends of British Imperialism*, p. 452.

43 James A. Bill, *The Eagle and the Lion: The Tragedy of American–Iranian Relations* (New Haven, CT: Yale University Press, 1988), p. 79.

44 Interviews with BP executives by the author in 1985.

45 Anthony Sampson, *The Seven Sisters* (London: Hodder & Stoughton, 1988 edition), pp. 128–9.

46 Ibid., p. 129.

47 A former British ambassador to the Gulf told this author that BP would never tell him what they were up to, or forewarn him of the potential political repercussions, until something went awry or they needed his intercession to help clinch a deal. Then they would show up at his residence expecting him to do as they asked.

48 Louis, *Ends of British Imperialism*, in particular Essay 17, with Ronald Robinson, 'The Imperialism of Decolonization', pp. 451–502.

49 Ibid., p. 461.

50 Norton Moore, *The Arab–Israeli Conflict*, p. 1084.

51 For example, J.B. Kelly, 'The British Position in the Persian Gulf', *The World Today*, June 1964; D.C. Watt, 'Britain and the Future of the Persian Gulf States', *The World Today*, November 1964; Elizabeth Monroe, *Britain's Moment in the Middle East*.

52 Richard Crossman, *The Diaries of a Cabinet Minister*, Vol. 1 (London: Hamilton and Cape, 1975), pp. 94–5.

53 See interview in Avi Shlaim, Peter Jones and Keith Sainsbury, *British Foreign Secretaries since 1945* (London: David and Charles, 1977), p. 197; and Michael Stuart, 'British Foreign Policy Today', *Australian Outlook*, Vol. 20 (1966), p. 109.

54 'Plowden Report', *Miscellaneous Report* No. 5 (1964), Cmnd. 2276, pp. 2–3, paragraph 9.

55 William Luce in Donald Hawley, *The Trucial States* (London: Allen & Unwin, 1970), p.189. See also White Paper on 'Fuel Policy', October 1965, Cmnd. 2798.

56 Gary Sick, *All Fall Down: America's Tragic Encounter with Iran* (New York: Random House, 1985), pp. 13–21.

57 See Easa Saleh Al-Gurg, *The Wells of Memory: An Autobiography* (London: John Murray, 1998), Chapter 1; and Mohammed Morsy Abdullah, *The United Arab Emirates: A Modern History* (London: Croom Helm, 1978), pp. 282–3.

58 Interview with Sir Anthony Parsons, the British Ambassador to Tehran in the 1970s,

conducted by the author in 1985; and Anthony Parsons, *The Pride and the Fall: Iran 1974–79* (London: Cape, 1984).

59 'The next five years and beyond', Prime Minister's anniversary statement printed in the *Sunday Times*, 29 April 1984.

60 'The Queen's Speech', *Financial Times*, 7 November 1985.

61 24 May 1985, *House of Commons Debates*, Vol. 79, Col. 1281.

62 12 June 1985, *House of Commons Debates*, Vol. 80, Col. 904.

63 Bridget Bloom, 'Heseltine faces constraints', *Financial Times*, 13 November 1985.

64 Minister of Defence Michael Heseltine, 12 June 1985, *House of Commons Debates*, Vol. 80, Col. 902.

65 Foreign Minister Francis Pym, 24 March 1980, *House of Commons Debates*, Vol. 981, Col. 406.

66 Minister of State at the FCO Douglas Hurd, *Verbatim Service*, edited transcript of interview with the BBC Arabic Service, 3 March 1981.

67 Speech to the Middle East Association, *FCO Verbatim Service*, 28 March 1985.

68 As revealed in the subsequent Scott Inquiry.

69 Geoffrey Howe, 18 December 1985, *House of Commons Debates*, Vol. 89, Col. 296; Timothy Renton, 17 January 1986, Written Answer, *House of Commons Debates*, Vol. 89, Col. 735.

70 Douglas Hurd interview, *FCO Verbatim Service*, 14 March 1981.

71 Statement issued by Geoffrey Howe, 14 October 1985, British Information Service (USA), *Policy Statements*, 14 November 1985.

72 Compiled by the author as a result of interviews with officials in May 1985, June and December 1986 and June 1987.

73 Richard Luce, 27 June 1984, *House of Commons Debates*, Vol. 62, Col. 983; Robert Fisk, 'Can Reagan really quench the flames?', *The Times*, 30 May 1984; Jon Connell, 'Allies wary of US moves on Gulf shipping', *Sunday Times*, 31 May 1987; D.C. Watt, 'Letting the side down', *The Times*, 5 August 1987; Lawrence Freedman, 'Avoiding British entanglement with the US in the Gulf', *Independent*, 13 August 1987.

74 Commission of the European Communities, *Review of Member States' Energy Policies*, Com (84), 88 Final (Brussels: EC, 1984), p. 157.

75 Rosemary Hollis, 'The U.S. Role', in Lawrence Potter and Gary Sick, eds, *Iran, Iraq and the Legacies of War* (New York: Palgrave, 2004), pp. 197–9.

76 For the full order of battle see Edward Foster and Rosemary Hollis, *War in the Gulf: Sovereignty, Oil and Security*, Whitehall Paper No. 8 (London: RUSI, 1991), pp. 162–73.

77 See General Sir Peter de la Billière, *Storm Command* (London: HarperCollins, 1992).

78 Rosemary Hollis, *Gulf Security: No Consensus*, Whitehall Paper No. 20 (London: RUSI, 1993), pp. 54–5.

79 Ibid., p. 26.

80 Ibid., and *RUSI International Security Review 1994* (London: RUSI, 1994), p. 257.

81 Douglas Jehl, 'Report says Saddam destroyed arms in '90s', *International Herald Tribune*, 7 October 2004.

82 For a discussion of Iraq's motives in seeming to retain a WMD capability see Raad Alkadiri, 'Iraq: the Dilemma of Sanctions and Confrontation', in Rosemary Hollis, ed., *Managing New Developments in the Gulf* (London: Royal Institute of International Affairs, 2000). After the revelations of the Iraq Survey Group in 2004, there was speculation that the Iraqi subterfuge had been designed to deter the Iranians in particular.

83 For a summary of the legal position see FCO memo to the British Prime Minister,

'Iraq: Legal Background', 8 March 2002, www.downingstreetmemo.com/iraqlegal-backtext.html.

84 See Gary Sick, 'US Policy in the Gulf: Objectives and Prospects', in Hollis, *Managing New Developments in the Gulf*, p. 37.

85 The most notable and disastrous attempted coup was routed in 1996, as noted in Memo from Overseas and Defence Secretariat, Cabinet Office, 'Iraq Options Paper', 8 March 2002, paragraph 13, www.downingstreetmemo.com/iraqoptions.html. For a discussion of differences within the administration of George W. Bush over Iraqi opposition groups see memo from Christopher Meyer, UK Ambassador to Washington, to David Manning, foreign policy adviser to Tony Blair, 18 March 2002, www.downingstreet-memo.com/meyertext.html.

86 Said Aburish, *Saddam Hussein: The Politics of Revenge* (London: Bloomsbury, 2000), pp. 337–9.

87 Former diplomat Carne Ross describes how distrust of the Iraqi regime and a determination to prevent it rearming permeated the judgment of the British members of the UN team monitoring Iraqi contracts under the oil-for-food scheme. See Carne Ross, 'War Stories', *FT Magazine*, 29 January 2005.

88 An investigation headed by former chairman of the US Federal Reserve, Paul Volker, in 2004–05 led to accusations against key individuals involved in the implementation of the oil-for-food programme, who in turn claimed the charges were politically motivated. See, for example, Mark Turner, 'Oil-for-food inquiry claims Sevan took $150,000 in payments', *Financial Times*, 9 August 2005. Also, citing weapons inspector Charles Duelfer, see Stephen Fidler and Thomas Catan, 'Saddam ran kickbacks scheme, says report', *Financial Times*, 8 October 2004.

89 Eric Herring, 'Power, Propaganda and Indifference: An Explanation of the Maintenance of Economic Sanctions on Iraq despite their Human Cost', in Tareq Y. Ismael and William W. Haddad, *Iraq: The Human Cost of History* (London: Pluto Press, 2004), p. 40.

90 Anthony H. Cordesman and Ahmed S. Hashim, *Iraq: Sanctions and Beyond* (Boulder, CO: Westview Press, 1997).

91 See Gary Sick, 'US Policy in the Gulf: Objectives and Prospects', in Hollis, *Managing New Developments in the Gulf*, p. 37.

2 NEW LABOUR WORLDVIEW AND THE MIDDLE EAST

1 Prime Minister's speech at the Lord Mayor's Banquet, 1997.

2 Kevin Morrison and Steve Johnson, 'Oil imports exceed exports for the first time in 11 years', *Financial Times*, 11 August 2004.

3 John Coles, *Making Foreign Policy: A Certain Idea of Britain* (London: John Murray, 2000), pp. 179–80.

4 Ferdinand Mount, 'Britain: Return to the Eighteenth Century?', in Wm. Roger Louis, ed., *Still More Adventures with Britannia* (London and New York: I.B. Tauris, 2003), p. 344.

5 Anthony Sampson, *Who Runs This Place? The Anatomy of Britain in the 21st Century* (London: John Murray, 2004), pp. 346–7.

6 Cited in Bruce Anderson, 'Tough at the Toff', *FT Magazine*, 29 May 2004. Worsthorne's book is *In Defence of Aristocracy* (London: Harper Collins, 2004).

7 Nick Cohen, *Pretty Straight Guys* (London: Faber & Faber, 2003).

8 CBI, 'Global trade, global gain: the CBI's international trade policy', *International Brief*, July 2000, p. 2.

9 Trade Partners UK, 'Shoulder to shoulder: now is the time to strengthen UK–US trade links', *Overseas Trade, USA Special Issue*, 2001, p. 5.

10 For discussion of two facets of the US–UK military relationship see Richard Norton-Taylor, 'It's hard to control what the American military do to us', *Guardian*, 5 April 2001; Dan Roberts and Peter Spiegel, 'Blair looks for US aid on defence technology', *Financial Times*, 12 July 2003.

11 Admiral Sir Michael Boyce, 'UK Strategic Choices Following the Strategic Defence Review and the 11th September', RUSI Annual Chief of Defence Staff Lecture, 11 December 2001.

12 Douglas Hurd speaking at Chatham House on 'Britain and the United States', May 2003; and Douglas Hurd, 'The penny-farthing's little wheel', *Financial Times*, 16 April 2003.

13 Stephen Fidler, 'A special relationship? The US and UK spying alliance is put under the spotlight', *Financial Times*, 6 July 2004, and 'The human factor: "All is not well in clandestine intelligence collection"', *Financial Times*, 7 July 2004.

14 Fidler, 'The human factor'.

15 Malcolm Rifkind, 'Whispering in Bush's ear has got him nowhere. Blair must find his voice on Iraq', *Independent on Sunday*, 23 May 2004.

16 Zbigniew Brzezinski, 'America's policy blunders were compounded by Britain', *Financial Times*, 6 August 2004. This was the thrust of the public letter to Tony Blair by 52 British former ambassadors and high commissioners, published in the *Independent on Sunday* and the *Guardian Online* on 27 April 2004.

17 Brian Groom and David Wolffe, 'Blair charm offensive wins over president', *Financial Times*, 24 February 2001; Philip Stephens, 'The unbending faith of two men on a moral mission', *Financial Times*, 14 November 2003.

18 Quentin Peel, 'Bush's quarrelling coterie', *Financial Times*, 2 April 2001; Frances FitzGerald, 'How hawks captured the White House', *Guardian*, 24 September 2002; Bryan Burrough, Evgenia Peretz, David Rose and David Wise, 'The path to war', *Vanity Fair*, May 2004.

19 Timothy Garton Ash, 'Gambling on America', *Guardian*, 3 October 2002; Roy Denman, 'Blair fails to bond Britain to Europe or the US', *International Herald Tribune*, 28 March 2003; Roger Cohen, 'Embattled Blair still hopes to be an EU–US bridge', *International Herald Tribune*, 8 May 2004.

20 Peter Hain explains Britain's stance in the debate on a European constitution, in James Blitz and Christopher Adams, 'Commission viewed as pillar of EU architecture', *Financial Times*, 15 November 2002.

21 Sebastian Mallaby, 'Insults back and forth over the Atlantic', *International Herald Tribune*, 14 May 2002; Francis Fukuyama, 'The transatlantic rift', *Guardian*, 7 September 2002; Gerard Barker, 'Past decade's historic changes erode US enthusiasm for united Europe', *Financial Times*, 7 November 2002.

22 George Parker, 'Choice on euro seen as test of the UK's commitment to European Union', *Financial Times*, 7 November 2002.

23 Roger Blitz, 'War shakes public's faith in the rest of Europe', *Financial Times*, 28 April 2003.

24 Cook's Opening Statement, at a press conference on the FCO Mission Statement, 12 May 1997, released by the Foreign Office at the time, and Foreign Office Annual Report to Parliament, 1998, Cm. 3903.

25 Ibid.

26 See Andrew Rawnsley, *Servants of the People: The Inside Story of New Labour* (London:

Penguin, 2001), chapter 10. Cook was also hounded by the press over aspects of his private life.

27 In their critique of the New Labour efforts to make British policy more ethically defensible, Dunne and Wheeler reject this argument on the grounds that the actual economic interests at stake in arms sales are 'so small' and taxpayers are actually subsidizing arms exports: Tim Dunne and Nicholas J. Wheeler, 'Blair's Britain: A Force for Good in the World?', in Karen E. Smith and Margot Light, eds, *Ethics and Foreign Policy* (Cambridge: CUP, 2001), p.182.

28 Ibid., pp. 170–71.

29 Christopher Adams and Jimmy Burns, 'Security fears swayed SFO to call off inquiry', *Financial Times*, 16 December 2006; David Leigh and Rob Evans, 'Brutal politics lesson for corruption investigators', *Guardian*, 16 December 2006.

30 Will Woodward and David Leigh, 'Saudi inquiry decision faces legal challenge', *Guardian*, 16 December 2006.

31 Cm. 3999 (London: The Stationery Office, 1998), p. 4, paragraph 19. The phrase recurs at p. 53, paragraph 201.

32 Ibid., p. 4, paragraph 17.

33 Ibid., p. 6, paragraph 14.

34 Ibid., p. 6, paragraph 13.

35 Rawnsley, *Servants of the People*, p. 177.

36 'Doctrine of the International Community', Speech by the Prime Minister, Tony Blair, to the Economic Club of Chicago, 22 April 1999, www.fco.gov.uk.

37 See for example, essays in Smith and Light, eds, *Ethics and Foreign Policy*.

38 Prime Minister's speech at the Lord Mayor's Banquet, 1997. I am indebted to Ben Rawlence for drawing my attention to this early demonstration of Blair's emphasis on values. See also Ben Rawlence, 'Tony Blair is the original neocon', *Guardian*, 23 October 2004.

39 15 December 1998, www.number10.gov.uk – Prime Minister's Speeches – 1998 – Foreign Affairs.

40 Foreign and Commonwealth Service, Verbatim Service VS04/98.

41 Ibid.

42 See Chapter 8, 'The United Kingdom', in Richard Youngs, ed., *Survey of European Democracy Promotion Policies 2000–2006* (Madrid: FRIDE, 2006).

43 Fred Halliday, *Nation and Religion in the Middle East* (London: Saqi Books, 2000), pp. 214–16; Rodney Wilson, 'The Challenges of the Global Economy for Middle Eastern Governments', in Toby Dodge and Richard Higgott, eds, *Globalization and the Middle East: Islam, Economy, Society and Politics* (London: Royal Institute of International Affairs, 2002); Charles Tripp, 'States, Elites and the "Management of Change"', in Hassan Hakimian and Ziba Moshave, eds, *The State and Global Change: The Political Economy of Transition in the Middle East and North Africa* (Richmond: Curzon, 2001); and Phil Marfleet, 'Religious Activism', in Ray Kiely and Phil Marfleet, eds, *Globalisation and the Third World* (London/New York: Routledge, 1998), p. 207, quoted in Wilson, 'The Challenges of the Global Economy', p. 201.

44 For details and analysis see Rosemary Hollis, 'Europe and the Middle East', in Louise Fawcett, ed., *The International Relations of the Middle East* (Oxford: Oxford University Press, 2005); and George Joffé, ed., *Perspectives on Development: The Euro-Mediterranean Partnership* (London and Portland, OR: Frank Cass, 1999).

45 Speech by Tony Blair, Prime Minister, Labour Party Conference, Brighton, 2 October 2001.

46 Quoted on American Embassy website, London.

47 Peter Hain address, 'New Policies for a New World', RUSI/*Guardian* Conference, 30 October 2001.

48 Ewen MacAskill and Patrick Wintour, 'How Blair's Syria gamble failed', *Guardian*, 1 November 2001.

49 Staff from Despatches, 'Blair draws rebuke from Syria in Mideast tour', *International Herald Tribune*, 1 November 2001; Patrick Wintour, 'Blair gets a public lecture on the harsh realities of the Middle East', *Guardian*, 1 November 2001; Andrew Parker, 'Assad tells Blair that Arab anger is growing', *Financial Times*, 1 November 2001.

50 Paul Waugh, 'Blair is greeted by Israeli defiance', *Independent*, 2 November 2001.

51 Andrew Parker, Harvey Morris and Brian Groom, 'Blair warns of rift with Arabs', *Financial Times*, 2 November 2001.

52 Prime Minister's Iraq Statement to Parliament, 24 September 2002, www.number10. gov.uk.

53 Labour Party press release, Speech by Tony Blair, Labour Party Conference, Winter Gardens, Blackpool, 1 October 2002.

54 *The Strategic Defence Review: A New Chapter*, Public Discussion Paper, Ministry of Defence, Crown Copyright 02/02 C85.

55 Rob Evans and Alexi Mostrous, 'Spy planes, clothes scanners and secret cameras: Britain's surveillance future', *Guardian*, 2 November 2006; Shami Chakrabarti, 'Give us good policing and fair trials – not rhetoric on stilts', *Guardian*, 12 August 2006.

56 Foreign and Commonwealth Office, *UK International Priorities: A Strategy for the FCO*, Cm 6052 (December 2003), p. 1.

57 Julian Borger, 'Condoleezza: Bush and Blair's branch of freedom is key to more secure world', *Guardian*, 15 November 2003.

58 Ibid.

59 Meeting attended by the author. The Directorate has since been wound up.

60 'UK Foreign Office Reaches Out for Arab Reform', *Gulf States Newsletter*, Vol. 27, No. 716, 8 August 2003, p. 5.

61 Jack Straw, 'Launch of the Civility Programme on Middle East Reform', 1 March 2004, http://fpc.org.uk/articles/242.

62 Derek Hopwood, 'Earth's Proud Empires Pass Away: Britain's Moment in the Middle East', 26th George Antonius Lecture, Middle East Centre, St Antony's College, Oxford, 7 June 2001.

3 NEW LABOUR: NEW POLICY-MAKING PROCESS

1 Speech by the Prime Minister Tony Blair to the Economic Club of Chicago, Hilton Hotel, Chicago, 22 April 1999, posted by the Foreign Office as 'Doctrine of the International Community'.

2 Bernard Porter, *Britain, Europe and the World 1850–1986: Delusions of Grandeur* (London: Allen & Unwin, 1987), p. 1.

3 Alan Chong and Jana Vancic, eds, 'The Image, the States and International Relations', Proceedings from the conference on 24 June 1999 at the LSE, *European Foreign Policy Unit (EFPU) Working Papers* No. 2001/2 (London: LSE, 2001), p. 4.

4 Ibid., p. 15.

5 Ibid., p. 18.

6 Dennis Kavanagh, *The Reordering of British Politics: Politics after Thatcher* (Oxford: Oxford University Press, 1997), p. 220.

7 Peter Mandelson and Roger Liddle, *The Blair Revolution* (London: Faber & Faber, 1996), and *The Blair Revolution Revisited* (London: Politico's, 2004).

8 Chris Blackhurst, 'Whitehall alarm over Mandelson's meetings in Syria', *Independent*, 16 February 2001.

9 He returned to a Cabinet position, in the House of Lords, in 2008 after Gordon Brown had become prime minister.

10 Nicholas Wyatt and Simon Taylor, 'Trade role elevates Mandelson to Europe's inner circle', *Guardian*, 13 August 2004.

11 See for example Andrew Rawnsley, *Servants of the People: The Inside Story of New Labour* (London: Penguin Books, 2001); James Naughtie, *The Rivals: The Intimate Story of a Political Marriage* (London: Fourth Estate, 2001); and Philip Stephens, *Tony Blair: The Price of Leadership* (London: Politico's, 2004).

12 Rawnsley, *Servants of the People*, p. 38.

13 Quoted in ibid., p. 52.

14 Kavanagh, *The Reordering of British Politics*, pp. 233–6.

15 Stephens, *Tony Blair*, p. 101.

16 Ibid., p. 7.

17 See, for instance, Kamal Ahmed, 'Unease as Blair lays soul bare', *Observer*, 4 May 2003.

18 Stephens, *Tony Blair*, pp. 126–7.

19 Blair's Chicago speech, 22 April 1999.

20 It was these early demonstrations of Blair's outlook that informed the argument developed by Ben Rawlence and discussed with the author; see also Ben Rawlence, 'Tony Blair is the original neocon', *Guardian*, 23 October 2004.

21 Speech by Tony Blair, Prime Minister, Labour Party Conference, Brighton, 2 October 2001.

22 Philip Stephens, 'The intelligence furore will prove a footnote in history', *Financial Times*, 6 June 2003.

23 James Blitz, 'The secretary of state for detail', *FT Magazine*, 24 July 2004.

24 John Coles, *Making Foreign Policy: A Certain Idea of Britain* (London: John Murray, 2000), p. 85.

25 Ibid., pp. 90–91.

26 Nicholas Timmins, 'Time for Whitehall to call in the removal men', *Financial Times*, 31 July 2000; Nicholas Timmins, John Mason and Jean Eaglesham, 'Ministers and mandarins wrestle with Whitehall reorganisation', *Financial Times*, 15 June 2001; Jean Eaglesham, 'Industry concern at Whitehall practice', *Financial Times*, 16 August 2004.

27 Peter Hennessy, Rosaleen Hughes and Jean Seaton, *Ready, Steady, Go! New Labour and Whitehall*, Fabian Society, April 1997.

28 Quoted in Christopher Adams and Sue Cameron, 'A message from the mandarins: Tony Blair's "coffee table" government leaves some in Whitehall in the cold', *Financial Times*, 1 May 2004.

29 A charge acknowledged by Peter Mandelson in Mandelson and Liddle, *The Blair Revolution Revisited*, and discussed by Andrew Rawnsley at length; see, for example, *Servants of the People*, pp. 52–3.

30 Report of a Committee of Privy Counsellors, *Review of Intelligence on Weapons of Mass Destruction*, HC898, London: Stationery Office, July 2004, p. 148.

31 Channel Four TV, 'Tony Blair: President or King?', 5 May 2002; and Nicholas Watt, 'Into the limelight: Jonathan Powell', *Guardian*, 23 February 2002.

32 Their formal position was not clear anyway: Andrew Grice, 'Clouds gather over Blair's team of "blue sky" advisers', *Independent*, 10 January 2002.

33 Brian Groom, 'The rise of the unelected', *Financial Times*, 22 September 2001; Jackie Ashley, 'Quiet rise of the king of Downing Street', *Guardian G2*, 14 July 2004.
34 'Spinners, fixers and the prince of wonks', *Guardian*, 23 February 2002.
35 Quoted in Coles, *Making Foreign Policy*, p. 111.
36 Nicholas Watt, 'The lost Straw', *Guardian G2*, 4 January 2002; Jackie Ashley, 'Duty bound but loth to keep taking the tablets', *Guardian*, 28 January 2002; and Anthony Sampson, *Who Runs This Place? The Anatomy of Britain in the 21st Century* (London: John Murray, 2004), Chapters 8 and 10.
37 Coles, *Making Foreign Policy*, p. 118.
38 Peter Hain, *The End of Foreign Policy? British Interest, Global Linkages and Natural Limits* (London: Fabian Society, Green Alliance and Royal Institute of International Affairs, 2001).
39 Andrew Parker, 'Blair to give higher priority to foreign policy', *Financial Times*, 20 June 2001.
40 Robert Shrimsley and Rosemary Bennett, 'Symons' appointment ends battle over trade brief', *Financial Times*, 20 June 2001.
41 Andrew Parker, 'Blair set to give higher priority to foreign policy', *Financial Times*, 20 June 2001.
42 Watt, 'Into the limelight'.
43 'Organisation changes in London take shape', FCO *News&Views*, Issue 51, April 2004, p. 2.
44 Other toolkits dealt with the Rule of Law, Peacebuilding and Human Rights.
45 Elie Khedourie, 'The Chatham House Version', in *The Chatham House Version and Other Middle Eastern Studies* (Chicago: Ivan Dee, 1970, reprinted 2004), pp. 351–94.
46 Jean Eaglesham, 'Iraq war shifts voters' priorities', *Financial Times*, 20 August 2004.

4 BRITAIN'S ROLE IN THE PEACE PROCESS: 1997–2001

1 Ned Temko, 'Peace: can Blair deliver?' *Observer*, 6 August 2006.
2 See www.fco.gov.uk/texts/1997/jul/08/mespeech.txt.
3 Ibid.
4 Discussed in Rosemary Hollis, 'Europe and the Middle East', in Louise Fawcett, ed., *International Relations of the Middle East* (Oxford: Oxford University Press, 2009), pp. 331–48.
5 Franco-British Council, 'French and British views of the situation in the Middle East', Report of a Seminar, July 2002, p. 11, www.francobritishcouncil.org.uk.
6 Key points of a speech by the Foreign Secretary, Mr Robin Cook, at a reception to mark 50th anniversary of the Anglo-Arab Association, Foreign Office, London, 5 March 1998, 'The Arab–British Partnership', *Verbatim Service* VSO04/98.
7 Robin Cook, *The Point of Departure* (London: Pocket Books, 2004), p. 176.
8 Interviews with British officials in October 1998.
9 As meticulously documented by Avi Shlaim, *Lion of Jordan: The Life of King Hussein in War and Peace* (London: Allen Lane, 2007).
10 As Prince Hassan once complained to the author.
11 The story of the succession is recounted authoritatively by Marwan Muasher, who was serving as Jordanian ambassador to Washington at the time of King Hussein's death, in his book *The Arab Center: The Promise of Moderation* (New Haven, CT and London: Yale University Press, 2008), pp. 72–101.

12 In conversations with the author, Jordanians joked that the Americans were their new colonial masters.

13 25 March 1999, EU's Berlin Declaration, http://www.europarl.europa.eu/summits/ber1_en.htm (Part IV).

14 Kevin Maguire, Ewen MacAskill and Michael White, 'Charmer who woos Labour donors', *Guardian*, 26 June 2000.

15 Afif Safieh, 'Anatomy of a Mission: London 1990–2005', speech at Chatham House, 13 July 2005.

16 For example the FCO brought a group of British academics, including the author, to Damascus for a series of meetings (26 February to 1 March 2000).

17 *Middle East International*, 29 October 1999, pp. 11–12.

18 Extracts from a speech by FCO Minister of State, Peter Hain, Westminster Hall, London, 24 October 2000, FCO – News – Adjournment debate on the Middle East, www.fco.gov.uk, 25 October 2000.

19 For an account that holds Israel and the US principally responsible for the failure see Patrick Seale, 'Obituary of the Syrian Track', *Middle East International*, No. 625, 19 May 2000, pp. 20–22.

20 In a foretaste of the raid of 12 July 2006, on 7 October 2000 Hizbullah captured three Israeli soldiers in the Sheba Farms area – abducted, it said, to trade against Lebanese prisoners held in Israel.

21 Finding of a Chatham House workshop on Palestinian Refugees in the Middle East Peace Process: Scenario-Building Exercise, 22–24 July 2000, Narrative Report, http://www.chathamhouse.org.uk/files/9857_220700report.pdf.

22 For example, Shlomo ben Ami, *The Israeli–Arab Tragedy* (Oxford University Press, 2006), and Robert Malley and Hussein Agha, 'Camp David: The Tragedy of Errors', *New York Review of Books*, 48(13), 9 August 2001.

23 For example, Khalil Shikaki speaking at Chatham House on 4 May 2001 on 'Palestine and Israel: Conflict or Peace?'.

24 Aaron David Miller, 'Israel's lawyer', *Washington Post*, 23 May 2005.

25 Edited transcript of briefing given by FCO Minister of State, Peter Hain, London, 11 September 2000, FCO news – 'Progress on Iraq and the Middle East Peace Process', www.fco.gov.uk/news 11 September 2000.

26 Ibid.

27 Ibid.

28 Extracts from a speech by FCO Minister of State, Peter Hain, London, 24 October 2000, FCO – News – Adjournment debate on the Middle East, www.fco.gov.uk/news 25 October 2000.

29 Ibid.

30 Wilton Park Conference, June 2001.

31 Graham Usher, 'Arafat Besieged', *Middle East International*, No. 652, 15 June 2001, pp. 4–6.

32 Richard Wolffe, 'Bush pressed over Mideast crisis', *Financial Times*, 17 August 2001; Joseph Fitchett, 'Europeans take lead in Mideast from U.S.', *International Herald Tribune*, 31 August 2001.

5 THE ROAD TO WAR IN IRAQ

1 *Review of Intelligence on Weapons of Mass Destruction*, Report of a Committee of Privy Counsellors, Chaired by The Lord Butler of Brockwell, HC 898, July 2004, paragraph 611 (hereafter *Butler Report*).
2 Ibid., paragraph 427.
3 Ibid., paragraph 472.
4 See Rosemary Hollis, 'Getting out of the Iraq Trap', *International Affairs*, Vol. 79, No. 1 (January 2003), pp. 23–35.
5 An investigation headed by former chairman of the US Federal Reserve, Paul Volker, in 2004–05, led to accusations against key individuals involved in the implementation of the oil-for-food programme, who in turn claimed the charges were politically motivated. See, for example, Mark Turner, 'Oil-for-food inquiry claims Sevan took $150,000 in payments', *Financial Times*, 9 August 2005. Also, citing weapons inspector Charles Duelfer, see Stephen Fidler and Thomas Catan, 'Saddam ran kickbacks scheme, says report', *Financial Times*, 8 October 2004.
6 Eric Herring, 'Power, Propaganda and Indifference: An Explanation of the Maintenance of Economic Sanctions on Iraq Despite Their Human Cost', in Tareq Y. Ismael and William W. Haddad, *Iraq: The Human Cost of History* (London: Pluto Press, 2004), p. 40.
7 The Conservative government had suffered embarrassment when the former trade minister Alan Clark had revealed in the trial of executives of Matrix Churchill – accused of breaking the official embargo on arms sales to Iraq in the 1980s – that it had dropped the ban on sales to Baghdad without telling parliament. John Major set up the Scott Inquiry on arms sales to Iraq and when the resulting report by Appeal Court Justice Sir Richard Scott was issued, Robin Cook pounced on it to subject the Conservatives to scathing criticism. See Cook's own account, in Robin Cook, *The Point of Departure* (London: Pocket Books, 2004), pp. 116–19; and Hansard, 15 February 1996, Column 1145, www.publications.parliament.uk/pa/cm199596/cmhansrd/vo960215/debtext/ 60215-05.htm.
8 John Reid, 'Gulf Security: UK Policy and Implications of the Strategic Defence Review', in *The Gulf: Future Security and British Policy* (Abu Dhabi: Emirates Center for Strategic Studies and Research, 2000), pp. 13–14.
9 Philip Stephens, *Tony Blair: The Price of Leadership* (London: Politico's, 2004), p. 177.
10 Ibid.
11 Ibid.
12 Letter to President Clinton on Iraq, 26 January 1998, www.newamericancentury.org/iraqclintonletter.htm.
13 Milan Rae, 'British Policy Towards Economic Sanctions on Iraq, 1990–2002', in Ismael and Haddad, eds, *Iraq: The Human Cost of History*, p. 98.
14 John Kampfner, *Blair's Wars* (London: Simon & Schuster, 2004), pp. 30–31.
15 This sort of rumour was typically circulated by Arab diplomats in London who seemed to assume, like many in the Arab world, that if the US and Britain wanted to eliminate Saddam Hussein they could do so.
16 See Rae, 'British Policy', p. 102, and FCO Minister of State Peter Hain's defence of Resolution 1284, at a briefing on 'Progress on Iraq and the Middle East Peace Process', www.fco.gov.uk/news, 11 September 2000.
17 'Iraq/Security Council – Address by HE Alain Dejammet, Ambassador, Permanent Representative of France to the UN', 17 December 1999, and 'Iraq/Adoption of the

Security Council Resolution – Communiqué issued by the Ministry of Foreign Affairs', 17 December 1999, New York, www.ambafrance.org.uk 17 December 1999.

18 Charles Duelfer, '1920s in Germany, 1990s in Iraq: Disarmament Fails Again', *International Herald Tribune*, 16 June 2000. This trend in the US was apparent to the author at a number of off-the-record meetings at Chatham House and in the United States at this time.

19 Hain, 'Progress on Iraq and the Middle East Peace Process'.

20 House of Commons, *Hansard*, Written Answers for 1 November 2000, Col. 511W.

21 Carne Ross, 'War stories', *FT Magazine*, 29 January 2005.

22 That certainly was the tenor of the arguments rehearsed in the 'Iraq Options Paper' of 8 March 2002, www.downingstreetmemo.com/iraqoptions.html (see below).

23 Hain, 'Progress on Iraq and the Middle East Peace Process'.

24 Peter Ricketts, memo to Jack Straw, 'Iraq: Advice for the Prime Minister', 22 March 2002, paragraph 6, www.downingstreetmemo.com/rickettstext.html.

25 Gary Sick, 'US Policy in the Gulf: Objectives and Prospects', in Rosemary Hollis, ed., *Managing New Developments in the Gulf* (London: Royal Institute of International Affairs, 2000), p. 37.

26 Kenneth H. Bacon, Assistant Secretary of Defense for Public Affairs, Department of Defense Briefing, 28 October 1999, cited in Sick, 'US Policy in the Gulf', p. 38.

27 Patrick Clawson, Stephen Solarz and Paul Wolfowitz, cited by Sick, 'US Policy in the Gulf', p. 39.

28 Prime Minister's Mansion House Speech, 13 November 2000, www.number10.gov.uk.

29 Richard Beeston, 'Sanctions on Iraq "could go in six months"', *The Times*, 20 November 2000 (cited by Rae, 'British Policy').

30 Rae, 'British Policy', p. 104.

31 Julian Borger, 'Bush decided to remove Saddam "on day one"', *Guardian*, 12 January 2004.

32 'Iraq Options Paper', paragraph 23.

33 Susan Cornwell, 'Attacks bring Bush and Blair "together"', *Daily Star* (Beirut), 19 February 2001.

34 Patrick Wintour and Martin Kettle, 'Blair's road to war', *Guardian*, 26 April 2003.

35 PM Statement Opening Iraq Debate, 18 March 2003, www.number10.gov.uk, 20 March 2003.

36 Philip Stephens, 'Unfinished business', *FT Magazine*, 30 April 2005.

37 Bob Woodward, *Bush at War* (New York: Simon & Schuster, 2003), pp. 60–61.

38 Bryan Burrough, Evgenia Peretz, David Rose and David Wise, 'The path to war', *Vanity Fair*, May 2004, p. 110.

39 Woodward, *Bush at War*, p. 203.

40 Paul Waugh and Andrew Grice, 'Mauled in Syria, frustrated in Israel, but Blair remains a man with a mission', *The Independent*, 2 November 2001.

41 Michael White, 'Blair's plea: Never forget the reasons for the bombing', *Guardian*, 30 October 2001; Warren Hoge, 'Blair exhorts British not to waver on war', *International Herald Tribune*, 31 October 2001; and Nicholas Watt, Julian Borger, Luke Harding, Duncan Campbell and Patrick Wintour, 'The other round the clock war', *Guardian*, 10 November 2001.

42 Brian Groom and Andrew Parker, 'Blair takes Arab relations plea to Washington', *Financial Times*, 7 November 2001.

43 Colin Powell, 'US Position on Terrorists and Peace in the Middle East', remarks

at University of Louisville, Kentucky, 19 November 2001, ww.state.gov/secretary/rm/2001/index.

44 See Seymour M. Hersh, *Chain of Command* (London: Penguin, 2005), pp. 169–70; Woodward, *Bush at War*, p. 329.

45 Suzanne Goldenberg, 'Blair refused three offers to stay out of Iraq', *Guardian*, 19 April 2004.

46 Hugo Young, 'Before long it may be Blair's moral fibre that's questioned', *Guardian*, 30 October 2001; Ewen MacAskill, Richard Norton-Taylor, Julian Borger and Ian Black, 'Clouds hang over special relationship', *Guardian*, 9 November 2001; Philip Stephens, 'Where zeal meets realpolitik', *Financial Times*, 9 November 2001.

47 Admiral Sir Michael Boyce, RUSI Annual Chief of Defence Staff Lecture, 10 December 2001, see *RUSI Journal*, Vol. 147, No. 1 (February 2002), pp. 3 and 4.

48 Richard Norton-Taylor, 'Both the military and the spooks are opposed to war', *Guardian*, 24 February 2003.

49 Max Boot, 'The Case for American Empire', *Weekly Standard*, 15 October 2001.

50 Ibid.

51 Philip H. Gordon and Jeremy Shapiro, *Allies at War: America, Europe, and the Crisis Over Iraq* (Washington: McGraw-Hill, 2004), p. 67; Michael Mann, *Incoherent Empire* (London: Verso, 2003), p. 201.

52 Robin Cook, *The Point of Departure* (London: Pocket Books, 2004), p. 104.

53 See *Butler Report*, Chapter 8, Summary of Conclusions, pp. 150–51, paragraphs 7–12, 'Iraq: The Policy Context'.

54 See also Blair's interview Emma Brockes, 'The bloke at No.10', *Guardian*, 26 April 2002.

55 See memo to Tony Blair from Sir David Manning, his foreign policy adviser, on 'Your Trip to the US', 14 March 2002, www.downingstreetmemo.com/manningtext.html and memo to Sir David Manning from Christopher Meyer, UK Ambassador to Washington, 18 March 2002, www.downingstreetmemo.com/meyertext.html.

56 Memo from Manning, 14 March 2002.

57 Hersh, *Chain of Command*, p. 176.

58 'Iraq Options Paper'.

59 Ibid., paragraph 1.

60 Ibid., paragraph 2.

61 Ibid., paragraph 10.

62 Ibid., paragraph 23.

63 Ibid., paragraph 33.

64 Ibid., paragraph 34.

65 Memo to Tony Blair from Jack Straw, 'Crawford/Iraq', 25 March 2002, www.downingstreetmemo.com/strawtext.html.

66 Transcript of 'Iraq: Prime Minister's Meeting, 23 July', prepared for David Manning at which were present the Prime Minister, David Manning, the Defence Secretary, the Foreign Secretary, the Attorney-General, Sir Richard Wilson, John Scarlett, Francis Richards, the Chief of Defence Staff, the Head of MI6 'C', Jonathan Powell, Sally Morgan and Alastair Campbell, www.downingstreetmemo.com/memoannote.html.

67 Wintour and Kettle, 'Blair's road to war'.

68 Cook, *The Point of Departure*, pp. 113–16.

69 'Cabinet Office Paper: Conditions for Military Action', dated 21 July 2002 and published by *The Times*, 12 June 2005, www.globalpolicy.org/security/issues/iraq.

70 Ibid., paragraph 3.

71 Transcript of 'Iraq: Prime Minister's Meeting, 23 July'.

72 Geoffrey Wheatcroft, 'Beware of counting on help from Blair', *International Herald Tribune*, 30 August 2002. General Wesley Clark told BBC Radio 4 on 20 August 2002 that 'Tony Blair's behaviour has left Americans automatically assuming that he will back any decision taken by President George Bush' – see Jean Eaglesham, 'Friendly fire risk "may undermine Iraq campaign"', *Financial Times*, 21 August 2002.

73 Christopher Adams, 'Prescott says cabinet divisions on war with Iraq are not serious', *Financial Times*, 17 August 2002; Michael White, 'Blair refuses ministers cabinet debate on Iraq', *Guardian*, 16 August 2002.

74 Glenn Frankel, 'Blair faces rising opposition to an attack on Iraq', *International Herald Tribune*, 7 August 2002.

75 Michael Quinlan, 'War on Iraq: a blunder and a crime', *Financial Times* 7 August 2002.

76 See, for example, Bruce Anderson, 'The US has got it right: the case for war is irresistible', *Guardian*, 13 August 2002; Martin Woollacott, 'One-sixth of Iraqis are exiles – and they want this war', *Guardian*, 16 August 2002; David Clark, 'Doing nothing about Saddam is not an option', *Guardian*, 26 August 2002.

77 James Blitz, 'Leap of faith', *FT Magazine*, 26 April 2003.

78 Prime Minister's Press Conference, Sedgefield, 4 September 2002, www.numberten. gov.uk.

79 Bob Woodward, *Plan of Attack: The Road to War* (London: Simon & Schuster, 2004); see Goldenberg, 'Blair refused three offers to stay out of Iraq'.

80 Bush speech to UN, http://news.bbc.co.uk/1/hi/world/middle_east/2254712.stm.

81 Patrick Wintour and Michael White, 'MPs from all sides unite to urge caution over taking on Saddam', *Guardian*, 25 September 2002.

82 *Iraq's Weapons of Mass Destruction: The Assessment of the British Government*, The Stationery Office, ID 114567, 9/2002, http://www.archive2.official-documents.co.uk/ document/reps/iraq/iraqdossier.pdf

83 *The Hutton Inquiry, 2003-4*, extracts from the report which appeared on the Hutton Inquiry website on 28 January 2004 (London and New York: Tim Coates, 2004), pp. 149–51; *Butler Report*, pp. 152–3; and Michael White, Richard Norton-Taylor and Ewen MacAskill, 'A litany of failure – but no one to blame', *Guardian*, 15 July 2004.

84 *Hutton Inquiry*; Patrick Wintour, 'Letter reveals Campbell's role in intelligence dossier', *Guardian*, 3 July 2003; and Cathy Newman, 'Campbell exposes No. 10 manoeuvres', *Financial Times*, 20 August 2003.

85 Mark Huband, 'MI6 attacked for dependence on poor sources', *Financial Times*, 15 July 2004.

86 *Butler Report*, p. 116, paragraph 472.

87 Tony Blair's interview with Philip Stevens and Cathy Newman, 'Hidden Saddam arsenal "will be found"', *Financial Times*, 28 April 2003.

88 Robin Cook, *The Point of Departure*, pp. 133 and 252–3.

89 FCO memo to the British Prime Minister, 'Iraq: Legal Background', 8 March 2002, www.downingstreetmemo.com/iraqlegalbacktext.html.

90 Stephens, *Tony Blair*.

91 Public opinion polls in the months preceding war showed a majority against, even if a second UN resolution was forthcoming: Krishna Guha, 'The gap in support for war may be down to Britons' distrust of President Bush', *Financial Times*, 28 January 2003.

92 In fact Chirac had added '*ce soir*' when he made the remark, but the government had traduced the original French, Roy Hattersley, 'Why we all love to hate the French', *Guardian*, 21 April 2003.

93 'Goldsmith's legal advice to Blair', *Guardian*, 29 April 2005.

94 Richard Norton-Taylor, 'The attorney who passed the buck', *Guardian*, 3 March 2005; and *Butler Report*, paragraphs 365–87.
95 PM Statement Opening Iraq Debate, 18 March 2003, www. number10.gov.uk, 20 March 2003.
96 Ibid.
97 Reprinted in the *Guardian*, 24 March 2005.
98 The title Robin Cook gave to his memoir, referring to his own resignation from the Cabinet (see note 7 above).

6 REAPING THE WHIRLWIND

1 Interviewed by Ghaith Abdul-Ahad, '"Welcome to Tehran" – how Iran took control of Basra', *Guardian*, 19 May 2007.
2 At the time of writing the inquiry was still ongoing. However, few commentators anticipated that it would concur with those critics who deemed the decision illegal under international law.
3 Jonathan Steele, 'This occupation is a disaster. The US must leave – and fast', *Guardian*, 21 April 2003.
4 Alan Travis, 'Blair reaps spoils of war with surge in support', *Guardian*, 22 April 2003.
5 Rajiv Chandrasekaran, *Imperial Life in the Emerald City: Inside Baghdad's Green Zone* (London: Bloomsbury, 2007), pp. 43–5.
6 Stephen Fidler and Gerard Barker, 'The best-laid plans? How turf battles and mistakes in Washington dragged down the reconstruction of Iraq', *Financial Times*, 4 August 2003.
7 Patrick Wintour, 'We were over-optimistic about regeneration, Blair adviser says', *Guardian*, 13 September 2007.
8 John Kampfner, *Blair's Wars* (London: Simon & Schuster, 2004), p. 334.
9 Christopher Adams, Peter Spiegel and James Drummond, 'Blair appoints special Baghdad envoy', *Financial Times*, 7 May 2003.
10 Briefing for British businessmen at the Arab British Chamber of Commerce, 26 June 2003.
11 Bob Woodward, *State of Denial: Bush at War, Part II* (New York and London: Simon & Schuster, 2006), pp. 196–200.
12 Julian Borger, 'US rethink on foreign troops', *Guardian*, 21 August 2003.
13 Guy Dinmore, James Politi and Mark Odell, 'Washington struggles to top up allied force in Iraq', *Financial Times*, 3 July 2003.
14 www.globalsecurity.org/military/ops/iraq_orbat.htm.
15 www.globalsecurity.org/military/ops/iraq_orbat_coalition.htm.
16 See *Iraq in Transition: Vortex or Catalyst?*, Chatham House Middle East Programme Briefing Paper, September 2004, http://www.chathamhouse.org.uk/files/3198_bp0904.pdf.
17 Ibid.
18 Woodward, *State of Denial*, pp. 275 and 305.
19 E. Eckholm, 'Return to what's left of Fallujah', *International Herald Tribune*, 6 January 2005.
20 Including that gathered by the author on a visit to Basra and Baghdad in March 2006.
21 See Andrew Anderson, *Bankrolling Basra* (London: Robinson, 2007) and evidence to the Foreign Policy Centre's Iraq Commission, June 2007.

22 As was the case when this author visited in March 2006.

23 Evidence to the *Iraq Commission*, from American Enterprise Institute (AEI), June 2007.

24 Co-chaired by James A. Baker III and Lee H. Hamilton, *The Iraq Study Group Report: The Way Forward – A New Approach* (New York: Vintage Books, 2006).

25 Ghaith Abdul-Ahad, '"Welcome to Tehran" – how Iran took control of Basra', *Guardian* 19 May 2007.

26 As discovered by this author on a visit to Tehran in May 2007.

27 Abdul-Ahad, '"Welcome to Tehran"'.

28 Walid Khaddouri, 'The Iraqi oil sector and the chaos over responsibilities', *Al-Hayat*, 10 August 2008.

29 Julian Borger, 'The inspector's final report', *Guardian G2*, 3 March 2004.

30 'Comprehensive Report of the Special Advisor to the Director of Central Intelligence on Iraqi WMD', 30 September 2004, www.cia.gov/cia/reports/iraq_wmd_2004.

31 www.iraqbodycount.net/database.

32 www.thelancet.com/webfiles/images/journals/lancet/s0140673606694919.pdf.

33 www.mod.uk/DefenceInternet/FactSheets/OperationsFactsheets/Operations InIraqBritishFatalities.htm and www3.brookings.edu/fp/saban/iraq/index.pdf.

34 Richard Norton-Taylor, 'Three British troops killed on Basra patrol', Guardian, 29 June 2007.

35 www.mod.uk/DefenceInternet/FactSheets/OperationsFactsheets/Operation-sInIraqBritishFatalities.htm.

36 Figures based on Department of Defense data, http://icasualties.org.

37 www3.brookings.edu/fp/saban/iraq/index.pdf.

38 Ibid.

39 James Risen, 'Back home, mental ills plague Iraq contractors', *International Herald Tribune*, 5 July 2007.

40 Jim Pickard and James Blitz, 'High cost of Iraq war surprised Whitehall', *Financial Times*, 22 August 2009.

41 Ibid.

42 Speech to the Los Angeles World Affairs Council, 1 August 2006, www.number10. gov.uk.

43 Blair's speech to business leaders in Dubai, 20 December 2006, http://www.number10. gov.uk/Page10661; and Daniel Dombey, 'Blair seeks closer ties with moderate Arabs', *Financial Times*, 20 December 2006.

44 Notably in a speech he made at the UN, New York, on 5 September 2000, http://www. unesco.org/dialogue/en/khatami.htm.

45 Adam Tarock, 'Iran–Western Europe: Relations on the Mend', *British Journal of Middle Eastern Studies*, Vol. 26, No. 1 (May 1999), p. 60.

46 The untimely death of Foreign Office Minister Derek Fatchett on 9 May meant that Britain could not follow up with the planned formal visit to Tehran.

47 Interviews conducted by the author, not for attribution, in September 1999. See also Ian Black, 'Britain joins rush to woo Tehran', *Guardian*, 8 September 1998.

48 In answer to a question from the author, following a presentation to an invited audience at Chatham House on 11 January 2000.

49 See in particular Secretary of State Madeleine Albright, 'Remarks at 1998 Asia Society Dinner', 17 June 1998, as released by the Office of the Spokesman, US Department of State, 18 June 1998.

50 Nicholas Watt, 'UK placates Iran with new envoy', *Guardian*, 24 September 2002.

51 Ian Traynor, 'Tehran agrees to freeze nuclear programme', *Guardian*, 27 November 2003.

52 http://www.armscontrol.org/factsheets/UNSC_1639_Iran.

53 House of Commons Foreign Affairs Select Committee, Global Security: Iran, Fifth Report of Session 2007-08, HC142.

54 A former Iranian official interviewed off the record by the author in Tehran in May 2007.

55 The Iranian authorities reacted with hostility to the launch of the BBC Persian television service in 2008. In 2009, when many Iranians came out on the streets to contest the official announcement of Ahmadinejad's re-election in June, the authorities singled out Britain for special criticism and alleged interference in their domestic politics.

56 Sudan was also on the list, but it is beyond the scope of this study.

57 Speech to the Washington Institute for Near East Policy, 26 November 1997; see summary at http://thewashingtoninstitute.com/templateC05.php?CID=1165.

58 US State Department, *Patterns of Global Terrorism*, April 1998.

59 The author went on two such trips.

60 Staff from Despatches, 'Blair draws rebuke from Syria in Mideast Tour', *International Herald Tribune*, 1 November 2001; Patrick Wintour, 'Blair gets a public lecture on the harsh realities of the Middle East', *Guardian*, 1 November 2001; Andrew Parker, 'Assad tells Blair that Arab anger is growing', *Financial Times*, 1 November 2001.

61 Ewen MacAskill, 'Assad calls Blair conference irrelevant', *Guardian*, 18 December 2002.

62 Richard Beeston, 'Syrian President accuses Blair of "ostrich" policy', *The Times*, 18 December 2002.

63 Will Woodward, 'First stop of Blair's farewell Africa tour: Gadafy's tent', *Guardian*, 30 May 2007.

64 Andrew Bolger, Daniel Dombey and Heba Saleh, 'US hits at decision to free Lockerbie bomber', *Financial Times*, 21 August 2009.

65 'King, Blair discuss debt relief for Jordan, peace process, Kosovo crisis', *Jordan Times*, 12 May 1999.

66 Amnesty International report, *Jordan: Security Measures Violate Human Rights* (MDE 16/001/2002), February 2002.

67 Amnesty International report, *Jordan: 'Your confessions are ready for you to sign': Detention and Torture of Political Suspects* (MDE 16/005/2006), July 2006, p. 33.

68 Paul Waugh, 'Jordan's king and Labour MPs warn Blair on Iraq attack', *Independent*, 30 July 2002.

69 Ibid.

70 Center for Strategic Studies, University of Jordan, report, *Revisiting the Arab Street*, February 2005, p. 14.

71 Ibid., table p. 14.

72 Ibid., p. 78.

73 Amnesty International, *Jordan: 'Your Confessions are Ready for You to Sign'*.

74 Julia Hall, 'Mind the Gap: Diplomatic Assurances and the Erosion of the Global Ban on Torture', Essay, *Human Rights Watch World Report 2008* (New York: HRW/Seven Stories Press).

75 Amnesty International, *Jordan: 'Your Confessions are Ready for You to Sign'*, p. 44.

76 Hall, 'Mind the Gap', p. 70.

77 Amnesty International, *Jordan: 'Your Confessions are Ready for You to Sign'*, p. 44.

78 http://ukinjordan.fco.gov.uk/en/working-with-jordan/defence.

79 Ibid.
80 International Monetary Fund, *Direction of Trade Statistics Yearbook*, 2004.
81 http://ukinegypt.fco.gov.uk/en/working-with-egypt/defence.
82 http://ukinegypt.fco.gov.uk/en/working-with-egypt/funding-opportunities.
83 Ahdaf Soueif, 'After September 11: Nile blues', *Guardian G2*, 6 November 2001.
84 Ibid.
85 Center for Strategic Studies, University of Jordan, *Revisiting the Arab Street*, p. 69.
86 Ibid., p. 70.
87 Ibid.
88 Ibid., pp. 14 and 26.
89 Ibid., p. 14.

7 REALPOLITIK AND THE PEACE PROCESS AFTER 9/11

1 Speech by Tony Blair, Labour Party Conference, Blackpool, 1 October 2002.
2 Ralph Atkins, 'Blair forced to avert veto by Israel on Straw's visit', *Financial Times*, 26 September 2001.
3 Joint press conference: Tony Blair and Yasser Arafat – 15 October 2001, Prime Minister's Speeches – 2001 – Press conference with Yasser Arafat, http://www.number10.gov.uk/Page1630.
4 Harvey Morris and agencies, 'Blair to offer fresh ideas for Mideast peace', *Financial Times*, 30 October 2001.
5 Ibid.
6 Staff from Despatches, 'Blair draws rebuke from Syria in Mideast tour', *International Herald Tribune*, 1 November 2001; Patrick Wintour, 'Blair gets a public lecture on the harsh realities of the Middle East', *Guardian*, 1 November 2001; Andrew Parker, 'Assad tells Blair that Arab anger is growing', *Financial Times*, 1 November 2001.
7 Ewen MacAskill and Patrick Wintour, 'How Blair's Syria gamble failed', *Guardian*, 1 November 2001.
8 Paul Waugh, 'Blair is greeted by Israeli defiance', *Independent*, 2 November 2001.
9 Harvey Morris, 'Gazans view Blair visit with cynicism', *Financial Times*, 1 November 2001.
10 Andrew Parker, Harvey Morris and Brian Groom, 'Blair warns of rift with Arabs', *Financial Times*, 2 November 2001.
11 Peter Mandelson, 'Bush must grasp the Middle East nettle', *Observer*, 18 November 2001.
12 Ed Vulliamy and Virginia Quirke, 'US commits to Palestine', *Observer*, 18 November 2001.
13 Nicholas Watt and Richard Norton-Taylor, 'Wounded Blair ready to rejoin the jet set', *Guardian*, 15 December 2001.
14 *Guardian*, 11 December 2001.
15 David Sobelman, Amnon Barzilai and Yossi Melman, 'German, British ministers stress need to end violence', *Haaretz*, 15 February 2002.
16 Julian Borger, 'Why president stopped listening to Powell', *Guardian*, 26 June 2002.
17 Text of the David Manning memo, 14 March 2002, www.downingstreetmemo.com/manningtext.html.
18 Ibid.
19 BBC Current Affairs, Radio 4 Documentary, 'Analysis: The Expired Mandate', broadcast 1 August 2002.

20 The Jordanians were instrumental in this, but understood that the Saudis would have more leverage. See Marwan Muasher, *The Arab Center: The Promise of Moderation* (New Haven, CT and London: Yale University Press, 2008), pp. 102–33.

21 Suzanne Goldenberg, 'Furious Arafat to miss summit', *Guardian*, 27 March 2002.

22 Michael White, 'Two minds on the Middle East', *Guardian*, 8 April 2002.

23 Prime Minister's Speeches, 2002, Statement by the Prime Minister Tony Blair to Parliament on the situation in the Middle East, 10 April 2002, www.number-10, gov.uk.

24 John Hooper and Richard Norton-Taylor, 'Secret UK ban on arms to Israel', 13 April 2002.

25 Blair shared this logic. Christopher Adams and Krishna Guha, 'Blair acts to prevent rift with US on Arafat', *Financial Times*, 26 June 2002.

26 Chris McGreal, 'UK monitors to help end Arafat siege', *Guardian*, 29 April 2002.

27 BBC, 'Analysis: The Expired Mandate'.

28 Bush had planned a speech to assuage concerns among allied Arab governments that would launch a new initiative, based on a vision for a two-state solution to the conflict, to commence with a new Middle East peace conference in July. However, Palestinian suicide attacks and interventions by Vice President Dick Cheney and Defense Secretary Donald Rumsfeld dissuaded him. Julian Borger, 'Why president stopped listening to Powell', *Guardian*, 26 June 2002. Christopher Adams and Richard Wolfe, 'Conflict that threatens to undo the special bond between Bush and Blair', *Financial Times*, 27 June 2006.

29 Adams and Wolfe, 'Conflict that threatens to undo the special bond between Bush and Blair'.

30 Cabinet Office Paper: Conditions for Military Action, 21 July 2002, revealed in *The Times*, 12 June 2005.

31 Press Conference with the UN Secretary-General, the US Secretary of State, Egyptian and Jordanian Foreign Ministers and the Permanent Representative of Saudi Arabia, at the UN Secretary General's residence, New York, 16 July 2002.

32 Press Conference by Quartet, 17 September 2002, www.un.org?News/briefings/docs/2002/Quartetpc.doc.htm.

33 Speech by Tony Blair, Labour Party Conference, Blackpool, 1 October 2002.

34 New Updates, 'The main point in the Blair vision', *Haaretz* (www.haaretzdaily.com), 4 October 2002.

35 Chris McGreal, 'Why was an unarmed Briton shot in the back?', *Guardian*, 7 May 2003.

36 Douglas Davis, 'Blair hosts Mitzna in London', *Jerusalem Post*, 10 January 2003.

37 Ewen MacAskill, 'Assad calls Blair conference irrelevant', *Guardian*, 18 December 2002.

38 Richard Beeston, 'Syrian President accuses Blair of "ostrich" policy', *The Times*, 18 December 2002.

39 Harvey Morris and James Blitz, 'Israeli ban scuppers Mideast talks', *Financial Times*, 7 January 2003.

40 Chris McGreal and Jonathan Steele, 'No peace till Israel quits West Bank, says Straw', *Guardian*, 14 January 2003.

41 Sharon Sadeh, 'Israel must not miss this historic chance for peace, says Blair', *Haaretz*, 16 May 2003.

42 'Britain in the World', PM Speech to Foreign Office Conference in London, 7 January 2003, www.pm.gov.uk.

43 Paul Taylor, 'US pushing Syria to abandon resistance', Reuters in *Gulf Times*, 15 April 2003.

44 Patrick Wintour and Chris McGreal, 'Bush will stand firm on Middle East road map', *Guardian*, 29 March 2003.
45 Najm Jjarrah, 'Bush Meets his Vassals', *Middle East International*, No. 702, 13 June 2003.
46 Patrick Wintour and Conal Urquhart, 'Sharon set to rebuff UK demands', *Guardian*, 14 July 2003.
47 Sidney Blumenthal, 'Bush, Blair – the betrayal, *Guardian*, 14 November 2003.
48 Harvey Morris, 'Tunnels and bridges divide while uniting', *Financial Times*, 6 February 2004.
49 Chris McGreal, 'Palestinian PM urges Blair to play fair', *Guardian*, 7 February 2004.
50 Ibid.
51 Brian Knowlton, 'Bush shifts views on the West Bank', *International Herald Tribune*, 15 April 2004.
52 Rosemary Hollis, 'Struggle Replaces Hope', *The World Today*, Vol. 60, No. 5 (May 2004).
53 Jonathan Freedland, 'Sharon's triumph is Blair's defeat', *Guardian*, 16 April 2004; and *Independent*, 27 April 2004.
54 'Blair should listen to the experts', *Financial Times*, 28 April 2004.
55 Gregory Khalil, 'A veto on the U.S. veto', *International Herald Tribune*, 20 July 2004; Chris McGreal, 'Israel lashes out at EU for backing UN vote on wall', *Guardian*, 22 July 2004.
56 Patrick Wintour, 'Alarm at US drift over Middle East', *Guardian*, 21 July 2007.
57 Conal Urquhart, 'US deal "wrecks Middle East peace"', 23 August 2004.
58 Tony Blair's speech to the Labour Party Conference, 28 September 2004, http://newsvote.bbc.co.uk.
59 Arnon Regular, 'Qureia hits out at UK's planned London conference', *Haaretz*, 24 December 2004.
60 Chris McGreal, 'Blair presses reluctant Abbas into London conference', *Guardian*, 28 February 2005.
61 Ewen MacAskill, 'Abbas pleads for direct talks with Israel', *Guardian*, 2 March 2005.
62 Christopher Adams and Roula Khalaf, 'Prospects for peace in region "best in years"', *Financial Times*, 2 March 2005.
63 Chris McGreal, 'Israelis pressure Straw over UK Hamas contacts', *Guardian*, 8 June 2005.
64 See Alan Seatter, giving evidence before the House of Commons, Foreign Affairs Select Committee, 28 November 2006, HC 114-I.
65 Harvey Morris, 'War that came from a clear blue sky', *Financial Times*, 22 July 2006.
66 Ewen MacAskill, Simon Tisdall and Patrick Wintour, 'United States to Israel: you have one more week to blast Hizbullah', *Guardian*, 19 July 2007.
67 BBC News, Politics, Blair 'working on Mid East plan', http://news.bbc.co.uk, 24 July 2006.
68 Guy Dinmore, 'No quick fix on Rice crisis mission', *Financial Times*, 22 July 2006.
69 For a transcript of the conversation see: '"Yo, Blair, how are you doing?" – overheard chat reveals the real special relationship', *Guardian*, 18 July 2006.
70 Andrew Rawnsley, 'It wasn't the "Yo" that was humiliating, it was the "No"', *Observer*, 23 July 2006.
71 E-mail to the author from a contact in Jerusalem, 27 July 2006.
72 Ismail Haniya, 'A policy of punishment', *Guardian*, 9 September 2006.
73 Christopher Adams and Andrew England, 'PM's Mideast tour marred by protests

over support for US', *Financial Times*, 12 September 2006; Hizbullah ministers did the right thing by publicly shunning Blair, Editorial, *Daily Star* (Lebanon), 12 September 2006; Therese Sfeir, 'Protests against Blair visit aim to topple government – Jumblatt', *Daily Star*, 12 September 2006.

74 Aluf Benn and Shmuel Rosner, 'Blair, Survival', www.haaretz.com, 19 September 2006.

75 Herb Keinon, 'Blair puts Palestinian issue center stage in Jerusalem', *Jerusalem Post*, 10 September 2006; Will Woodward and Rory McCarthy, 'Blair offers support for a Palestinian coalition', *Guardian*, 11 September 2006.

76 Michael Young, 'The indomitable illusion of a peace process', *Daily Star* (Lebanon), 14 September 2006;

77 Gonzalo Vina, 'Palestinians Facing an Internal "Crisis" Abbas Says', Bloomberg.com, 18 December 2006.

78 'Blair pushes for Mideast peace', *Gulf Daily News*, 18 December 2006.

79 Patrick Wintour, 'Blair makes one last push in Middle East with Palestinian funding plan', *Guardian Unlimited*, 19 December 2006, http://www.guardian.co.uk/politics/2006/dec/19/israel.foreignpolicy.

80 Tim McGirk and Jamil Hamad, 'Rice Visit Leaves Palestinians Gloomy', *Time Magazine*, 14 January 2007.

81 Ian Black, 'Arab leaders offer Israel guarded peace offer', *Guardian*, 30 March 2007.

82 Harvey Morris, 'Olmert calls Arab leaders to summit', *Financial Times*, 2 April 2007.

83 Ian Black, 'MPs criticise UK-backed financial boycott of Palestinian Authority', *Guardian*, 31 January 2007.

84 Hugh Williamson and Daniel Dombey, 'UK set to break ranks and deal with Hamas officials', *Financial Times*, 22 February 2007.

8 STILL FLYING THE FLAG: BRITAIN AND THE ARAB GULF STATES

1 Easa Saleh Al-Gurg, *The Wells of Memory: An Autobiography* (London: John Murray, 1998), p. 162.

2 Greg Jaffe, 'Desert maneuvers: Pentagon boosts U.S. military presence in the Gulf', *Wall Street Journal*, 24 June 2002; and Ewen MacAskill, 'Tehran the target of huge arms deal, says Rice', *Guardian*, 1 August 2007.

3 Anthony Sampson, *Who Runs This Place?* (London: John Murray, 2004), pp. 287–8.

4 Clive Leatherdale, *Britain and Saudi Arabia, 1925–1939: The Imperial Oasis* (London: Frank Cass, 1983).

5 Madawi Al-Rasheed, *A History of Saudi Arabia* (Cambridge: Cambridge University Press, 2002), pp. 91–100.

6 Leatherdale, *Britain and Saudi Arabia*.

7 Lieutenant H. H. Whitelock, Indian Navy, 'An Account of Arabs who Inhabit the Coast between Ras-el Kheimah and Abothubee in the Gulf of Persia generally called the Pirate Coast', Annual Report of 1835–6, Transactions of the Bombay Geographical Society, Vol. I (1844), p. 32.

8 General Treaty with the Arab Shaikhs for the Cessation of Plunder and Piracy by Land and Sea. Dated 8 January 1820, C.U. Aitchison, *A Collection of Treaties, Engagements and Sanads Relating to India and Neighbouring Countries*, Vol. XI (Calcutta: Indian Government, 1933).

9 Ibid., p. 245.

10 Ibid., pp. 252–3.

11 The same group also signed agreements to prohibit slave trading in the area, granting rights of search and seizure to the British government. In 1864 the Trucial States agreed to an additional article to the Maritime Truce, providing for the protection of telegraph lines and stations installed in the region by Britain. In 1879, meanwhile, a mutual agreement was entered into by the Rulers of the Trucial Coast, 'to combine mutually for the prevention of their subjects absconding for fraud from one territory and taking asylum in another', to be enforced, if necessary, by 'Her Britannic Majesty's Political Resident in the Persian Gulf'.

12 Aitchison, *A Collection of Treaties*, pp. 256–66.

13 Ibid., p. 261.

14 Rupert Hay, *The Persian Gulf States* (Washington, DC: Middle East Institute, 1959), pp. 66–7.

15 Leatherdale, *Britain and Saudi Arabia*, p. 1.

16 Ibid., pp. 234–6.

17 Ibid., pp. 233–9 and 252.

18 Ibid., pp. 258–60.

19 Ravinder Kumar, 'The Dismemberment of Oman and British Policy towards the Persian Gulf', *Islamic Culture*, Vol. 36, No. 1 (January 1962).

20 John E. Peterson, *Oman in the Twentieth Century* (London: Croom Helm, 1978), pp. 137–51; Husain M. Al-Baharna, 'The Consequences of Britain's Exclusive Treaties', in Brian Pridham, ed., *The Arab Gulf and the West* (London: Croom Helm, 1985), p. 19.

21 Agreement Regarding the Cessation of Territory by the Sultan of Oman, dated 20 March 1891, in Aitchison, *A Collection of Treaties*, pp. 317–18.

22 Rupert Hay, 'Great Britain's Relations with Yemen and Oman', *Middle East Affairs*, Vol. 11 (May 1960), p. 144. Sir Rupert Hay, as Political Resident in the Gulf at the time, acted on behalf of the British government in the conclusion of the treaty. See *Treaty Series* No. 44 (1952) Cmnd. 8633.

23 Secretary of State for Foreign Affairs to Sultan of Muscat and Oman, 25 July 1958. Reply also dated 25 July 1958. For full text see 'Oman: Insurgency and Development', *Conflict Studies*, No. 53 (January 1975), pp. 18–19.

24 J.G. Lorimer, *Gazetteer of the Persian Gulf, Oman and Central Arabia*, Vol. 1, Historical (Superintendent of Government Printing, Calcutta, 1905 and 1915), pp. 1027–30.

25 Aitchison, *A Collection of Treaties*, p. 263.

26 Ibid., pp. 265–6.

27 Elizabeth Monroe, 'British Bases in the Middle East: Assets or Liabilities?', *International Affairs*, Vol. 42, No. 1 (January 1966), p. 29.

28 White Paper (1961), Cmnd. 1409.

29 Lord Curzon to Secretary of State for India, Despatch No. 175 of 21 September 1899, India Office, Foreign Department, *Political and Secret Proceedings*.

30 Al-Gurg, *The Wells of Memory*, p.162.

31 Ibid., p. 138.

32 John Akehurst, *We Won a War: The Campaign in Oman, 1965–1975* (Salisbury: Russell, 1982).

33 *Statement of the Defence Estimates* 1985, Cmnd. 9430, Vol. I, p. 27; James Lunt, *Imperial Sunset: Frontier Soldiering in the Twentieth Century* (London: Macdonald, 1981); John Bulloch, 'Shifting sands in the Persian Gulf', *Daily Telegraph*, 2 December 1971.

34 'Ex-intelligence agents are said to have major roles in Oman', *New York Times*, 26 March 1985.

35 Interview with Lord Carrington in 'Oman and the UK', *MEED Special Report* (March 1982), p. 6.

36 John Reid, 'Gulf Security: UK Policy and Implications for the Strategic Defence Review', in *The Gulf: Future Security and British Policy* (Abu Dhabi: ECSSR, 2000), p. 11.

37 Geoffrey Jones, *Banking and Oil: The History of the British Bank of the Middle East*, Vol. 2 (Cambridge: Cambridge University Press, 1987).

38 Sinclair Road and Averil Harrison, 'Gulf Investment in the West: Its Scope and Implications', in B.R. Pridham, ed., *The Arab Gulf and the West* (Beckenham: Croom Helm, 1985), pp. 80–109.

39 'Promoting British Interests Abroad: Some Key Foreign Policy Statements, June 1983 to August 1984' *FCO News Department Compilation* (22 March 1984), p. 26.

40 Britain's adaptation to decline, as played out in the Arab Gulf states, was the subject of the author's PhD thesis. The research included extensive interviews conducted in the 1980s with British government officials, diplomats, businessmen, bankers, oil company executives, service personnel, including some who served in the Dhofar War, and many individuals who had lived and worked in the Arab Gulf states before and after the 1971 withdrawal. See Rosemary Hollis, 'From Force to Finance: Britain's Adaptation to Decline: Transforming Relations with Selected Arab Gulf States, 1965-85', PhD thesis, George Washington University, Washington, DC, 1988.

41 See, for example, Colin Narbrough, 'Heseltine flies the export flag in Saudi Arabia', *The Times*, 18 January 1993.

42 See Michael A. Palmer, *Guardians of the Gulf: A History of America's Expanding Role in the Persian Gulf, 1833-1992* (New York: Macmillan, 1992).

43 Michael Thomas, *American Policy Toward Israel: The Power and Limits of Beliefs* (London: Routledge, 2007), pp. 71–93.

44 Andrew Lorenz, 'BAe pulls it off: Saudi contract seals revival', *The Times,* 31 January 1993; and Stephen Martin, *The Economics of Offset: Defence Procurement and Countertrade* (Amsterdam: Harwood Academic Publishers, 1996), p. 233.

45 Ibid.

46 BAE Systems publicity material, briefings and conversations with BAE Systems staff and British officials, 1992–2002.

47 See Martin, *The Economics of Offset*, p. 233.

48 'Saudi banks help fund defence deal', Reuters, 13 April 1992.

49 'Saudi deal just in time to avoid Warton line's closure, BAe says', *Aerospace Daily*, 2 February 1993, Vol. 165, No. 22, p. 176.

50 Martin, *The Economics of Offset*, p. 233.

51 Masood Alam, 'UK expects over $100m UAE deals', *Gulf News*, 18 November 1997.

52 Ibid.

53 International Monetary Fund, *Direction of Trade Statistics Yearbook, 2003*.

54 Ibid.

55 Ibid.

56 John Reid, 'Gulf Security', pp. 11–12.

57 'New Labour Backs UN Resolutions on Iraq', *Kuwait Monthly Bulletin*, Kuwait Information Center, London, June 1997.

58 Ibid.

59 Stuart Laundy, 'UAE, UK sign agreement', *Gulf News*, 17 March 1998.

60 George Robertson, 'Welcome Address', in *The Gulf: Future Security and British Policy* (Abu Dhabi: ECSSR, 2000).

61 'Tony Blair in Kuwait', *Kuwait Monthly Bulletin*, Kuwait Information Center, London, January 1999.
62 Andrew Edgecliffe-Johnson, 'BAe hit as Saudi payments fall', *Financial Times*, 18 September 1998.
63 Paul Kelso, 'Saudi bomb victim's torture ordeal – and Britain's silence', *Guardian*, 31 January 2002.
64 Don Van Natta and Tim Golden, 'US helped two allies in exchange of suspects, officials say', *International Herald Tribune*, 5 July 2004; David Pallister, 'Saudi Britons "freed in swap"', *Guardian*, 5 July 2004.
65 Rachel Bronson, 'Don't back Saudi Arabia into a corner', *International Herald Tribune*, 16 August 2002.
66 Max Boot, 'The case for American empire', *The Weekly Standard*, 15 October 2001; and David Frum and Richard Perle, *An End to Evil: How to Win the War on Terror* (New York: Ballantine Books, 2003).
67 See 'Cohen Tours Gulf', *Gulf States Newsletter*, Vol. 25 No. 634, 17 April 2000; Jaffe, 'Desert Maneuvers'; Robin Allen, 'Gulf states keep lid on extent of defence ties', *Financial Times*, 18 February 2003.
68 Youssef Ibrahim, 'Don't play into the hands of the extremists', *International Herald Tribune*, 13 August 2002.
69 International Crisis Group, *Can Saudi Arabia Reform Itself?*, ICG Middle East Report No. 28, 14 July 2004, p. 8.
70 Jamie Wilson and Richard Norton-Taylor, 'British forces flex military muscle for £93m "desert war"', *Guardian*, 3 September 2001.
71 Paul Waugh and Andrew Grice, 'Mauled in Syria, frustrated in Israel, but Blair remains a man with a mission', *The Independent*, 2 November 2001.
72 Ed Blanche, 'Saudi Arabia's Dilemma', *Jane's Defence Weekly*, Vol. 36 No. 3, 3 October 2001.
73 'Inside Saudi Arabia: The Kingdom copes with the fallout from terrorism', Special report, *Business Week*, 26 November 2001.
74 Roula Khalaf, 'Saudis reconsider US links after terrorism lawsuit', *Financial Times*, 19 August 2002.
75 International Crisis Group, *Can Saudi Arabia Reform Itself?*, p. 9.
76 Hugh Pope, 'Why some Westerners struggle to stay as terrorist attacks mount', *Wall Street Journal*, 14 June 2004.
77 Andrew Clark, 'British Airways to axe Saudi Arabia service', *Guardian*, 12 January 2005.
78 David Leigh and Rob Evans, 'Arms firm's £60m slush fund', *Guardian*, 4 May 2004.
79 David Leigh and Rob Evans, 'BAE chairman named in "slush fund" files', *Guardian*, 5 May 2004.
80 As subsequently spelled out in http://www.publications.parliament.uk/pa/ld200708/ldjudgmt/jd080730/corner-1.htm.
81 Jimmy Burns, Christopherr Adams and Hugh Williamson, 'SFO chief disputes government line on BAE', *Financial Times*, 16, December 2006.
82 Michael Peel, '"People could die": how the inquiry into BAE's Saudi deal was brought to earth', *Financial Times*, 26 February 2007.
83 James Boxell, Roula Khalaf, Michael Peel and Peggy Hollinger, 'Saudis halt £10bn jet talks to end SFO probe', *Financial Times*, 28 November 2006.
84 'BAE allegations: investigators navigate the antiquated legal labyrinth', *Financial Times*, 8 June 2007.

85 Jimmy Burns, Michael Peel and Andrew Parker, 'Row threatens relations between UK and Qatar', *Financial Times*, 8 December 2001.

86 Michael Peel, 'Jersey payments probe with lessons for BAE investigations', *Financial Times*, 20 February 2007.

87 Richard Norton-Taylor, 'MPs' anger over withheld spy documents', *Guardian*, 30 January 2008; David Leigh and Rob Evans, 'A cover-up laid bare: court hears how SFO inquiry was halted', *Guardian*, 15 February 2008.

88 http://www.publications.parliament.uk/pa/ld200708/ldjudgmt/jd080730/corner-1. htm.

89 For his involvement see http://www.publications.parliament.uk/pa/ld200708/ ldjudgmt/jd080730/corner-1.htm, and for preceding speculations see David Leigh, Richard Norton-Taylor and Rob Evans, 'MI6 and Blair at odds over Saudi deals', *Guardian*, 16 January 2007; 'MI6 "shared Saudi deal concerns"', *Evening Standard*, 17 January 2007, www.thisislondon.co.uk/standard/article-23381978-mi6-shared-saudi-deal-concern.

90 'US envoy to Saudi Arabia interviewed on security, trade and cooperation', Saudi TV1 on 10 March 2006, BBC Monitoring, 10 March 2006.

91 Foreign Affairs Committee Report, *Foreign Policy Aspects of the War against Terrorism*, HC 573, 2 July 2006, p.4.

92 Ibid., p. 5.

93 AFP, 'Saudis use soft touch to "save" ex-militants', *Kuwait Times*, 28 April 2009.

94 Human Rights Watch report, *Human Rights and Saudi Arabia's Counterterrorism Response: Religious Counselling, Indefinite Detention, and Flawed Trials*, HRW, August 2009, www.hrw.org/node/84894.

95 HRW Press, 10 August 2009.

96 'Gulf Arab states ride the petrodollar boom', leader column, *Financial Times*, 28 December 2006.

97 'Saudi Ambassador opens economic conference in London, lauds bilateral relations', Saudi News Agency report, BBC Monitoring, 26 October 2007.

98 Stephen Fidler, 'Saudis confirm £4bn Typhoon deal', *Financial Times*, 18 September 2007.

99 Stephen Fidler, 'UK becomes largest exporter of arms', *Financial Times*, 18 June 2008.

100 Simeon Kerr, 'UK makes Gulf priority for trade development', *Financial Times*, 21 May 2007.

101 Ibid.

102 Simeon Kerr, 'Gulf Arabs flex muscles for global buy-outs as funds gain confidence', *Financial Times*, 12 July 2007.

103 Ibid.

104 Tony Blair, Speech to Business Leaders in Dubai, 20 December 2006, www.pm.gov. uk.

105 Steffen Hertog, 'The Current Crisis and Lessons of the 1980s', *Arab Reform Bulletin: Gulf Countries* (July/August 2009).

106 Paul Lewis, 'Too high, too fast: the party's over for Dubai', *Guardian*, 14 February 2009.

Index

Index

Index